Getting a Job in
America

*A step-by-step guide
to finding work in the USA*

ROGER JONES

7th edition

howtobook

By the same author

Getting a Job Abroad
How to Emigrate
How to Manage Your Career
How to Master Languages
Retire Abroad
Obtaining Visas and Work Permits
Teaching Abroad

Published by How To Books Ltd,
3 Newtec Place, Magdalen Road,
Oxford OX4 1RE, United Kingdom.
Tel: (01865) 793806. Fax: (01865) 248780.
email: info@howtobooks.co.uk
http://www.howtobooks.co.uk

First published 1992
Sixth edition 2001
Seventh edition 2003

© Copyright 2003 Roger Alan Jones

British Library Cataloguing in Publication Data.
A catalogue record for this book is available from
the British Library.

Cover design by Baseline Arts Ltd, Oxford

Produced for How To Books by Deer Park Productions
Typeset by Kestrel Data, Exeter
Printed and bound by Cromwell Press, Trowbridge, Wiltshire

NOTE: The material contained in this book is set out in good
faith for general guidance and no liability can be accepted
for loss or expense incurred as a result of relying in particular
circumstances on statements made in the book. The laws and
regulations are complex and liable to change, and readers should
check the current position with the relevant authorities before
making personal arrangements.

Getting a Job in
America

Contents

Illustrations

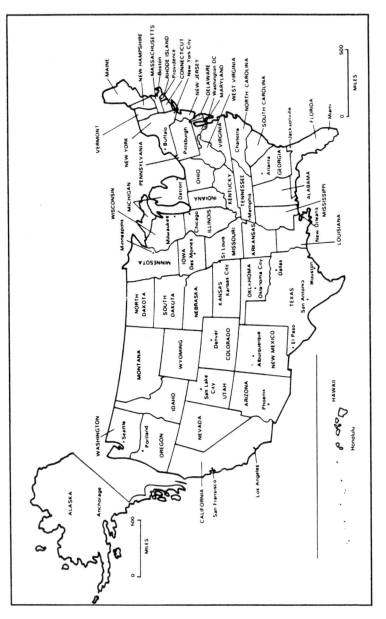

Fig. 1. Map of USA.

Preface
to the Seventh Edition

Although the US economy may be faltering as this book goes to press, the country continues to offer greater opportunities than most, so it is no wonder that many people from outside America are keen to go there to live and work either temporarily or on a permanent basis. However, most have only a hazy notion of how to set about it.

Do I simply turn up in the country and start job hunting? Or are there matters like work visas to be sorted out in advance? Where are the best places to look for jobs – newspapers, specialist journals, websites or recruitment agencies? What preparations do I need before leaving for America?

This handbook aims to answer such questions and many more. It looks at the immigration rules which decide whether or not you are eligible for a work permit. It explains how to set about finding work – whether you want a holiday job or a more permanent appointment. It also offers advice on how to set up your own business, as so many British and Irish people have done very successfully.

In addition, you will find an extensive reference section with hundreds of contacts – recruitment agencies, employers, specialist journals, immigration lawyers and consultants, professional and trade associations, federal and state government offices. Some of these sources may be able to offer you employment while others can provide advice on how to set about finding it.

Unfortunately, there can be no sure-fire guarantee of success; you may find that the immigration rules do not work in your favour. However, by paying heed to the advice in these pages you are getting off to the best of starts in your quest for work in the United States.

This new edition has been extensively revised in order to reflect modern day realities and, in particular, the growing importance of the Internet. More people than ever now have access to this powerful information tool, and will be able to exploit the hundreds of websites which appear in this book.

Although I have gone to great pains to ensure accuracy, the jobs market, in particular, is changing rapidly and information can quickly go out of date. I can only apologise for any inconvenience this may cause and urge you to let me know of any inaccuracies c/o How To Books or by emailing arle@ukonline.co.uk. Corrections can then be incorporated in any new editions.

ACKNOWLEDGEMENTS

I am grateful to a number of people and organisations who have helped me in the preparation of this book by supplying me with information, allowing me to use their facilities or offering ideas and criticism. They include the American Community School, Hillingdon; the American School in London; the British Library; Cheltenham Public Library; the Central Bureau; the Department of Social Security; Expat Network; Sanwar Ali of BCL Immigration Services; Sarah Eykyn; Tommy Grant; Richard S. Goldstein; Ira Levy of US Visa Consultants; the National Association of Temporary Services; the New York State Office in London; Frederick Pearce; Peter Rushworth; the US Department of Labor; the US Customs Service, London; the US Information Service, London; the US–UK Educational Commission; the Visa Branch of the US Embassy, London as well as publishers, recruitment agencies and the staff of How To Books.

1

Land of Opportunity

THE USA PAST AND PRESENT

The past

The United States has always been regarded as the land of opportunity, and over the centuries millions of Europeans have crossed the Atlantic to seek their fortunes in the New World. The Spanish were the first to settle there in what is now Florida, and were followed by the French in Maine in 1604. The English were not far behind; the settlement of Jamestown in Virginia was founded in 1607. Dutch, Swedish and German communities were also established around this time.

For two centuries or so the English and the Irish predominated. In 1780, for instance, three out of four Americans could claim English or Irish ancestry. But over the past hundred years the population has become much more diverse, with mass immigration from eastern and southern Europe, and more recently from Asia. American blacks are a special case: they were unwilling immigrants.

Money was not always the motivating factor. The Pilgrim Fathers sailed to America in order to be able to worship as they pleased; during the years of the Potato Famine tens of thousands of Irish families went there to escape starvation; from 1880 onwards there was large scale emigration of Jews escaping the pogroms of Eastern Europe; and in our own time Cubans and South East Asians have sought asylum in America in large numbers.

For every one of these unfortunates, the United States meant hope and freedom, and many were doubtless inspired by the words on the base of the statue of Liberty in New York City harbour:

> Give me your tired, your poor,
> Your huddled masses yearning to breathe free,
> The wretched refuse of your teeming shore.

Send these, the homeless tempest-tossed to me.
I lift my lamp beside the golden door.

The present

While the United States continues to open its door wide to refugees, the invitation does not extend to all comers. America, in common with most other countries, now places restrictions on immigration. The authorities are keen to protect the jobs of American citizens, and as a consequence employers are not allowed to offer jobs to outsiders ('aliens') if there is an American who can do the job just as well. So if you wish to take up employment you need to apply for a visa, and there is absolutely no guarantee that it will be granted.

For many immigrant categories a quota system is in operation, and when the annual quota is reached, applications in the pipeline are held over to the next fiscal year, often resulting in long waits. Yet currently there seem to be plenty of jobs to go around – particularly in the hi-tech industries – and employers are keen to have quota levels raised.

Interestingly enough, the United States is attracting over a million immigrants a year – a greater number than at any time in its history. Nearly eleven million newcomers have made their home here during the past decade – nearly twice as many as in the 1980s and almost three times as many as in the 1970s. The reasons are not hard to find. Many of its industries are the leaders in their particular field and so are its academic institutions. It remains one of the world's leading economies, politically it is the most powerful country on earth and it is a trendsetter in many ways. American commercial interests span the globe and our business culture is strongly influenced by them.

For natives of the UK and Ireland there is a special benefit: it is a home from home – almost. Americans speak English – more or less – whatever George Bernard Shaw might say; American law has its roots in English law; Americans think in terms of pounds, miles, feet and inches; the food is familiar even if chips are called 'French fries'; the natives are hospitable and it is a 'swell' place to visit.

WHY WORK IN THE USA?

People hoping to work in the United States need to be clear from the start what they hope to gain from the experience. Your

	(000s)
All countries	6,944.6
Europe	1,036.6
Austria	17.9
Hungary	12.1
Germany	58.9
Ireland	53.0
Italy	54.2
Norway	3.6
Sweden	8.2
Soviet Union	377.2
United Kingdom	117.2
Asia	2,141.2
China	303.4
Philippines	401.9
Vietnam	226.5
America	3,427.0
Canada	139.1
Mexico	1,800.8
Caribbean	753.8
Central America	387.6
South America	398.5
Africa	245.9
Oceania	36.3
Not specified	0.2

Fig 2. Immigration by leading country or region of
last residence 1991–1997.
(Source: US Immigration and Naturalization Service)

motives will often determine the kind of visa you apply for, and during the course of the application procedure you may well need to spell out your aims.

Here are some of the more usual reasons people give:

- To **finance a stay** in America. Students and young people in particular are almost invariably short of cash, so holidays or longer stays in the United States are only possible if they can find a means of financing themselves. What they do is immaterial: washing dishes, looking after children or waiting in restaurants are merely a means to an end. The important thing is to be there and to savour the country at first hand.

- To gain useful **work experience**. Some higher education courses require students to do a placement in a foreign country which could last from just a couple of months to over a year. Learning to work and survive in a different environment not only broadens one's outlook but could lead to excellent opportunities in the future in the international sphere.

- For **career development**. An increasing number of high level jobs nowadays call for people with international experience, who can work effectively in any part of the world and are equally at home in Birmingham, Bangkok or Bogota. Teachers and academics may also find that experience in a foreign country, apart from stimulating their ideas, also improves their status.

- To enjoy a **better work environment**. There are times when prospects at home look pretty bleak and people have an urge to look for greener pastures. In the 1960s and 1970s there was a considerable brain-drain from the British Isles to the United States, because R&D (research and development) facilities across the Atlantic were so much better funded. In certain areas, too, pay scales are much more generous.

- Because of **family ties**. If you have close relations in the United States, or you marry an American, you may have more compelling reasons than most to make your home there. You may also find that it is much easier for you to obtain the necessary documentation that will enable you to work.

- A **company transfer**. Some people do not specifically choose to go to the United States; they are asked to go there – to represent their company or their country, for instance, or to take control of a subsidiary firm. The move could represent a promotion and the prospect of higher earnings – in other words, you have an offer you can hardly refuse.

WHERE CAN I GO?

Clearly, people in the last category know precisely where they are to be located. Others may be in a position to choose, and for them a brief geography lesson is perhaps in order.

One mistake people tend to make is to think of America solely in terms of New York, Los Angeles and perhaps Washington, since these are the places that have the best media coverage. In fact, the United States is a semi-continent extending over 3.6 million square miles, which means it is almost twice the size of Europe. The scenery and climate are tremendously varied; and there are vast conurbations at one end of the spectrum and sparsely populated regions at the other.

In order to gain a better understanding of the country it is convenient to divide it into regions.

New England
Connecticut (CT): 4,872 sq m (area), 3.4 million (population), Hartford (capital)
Massachusetts (MA): 7,824 sq m, 6.3 million, Boston
Maine (ME): 30,995 sq m, 1.3 million, Augusta
New Hampshire (NH): 8,993 sq m, 1.2 million, Concord
Rhode Island (RI): 1,055 sq m, 1 million, Providence
Vermont (VT): 9,273 sq m, 600,000, Montpelier

Arguably the most English and historic part of the United States, some areas have experienced industrial decline in recent years. People here tend to be more formal and other Americans regard New Englanders as snobbish. The climate consists of cold winters (below freezing for three to four months of the year) and mild summers with rainfall on a par with the British Isles. The major centres of the area are Boston, Hartford (important for insurance) and New Haven (home to Yale University).

The Mid Atlantic Region
District of Columbia (DC): 63 sq m, 530,000

Delaware (DE): 1,932 sq m, 783,000, Dover
Maryland (MD): 9,837, 5.2 million, Annapolis
New Jersey (NJ): 7,468, 8.4 million, Trenton
New York (NY): 47,377 sq m, 19 million, Albany
Pennsylvania (PA): 44,888 sq m, 12.3 million, Harrisburg
Virginia (VA): 39,704 sq m, 7 million, Richmond
West Virginia (WV): 24,119 sq m, 1.8 million, Charleston

One of the major industrial centres of America and therefore a fruitful place for job hunting. New York State is the third most populous state, and the New York Metropolitan area is home to 18 million. Both New York City and Washington have considerable expatriate British communities – 50,000 in New York; 15,000 in Washington. Some 200 British firms have a Washington base. Other important centres are Baltimore, Buffalo, Philadelphia, Pittsburgh and Virginia Beach. In general the summers are warmer and the winters milder than those of New England, but inland you will encounter extremes.

The South
Alabama (AL): 50,767 sq m, 4.4 million, Montgomery
Arkansas (AR): 52,078 sq m, 2.6 million, Little Rock
Florida (FL): 54,153 sq m, 16 million, Tallahassee
Georgia (GA): 58,056 sq m, 8 million, Atlanta
Kentucky (KY): 39,669 sq m, 4 million, Frankfort
Louisiana (LA): 44,521 sq m, 4.5 million, Baton Rouge
Mississippi (MS): 47, 233 sq m, 2.8 million, Jackson
North Carolina (NC): 48,843 sq m, 8 million, Raleigh
South Carolina (SC): 30,203 sq m, 4 million, Columbia
Tennessee (TN): 41,155 sq m, 5.6 million, Nashville

This is *Gone with the Wind* country, where the pace of life tends to be slower, the cost of living lower and the climate warmer, though there can be plenty of snow inland in winter. Florida, which has a subtropical, somewhat humid climate, has expanded enormously in recent years and is perhaps the most promising place to seek work, particularly in the hotel and leisure industry. It has a large British community of more than 100,000 living principally in Tampa and Orlando, and its own newspaper the *Florida Brit*. The main centres are Atlanta, El Paso, Jacksonville, Kansas City, Miami, Nashville, New Orleans, Raleigh and Tampa.

The Mid West
Illinois (IL): 55,645 sq m, 12.4 million, Springfield
Indiana (IN): 35,932 sq m, 6 million, Indianapolis
Iowa* (IA): 55,965 sq m, 2.9 million, Des Moines
Kansas* (KS): 81,778 sq m, 2.7 million, Topeka
Michigan (MI): 56,954 sq m, 9.9 million, Lansing
Minnesota* (MN): 79,548 sq m, 4.9 million, St Paul
Missouri (MO) 68,945 sq m, 5.6 million, Jefferson City
Nebraska* (NE): 76,644 sq m, 1.7 million, Lincoln
North Dakota* (ND): 69,300 sq m, 640,000, Bismarck
Ohio (OH): 41,004 sq m, 11.4 million, Columbus
South Dakota* (SD): 75,952 sq m, 750,000, Pierre
Wisconsin (WI): 54,426 sq m, 5.3 million, Madison

The hub of this vast area is Chicago, the nation's third largest city, and the region contains some of the country's richest farmland as well as many important mining industrial centres. However, some of the activities of the area, notably the car industry in Detroit and agriculture on the Great Plains (the states marked with an asterisk), are in decline.

Other important centres are Cincinnati, Cleveland, Detroit, Milwaukee, Minneapolis St Paul, Omaha and St Louis. The temperatures are more extreme than in the UK and on the Great Plains winter temperatures of -40 degrees Celsius are not unusual.

The Rocky Mountains
Colorado (CO): 103,595 sq m, 4.3 million, Denver
Idaho (ID): 82,412 sq m, 1.3 million, Boise
Montana (MT): 145,388 sq m, 900,000, Helena
Utah (UT): 82,073 sq m, 2.2 million, Salt Lake City
Wyoming (WY): 96,989 sq m, 490,000, Cheyenne

Scenically stunning but sparsely populated, this is cowboy country. There may be job opportunities in some of the larger cities and in the National Parks. Colorado with dynamic cities like Denver and Colorado Springs is currently one of the fastest growing states of the Union. Salt Lake City is also an important and thriving centre.

The South West
Arizona (AZ): 113,508 sq m, 5.1 million, Phoenix
New Mexico (NM): 121, 335 sq m, 1.8 million, Santa Fe

Oklahoma (OK): 68,655 sq m, 3.4 million, Oklahoma City
Texas (TX): 262,017 sq m, 20.8 million, Austin

The oil industry gave this region a boost in the 1980s. Now the area is developing a substantial hi-tech industrial base and recruiting extensively from abroad. The main centres are Austin, Dallas-Fort Worth, Houston, Oklahoma City and Phoenix, San Antonio and Tucson. Summers in the South West can be uncomfortably hot, but air conditioning makes life bearable.

The West
Alaska (AK): 570,833 sq m, 626,000, Juneau
California (CA): 156,299 sq m, 33.9 million, Sacramento
Nevada (NV): 109,894 sq m, 2 million, Carson City
Oregon (OR): 96,184 sq m, 3.4 million, Salem
Washington (WA): 66,511 sq m, 5.9 million, Olympia

If California were a country it would rank among the top ten economies of the world. There is a large immigrant population in southern California since this is one of the largest industrial centres in the United States and is still expanding. The population of the Los Angeles Metropolitan Area numbers 13 million, and there is a sizeable British community here (consisting not only of film stars) which supports its own community newspaper, *The British Weekly* and TV channel. A monthly expatriate newspaper, *The Union Jack*, is also published in California and distributed nationwide. This is very much a home-from-home with British-style pubs and grocery shops.

Further north, in Washington State, is Seattle with its large aerospace industry. Apart from Los Angeles other important centres are Fresno, Long Beach, Portland, San Diego, San Francisco, San Jose, Santa Ana, Seattle, and – for gamblers and entertainers – Las Vegas. Alaska stands apart from the rest of the West; mining and oil are the mainstay of its economy and it has much of the old frontier atmosphere. It is also pretty cold in winter.

The Islands
Hawaii (HI) and various US Pacific and Caribbean territories (including Puerto Rico, Guam, American Samoa, Virgin Islands).
Hawaii (HI): 6,425 sq m, 1.2 million, Honolulu

One seldom associates these tropical islands with the United States. Employment opportunities here – apart from tourism – tend to be restricted.

So where should I make for?

The majority of newcomers head for New York or Los Angeles followed by San Francisco, Chicago and Miami, all of which have large multi-ethnic populations. However, you should not overlook the potential of other less popular locations since they may well offer both good employment or business prospects and a good quality of life.

Ten years ago Grant Thornton judged the different states of the Union according to four different criteria: education, healthcare, cost of living and transport. The top five in their quality of life rankings were North Dakota, Minnesota, Iowa, Connecticut and Massachusetts. New York State was ranked 31st, California 35th and Florida a lowly 44th. Yet the latter two are among the top three fastest growing states.

AM I ELIGIBLE TO WORK IN THE UNITED STATES?

One point you have to bear in mind throughout this book is that the United States has a well-educated population and is more or less self-sufficient in skilled people. The Federal Government therefore expects employers to recruit from this pool of talent wherever possible, rather than import staff from other countries. Not that the employers' choice is restricted to US citizens; nationals of other countries who have permanent resident status (and are known in bureaucratic parlance as 'resident aliens') are eligible to apply for any jobs that are going.

However, you do not have to be a resident alien in possession of an **Alien Registration Receipt Card** (sometimes called the '**green card**') in order to work in the United States. A good many foreigners work for periods ranging from a few months to several years on temporary permits. There are certain restrictions: any employer wishing to recruit will normally have to demonstrate to the State authorities that he is unable to recruit the right kind of person locally. If he fails to convince them, they may well refuse his request for labour certification without which he cannot employ a non-US resident for a particular job.

	Resident population April 1 2000	State rank April 1 2000	Numeric change 1990–2000	Percent change 1990–2000
United States	281,421,906	(X)	32,712,033	13.2
Alabama	4,447,100	23	406,513	10.1
Alaska	626,932	48	76,889	14.0
Arizona	5,130,632	20	1,465,404	40.0
Arkansas	2,673,400	33	322,675	13.7
California	33,871,648	1	4,111,627	13.8
Colorado	4,301,261	24	1,006,867	30.6
Connecticut	3,405,565	29	118,449	3.6
Delaware	783,600	45	117,432	17.6
District of Columbia	527,059	(X)	−34,841	−5.7
Florida	15,982,378	4	3,044,452	23.5
Georgia	8,186,453	10	1,708,237	26.4
Hawaii	1,211,537	42	103,308	9.3
Idaho	1,293,953	39	287,204	28.5
Illinois	12,419,293	5	988,691	8.6
Indiana	6,080,485	14	536,326	9.7
Iowa	2,926,324	30	149,569	5.4
Kansas	2,688,418	32	210,844	8.5
Kentucky	4,041,769	25	356,473	9.7
Louisiana	4,468,976	22	249,003	5.9
Maine	1,274,923	40	46,995	3.8
Maryland	5,296,486	19	515,018	10.8
Massachusetts	6,349,097	13	332,672	5.5
Michigan	9,938,444	8	643,147	6.9
Minnesota	4,919,479	21	544,380	12.4
Mississippi	2,844,658	31	271,442	10.5
Missouri	5,595,211	17	478,138	9.3
Montana	902,195	44	103,130	12.9
Nebraska	1,711,263	38	132,878	8.4
Nevada	1,998,257	35	796,424	66.3
New Hampshire	1,235,786	41	126,534	11.4
New Jersey	8,414,350	9	684,162	8.9
New Mexico	1,819,046	36	303,977	20.1
New York	18,976,457	3	986,002	5.5
North Carolina	8,049,313	11	1,420,676	21.4
North Dakota	642,200	47	3,400	0.5
Ohio	11,353,140	7	506,025	4.7
Oklahoma	3,450,654	27	305,069	9.7
Oregon	3,421,399	28	579,078	20.4
Pennsylvania	12,281,054	6	399,411	3.4
Rhode Island	1,048,319	43	44,855	4.5
South Carolina	4,012,012	26	525,309	15.1
South Dakota	754,844	46	58,840	8.5
Tennessee	5,689,283	16	812,098	16.7
Texas	20,851,820	2	3,865,310	22.8
Utah	2,233,169	34	510,319	29.6
Vermont	608,827	49	46,069	8.2
Virginia	7,078,515	12	891,157	14.4
Washington	5,894,121	15	1,027,429	21.1
West Virginia	1,808,344	37	14,867	0.8
Wisconsin	5,363,675	18	471,906	9.6
Wyoming	493,782	50	40,194	8.9

X Not applicable.

Fig. 3.   USA resident populations by state (2000 census)
(Source: US Census Bureau).

The important matter of visas is treated at length in Chapter 2. It's a good idea to work through that chapter to find out what type of visa you will need in order to work in the United States. While it is now possible to move freely across borders within the European Union in search of a job, there is no open jobs market for British people – or indeed any non-American – in the United States, except for those with residential status.

Certain kinds of people are more welcome than others. You may have outstanding ability in your field or be able to offer skills that are much in demand. Certain areas of the United States are experiencing a shortage of computer experts, electronics engineers, nurses and paramedics, and this shortage is being overcome by recruitment from abroad.

Your own connections can be crucial as well. You may be able to gain permanent residence on the strength of close family relationships; or you may be transferred to the United States by your firm or organisation. Entrepreneurial skills can also gain you access to the country and America welcomes investors.

WILL AMERICA SUIT ME?

Assuming there will be no problem in getting the necessary permission to work in the United States, you still need to consider whether a job on the other side of the Atlantic will really suit you. For, while most newcomers take to the United States like ducks to water, there are some who do not. They are irritated by the exuberance of many Americans, complain about the materialism they see around them, dislike the television programmes and the extremes of climate, and long for a pint of real ale and fish and chips.

Going to live and work in a strange location inevitably calls for adaptability; you must be prepared to meet the local people on their own terms. Fortunately, the American way of life is not as different from ours as that of, say, Mexico or Yemen, but even slight differences can irritate some people. You may dislike one part of the country and feel very much at home in another. There is, after all, considerable regional variety; if you dislike the formality of the east coast, you may feel more at home on the west coast where people are more casual.

It is unwise to take everything for granted. Public transport is a case in point: in much of the country public transport systems are

Average Monthly Temperature and Rainfall

T, temperature in Fahrenheit; P, precipitation in inches; L, less than 0.5 inch

Station	Jan T	Jan P	Feb T	Feb P	Mar T	Mar P	Apr T	Apr P	May T	May P	June T	June P	July T	July P	Aug T	Aug P	Sept T	Sept P	Oct T	Oct P	Nov T	Nov P	Dec T	Dec P
Albany	21	2.4	23	2.3	34	3.0	47	2.9	58	3.3	67	3.3	71	3.0	69	3.3	61	3.2	51	2.9	39	3.0	26	3.0
Albuquerque, N.M.	35	0.4	39	0.4	46	0.5	55	0.5	64	0.5	75	0.5	79	1.3	76	1.5	69	0.9	57	0.9	44	0.4	36	0.5
Anchorage, Alas.	13	0.8	18	0.9	24	0.7	35	0.7	46	0.6	54	1.1	58	2.0	56	2.1	48	2.5	35	1.7	22	1.1	14	1.1
Asheville, N.C.	37	3.5	39	3.6	46	5.1	56	3.8	63	4.2	70	4.2	73	4.4	72	4.8	70	4.0	56	3.3	46	3.4	39	3.5
Atlanta, Ga.	42	4.9	45	4.4	53	5.9	62	4.4	69	4.0	76	3.4	79	4.7	78	3.4	73	3.2	62	2.5	52	3.4	45	4.2
Atlantic City, N.J.	33	3.3	35	3.2	42	3.7	51	3.1	60	2.9	68	2.9	74	3.9	74	4.5	68	2.7	58	2.8	48	3.5	38	3.5
Baltimore, Md.	33	3.0	35	3.0	43	3.7	54	3.4	63	3.4	72	3.8	77	3.9	76	4.6	69	3.5	57	3.1	46	3.1	37	3.4
Barrow, Alas.	-14	0.2	-20	0.2	-16	0.2	-2	0.2	19	0.2	33	0.4	39	0.9	38	1.0	31	0.6	14	0.6	-1	0.3	-13	0.2
Birmingham, Ala.	44	5.2	46	4.7	54	6.6	63	5.0	70	4.5	77	3.7	80	5.1	80	3.9	74	4.3	62	2.7	52	3.6	45	5.0
Bismarck, N.D.	7	0.5	15	0.5	26	0.7	43	1.5	55	2.2	64	3.0	70	2.0	69	1.7	57	1.4	46	0.8	29	0.5	15	0.5
Boise, Ida.	30	1.6	36	1.1	41	1.0	49	1.2	57	1.2	66	1.0	75	0.3	72	0.4	63	0.6	52	0.8	40	1.3	32	1.3
Boston, Mass.	30	4.0	31	3.7	38	4.1	49	3.7	59	3.5	68	2.9	74	2.7	72	3.7	65	3.4	55	2.9	45	4.2	34	4.9
Buffalo, N.Y.	24	3.0	25	2.4	33	3.0	45	3.0	56	2.9	66	2.3	71	3.0	69	3.2	62	3.4	52	2.9	40	3.6	29	3.4
Burlington, Vt.	17	1.9	18	1.7	29	2.2	43	2.8	55	3.0	65	3.6	70	3.4	67	3.9	59	3.2	48	2.8	37	2.8	23	2.4
Caribou, Me.	11	2.4	13	2.1	24	2.4	37	2.6	50	2.9	60	3.0	68	4.0	66	4.0	54	3.8	43	3.1	31	3.2	16	3.1
Charleston, S.C.	49	3.3	51	3.4	57	4.4	66	2.6	73	4.4	79	5.5	82	7.3	81	6.5	77	4.9	68	2.9	59	2.2	52	2.1
Chicago, Ill.	21	1.6	26	1.3	36	2.6	49	3.7	59	3.2	69	4.1	73	3.6	72	3.4	65	3.4	54	2.3	40	2.1	28	2.1
Cleveland, Oh.	26	2.5	27	2.2	37	3.0	48	3.4	58	3.3	68	3.5	72	3.4	70	3.4	64	2.9	54	2.5	42	2.8	31	2.8
Columbus, Oh.	27	2.8	30	2.2	40	3.2	51	3.4	61	3.8	70	4.0	74	4.0	72	3.7	66	2.8	55	1.9	42	2.6	32	2.6
Dallas-Ft. Worth, Tex.	44	1.7	49	1.9	56	2.4	66	3.6	74	4.3	82	2.6	86	2.0	86	1.8	79	3.3	68	2.5	56	1.7	46	1.7
Denver, Col.	30	0.5	34	0.7	38	1.2	47	1.8	57	2.5	67	1.6	73	1.9	71	1.5	63	1.1	52	1.0	39	1.1	33	0.6
Des Moines, Ia.	19	1.0	25	1.1	35	2.2	51	3.2	62	4.0	72	4.2	76	3.2	74	4.1	65	3.1	54	2.2	39	1.5	25	1.5
Detroit, Mich.	23	1.9	26	1.7	35	2.5	47	3.2	58	2.8	68	3.4	72	3.1	71	3.2	63	2.3	52	2.1	40	2.3	29	2.5
Dodge City, Kan.	30	0.5	35	0.5	42	1.5	54	1.8	64	3.3	75	3.0	80	3.1	78	2.5	69	1.9	58	1.3	43	0.8	34	0.5
Duluth, Minn.	6	1.2	12	0.9	23	1.8	38	2.2	50	3.2	59	4.0	65	4.0	63	4.1	54	3.3	44	2.2	28	1.7	14	1.3
Eureka, Cal.	47	7.0	49	5.2	48	5.1	48	2.9	52	1.6	55	0.6	56	0.1	57	0.4	57	0.7	54	2.7	51	5.9	48	6.2
Fairbanks, Alas.	-13	0.5	-4	0.5	9	0.4	30	0.3	48	0.6	59	1.3	62	1.8	57	1.9	45	1.1	25	0.7	4	0.7	-10	0.7
Fresno, Cal.	46	2.0	51	1.9	54	2.1	60	1.2	68	0.3	75	0.1	81	L	79	L	74	0.2	65	0.4	53	1.2	45	1.6
Galveston, Tex.	54	3.0	56	2.3	62	2.1	69	2.6	76	3.3	81	3.5	83	4.4	83	4.4	80	5.8	73	2.6	63	3.2	57	3.6
Grand Junction, Col.	26	0.6	34	0.5	42	0.8	52	0.7	62	0.8	72	0.4	79	0.5	76	0.9	67	0.7	55	0.9	40	0.6	28	0.6
Gr. Rapids, Mich.	22	0.9	24	1.5	33	2.5	46	3.3	58	3.0	67	3.4	71	3.0	70	3.5	62	3.1	51	2.9	39	2.9	29	2.6
Hartford, Conn.	25	3.5	28	3.2	37	4.2	49	4.0	59	3.4	69	3.4	73	3.1	71	4.0	63	3.9	52	3.5	42	4.1	29	4.2
Helena, Mon.	18	0.7	26	0.4	32	0.7	42	1.0	52	1.7	60	2.0	68	1.0	66	1.2	56	0.8	45	0.7	31	0.5	23	0.6
Honolulu, Ha.	73	3.8	73	2.7	74	3.5	76	1.5	78	1.2	79	0.5	80	0.5	81	0.6	81	0.6	80	1.9	77	3.2	74	3.4
Houston, Tex.	51	3.2	55	3.3	61	2.7	69	4.2	75	4.7	81	4.0	83	3.3	83	3.7	78	4.9	70	3.7	60	3.4	54	3.7
Huron, S.D.	11	0.4	18	0.8	29	1.2	46	2.0	57	2.7	68	3.3	74	2.3	72	2.0	61	1.4	49	1.4	32	0.7	19	0.5
Indianapolis, Ind.	26	2.7	30	2.5	40	3.6	52	3.7	63	3.7	72	4.0	75	4.3	73	3.5	67	2.7	55	2.5	42	3.0	32	3.0
Jackson, Miss.	46	5.0	49	4.9	56	5.9	65	5.9	73	4.8	79	2.9	82	4.4	81	3.7	76	3.6	65	2.6	55	4.2	49	5.4
Jacksonville, Fla.	53	3.1	55	3.5	61	3.7	68	3.3	74	4.9	79	5.4	81	6.5	81	7.2	78	7.3	70	3.4	61	1.9	55	2.6
Juneau, Alas.	22	3.7	28	3.7	31	3.3	39	2.9	46	3.4	53	3.0	56	4.1	55	5.0	49	6.4	42	7.7	33	5.2	27	4.7
Kansas City, Mo.	26	1.0	32	1.0	42	2.1	55	2.7	65	3.4	76	4.1	79	3.5	77	3.2	68	3.3	58	2.5	43	1.2	32	1.1
Knoxville, Tenn.	38	4.7	42	4.2	50	5.5	60	3.9	67	3.7	74	4.0	78	4.3	77	3.0	72	3.0	60	2.7	49	3.8	41	4.6
Lander, Wyo.	20	0.5	26	0.6	32	1.1	42	2.2	53	2.7	62	1.5	71	0.7	69	0.5	58	0.9	47	1.2	31	0.8	23	0.5
Lexington, Ky.	32	3.6	35	3.3	44	4.8	55	4.0	64	4.2	72	4.3	76	5.0	75	4.0	69	3.3	57	2.3	45	3.3	36	3.8
Little Rock, Ark.	40	3.9	44	3.8	52	4.7	62	5.4	71	5.3	79	3.7	82	3.6	81	3.1	74	4.3	63	2.8	51	4.4	43	4.2

Fig. 4.   Average monthly temperature and rainfall, based on a 30-year period (National Climatic Data Center US Department of Commerce).

City	Jan T	Jan R	Feb T	Feb R	Mar T	Mar R	Apr T	Apr R	May T	May R	Jun T	Jun R	Jul T	Jul R	Aug T	Aug R	Sep T	Sep R	Oct T	Oct R	Nov T	Nov R	Dec T	Dec R
Los Angeles, Ca.	57	3.7	59	3.0	60	2.4	62	1.2	66	0.2	69	L	74	L	75	0.1	73	0.3	69	0.2	63	1.9	58	2.0
Louisville, Ky.	33	3.4	36	3.2	45	4.7	57	4.1	65	4.2	74	3.6	78	4.1	76	3.3	70	3.6	58	2.6	48	3.5	37	3.5
Marquette, Mich.	12	2.0	14	1.9	23	2.8	37	3.6	50	4.0	60	3.9	65	3.2	63	3.3	54	3.9	44	3.9	30	2.9	18	2.4
Memphis, Tenn.	40	4.6	44	4.3	52	5.4	63	5.8	71	5.1	81	3.6	82	4.0	81	3.3	74	3.6	63	2.5	51	4.2	43	4.9
Miami, Fla.	67	2.1	68	2.1	72	1.9	75	3.1	79	6.5	81	9.2	83	7.0	83	7.1	82	8.1	78	8.1	73	2.7	69	1.9
Milwaukee, Wis.	19	1.6	23	1.3	32	2.6	45	3.4	55	2.6	68	4.1	73	3.5	69	3.1	62	2.6	51	2.3	37	2.0	25	2.0
Minneapolis, Minn.	11	0.8	18	0.9	29	1.7	46	2.1	59	3.2	68	4.1	73	3.5	71	3.6	62	2.5	50	1.9	33	1.3	19	0.9
Mobile, Ala.	51	4.6	54	4.9	60	6.5	68	5.4	75	5.5	81	6.8	82	7.7	82	6.8	78	6.6	69	2.7	59	3.7	53	5.4
Moline, Ill.	20	1.6	25	1.3	36	2.8	50	4.0	61	4.2	71	4.3	75	4.9	73	3.8	65	3.7	54	2.7	39	2.0	26	1.9
Nashville, Tenn.	37	4.5	40	4.0	49	5.6	60	4.8	68	4.6	76	3.7	79	3.8	79	3.4	72	3.4	60	2.3	47	3.6	41	4.6
Newark, N.J.	31	3.1	33	3.1	41	4.2	52	3.6	62	3.6	72	2.9	77	3.8	76	4.3	68	3.7	57	3.1	47	3.6	36	3.4
New Orleans, La.	52	5.0	55	5.2	61	4.7	69	4.5	75	5.1	80	4.6	82	6.7	82	6.0	79	5.9	69	2.7	60	4.1	55	5.3
New York, N.Y.	32	3.2	33	3.1	41	4.2	53	3.8	62	3.8	71	3.2	77	4.0	76	4.3	68	3.7	58	3.4	47	4.1	36	3.8
Nome, Alas.	9	0.8	3	0.5	7	0.6	18	0.6	36	0.5	45	1.2	51	2.2	50	3.1	42	2.3	28	1.3	16	0.9	4	0.7
Norfolk, Va.	40	3.7	41	3.3	49	3.9	58	2.9	67	3.8	76	3.5	78	5.3	78	5.3	72	4.1	61	3.1	52	2.9	44	3.2
Okla. City, Okla.	36	1.0	41	1.3	49	2.1	60	2.9	68	5.3	77	3.9	82	3.0	81	2.4	74	4.1	62	2.7	49	1.5	40	1.2
Omaha, Neb.	19	0.8	25	0.9	35	1.9	50	2.9	62	4.3	71	4.1	76	3.6	74	4.1	64	4.5	54	2.1	38	1.3	26	0.9
Pago Pago, Amer. Samoa	81	13	81	13	81	11	81	11	80	11	80	8.6	79	6.5	79	7.1	79	6.7	80	11	80	11	81	14
Philadelphia, Pa.	31	3.2	33	2.8	42	3.9	53	3.5	63	3.2	72	3.9	77	3.9	75	4.1	68	3.4	57	2.8	46	3.3	36	3.5
Phoenix, Ariz.	52	0.7	56	0.6	61	0.8	68	0.3	77	0.1	86	0.2	92	0.7	90	1.0	85	0.6	73	0.6	61	0.5	53	0.8
Pittsburgh, Pa.	27	2.9	29	2.4	39	3.6	50	3.3	60	3.5	68	3.3	72	3.8	71	2.8	64	2.8	53	2.5	42	2.3	31	2.6
Portland, Me.	22	3.8	23	3.6	32	4.0	43	3.9	53	3.3	62	3.1	68	2.8	67	2.8	59	3.3	49	3.8	38	4.7	26	4.5
Portland, Ore.	39	6.2	43	3.9	46	3.6	50	2.3	57	2.1	63	1.5	67	0.5	67	1.1	63	1.6	54	3.1	46	5.2	41	6.4
Providence, R.I.	28	4.1	29	3.7	37	4.3	48	4.0	58	3.8	67	2.8	73	3.0	71	4.4	64	3.8	53	3.8	43	4.2	32	4.5
Raleigh, N.C.	40	3.6	42	3.4	49	3.7	59	2.9	67	3.7	74	3.7	78	4.4	77	4.4	71	3.3	60	2.7	50	2.9	42	3.1
Rapid City, S.D.	21	0.4	26	0.6	33	1.0	45	2.0	56	2.8	65	3.3	74	2.1	73	2.1	61	1.0	50	0.8	35	0.5	26	0.5
Reno, Nev.	32	1.2	37	1.0	41	0.7	46	0.5	55	0.7	62	0.3	71	0.3	67	0.3	61	0.3	50	0.3	40	0.6	33	1.2
Richmond, Va.	37	3.2	39	3.1	47	3.3	58	2.9	66	3.5	74	3.6	78	5.1	77	5.0	70	3.5	59	3.3	49	3.3	40	3.4
St. Louis, Mo.	29	1.7	34	2.1	43	3.3	56	3.6	66	3.5	75	3.7	78	3.7	77	2.6	70	2.7	58	3.1	45	2.5	34	2.2
Salt Lake City, Ut.	29	1.4	34	1.9	41	1.7	49	2.2	59	1.5	68	1.0	78	0.7	77	0.9	65	0.9	53	1.1	40	1.2	30	1.4
San Antonio, Tex.	50	1.6	54	1.6	62	1.3	70	2.7	76	3.7	82	3.0	85	1.9	84	2.7	79	3.8	70	2.9	60	2.3	53	1.4
San Diego, Cal.	58	2.1	58	1.4	59	1.6	61	0.8	63	0.2	66	0.1	70	L	72	0.1	71	0.2	68	0.1	62	1.1	57	1.4
San Francisco, Cal.	49	4.7	52	3.2	53	2.6	55	1.5	58	0.3	61	0.1	62	L	63	0.1	64	0.2	61	1.1	55	2.4	49	3.6
San Juan, P.R.	73	3.0	77	3.0	78	2.3	80	3.6	79	5.6	80	4.7	82	4.9	82	5.9	81	6.0	81	5.9	80	5.6	78	4.7
Sault Ste. Marie, Mich.	13	2.2	14	1.7	24	2.3	38	2.4	50	3.0	58	3.3	64	3.0	63	3.7	55	3.2	45	2.3	33	3.2	20	2.6
Savannah, Ga.	49	3.1	52	3.2	58	3.8	66	3.2	73	4.6	79	5.7	81	7.4	81	6.7	77	5.2	67	2.0	58	1.9	51	2.8
Seattle, Wash.	39	6.0	43	4.2	44	3.6	48	2.4	55	1.6	60	1.5	65	0.7	65	1.3	60	2.0	52	3.6	45	5.6	41	6.3
Spokane, Wash.	26	2.5	32	1.6	38	1.4	46	1.1	54	1.4	62	1.2	70	0.5	68	0.7	60	1.2	48	1.1	35	2.1	29	2.5
Springfield, Mo.	32	1.6	36	2.1	45	3.4	56	4.0	65	4.3	73	4.7	78	4.7	77	2.8	70	4.2	58	3.2	45	2.9	36	2.6
Syracuse, N.Y.	23	2.6	24	2.7	33	3.1	46	3.3	57	3.2	66	3.6	71	3.8	69	3.6	62	3.3	51	3.1	41	3.5	28	3.2
Tampa, Fla.	60	2.2	61	3.0	66	3.5	72	1.8	77	3.4	81	5.3	82	7.4	82	7.6	81	6.2	74	2.3	67	1.9	61	2.1
Washington, D.C.	31	2.8	34	2.6	42	3.4	53	3.1	62	3.6	71	4.2	76	3.8	74	4.2	67	3.0	55	3.0	45	3.0	35	3.1
Wilmington, Dal.	31	3.1	33	3.0	42	3.9	52	3.4	62	3.2	71	3.5	76	3.9	75	4.0	68	3.6	56	2.9	48	3.3	36	3.5

rudimentary or completely non-existent. The car is king, and if you cannot drive you will be at something of a disadvantage. Another difference is that there is no government funded health service except for the old and handicapped; you will need to pay for medical treatment, or better, insure yourself against illness.

Though the language may sound reasonably familiar, it is perhaps wiser to regard the United States as a foreign country with different values and different customs. Even things which sound similar may be different: an American gallon, for instance, is less than the Imperial equivalent. Driving rules are different as well, with speed limits normally lower than those in Europe. The high-speed car chases you see in films are definitely not typical of the United States.

Will my family like living there?

If you have a family, you need to consider the implications of a move to the United States with care. What may be an exciting challenge for you could turn out to be a mild form of torture for them.

Your spouse

This is most frequently a wife, but sometimes the wife is the main breadwinner and the accompanying spouse is male.

Problems can arise when both partners want to pursue their own careers. You need to discuss whether your spouse is prepared to give up his or her job in order to accompany you to the United States, or whether you should settle for a bachelor existence with holidays and the occasional weekend spent together.

There are also financial considerations. If your spouse gives up her/his job you are probably faced with the matter of living on one income instead of two. There is no guarantee that your spouse will be granted the type of visa that will enable him/her to work in America.

Some spouses may relish a life away from the workplace, but for others who are used to a busy existence time may hang heavy. While you may have plenty of colleagues with whom to socialise at work, your spouse has to go out and make his/her own social contacts. If they cannot drive or do not have the use of a car, this can be a problem in suburbia and in remote areas.

Fortunately, in most areas there are clubs to join and adult education classes to attend. Organisations such as the Women's

Economics/finance	$40,577
Business administration	$38,449
Management information systems	$45,585
Computer Science	$52,723
Information sciences	$45,182
Computing engineering	$53,924
Civil engineering	$40,616
Chemical engineering	$51,073
Petroleum engineering	$53,878
English	$31,501
Sociology	$28,812
Psychology	$30,338
History	$30,375
Political Science	$30,375

Fig. 5.   Starting salaries for new graduates 2001
(National Association for Colleges and Employers).

Corona Society and Christians Abroad may also be able to find a contact to look after your spouse in the initial stages.

Your children
If you are planning to live in the United States for several years, or possibly for ever, you will doubtless want to take your children with you. However, if they are into their teens consideration has to be given to their education. The American education system differs fundamentally from the British system, and if crucial examinations are looming up and you want them to go on to further or higher education in the UK, you need to consider their future carefully.

There are various options:

- enable them to continue at their present school

	Median weekly earnings ($) 2000		
	Total	Men	Women
Managerial and professional specialty	827	976	702
Executive, administrative, and managerial	820	981	674
Professional specialty	833	972	725
Technical, sales and administrative support	505	661	446
Technicians and related support	637	747	524
Sales occupations	558	679	410
Administrative support	467	588	443
Service occupations	357	418	317
Private household	258	(1)	251
Protective service	619	646	507
Service, except private household and protective	329	359	314
Precision production, craft, and repair	608	623	421
Mechanics and repairers	660	660	644
Construction trades	593	595	(1)
Other precision production, craft, and repair	566	624	402
Operators, fabricators, and laborers	445	488	348
Machine operators, assemblers, and inspectors	428	495	349
Transportation and material moving occupations	528	548	399
Handlers, equipment cleaners, helpers, and laborers	378	395	320
Farming, forestry and fishing	320	329	279

(1) *Data not shown where base is less than 100,000*

Fig. 6. Median usual weekly earnings (in dollars) of full-time wage and salary workers (Bureau of Labor Statistics, US Department of Labor).

State	dollars 1990	1999	State	dollars 1990	1999
United States	**17,146**	**24,297**			
Alabama	14,097	20,068	Missouri	15,611	22,469
Alaska	19,937	24,978	Montana	13,785	19,590
Arizona	15,247	21,855	Nebraska	16,071	23,805
Arkansas	12,988	19,412	Nevada	18,112	26,205
California	19,027	25,100	New Hampshire	18,450	26,732
Colorado	17,251	26,801	New Jersey	21,503	30,251
Connecticut	23,279	31,797	New Mexico	13,396	19,396
Delaware	18,612	25,714	New York	19,899	28,072
District of Columbia	22,921	31,457	North Carolina	15,257	22,424
Florida	17,731	24,201	North Dakota	14,320	20,842
Georgia	15,537	23,225	Ohio	16,442	23,018
Hawaii	19,428	24,305	Oklahoma	14,264	19,800
Idaho	14,071	20,419	Oregon	16,003	22,964
Illinois	18,042	26,519	Pennsylvania	17,433	24,498
Indiana	15,398	22,223	Rhode Island	17,795	25,686
Iowa	15,295	22,252	South Carolina	14,199	20,491
Kansas	16,009	22,880	South Dakota	14,846	22,443
Kentucky	13,623	19,930	Tennessee	15,193	22,626
Louisiana	13,681	20,061	Texas	15,600	23,223
Maine	15,414	21,530	Utah	13,219	20,013
Maryland	19,712	26,686	Vermont	15,838	22,308
Massachusetts	19,915	29,589	Virginia	17,899	25,010
Michigan	16,589	23,684	Washington	17,761	26,203
Minnesota	17,328	26,003	West Virginia	12,997	18,377
Mississippi	11,927	18,241	Wisconsin	15,817	23,213
			Wyoming	16,077	22,244

Fig. 7. Disposable personal income per capita by state (US Bureau of Economic Analysis).

Metropolitan area	1997	1998	1999
U.S., all areas	**121.8**	**128.4**	**133.3**
Albuquerque, NM	126.7	128.2	130.3
Atlanta, GA	108.4	115.4	123.7
Atlantic City, NJ	109.7	112.8	117.0
Aurora-Elgin, IL	141.8	146.2	151.9
Austin-San Marcos, TX	(NA)	121.1	128.6
Baltimore, MD	118.2	120.6	127.4
Birmingham, AL	118.9	122.7	127.1
Boise City, ID	102.5	109.2	123.9
Boston, MA	229.0	258.4	290.0
Bradenton, FL	94.9	107.3	117.2
Charleston, SC	103.6	120.0	131.7
Charlotte-Gastonia-Rock Hill, NC-SC	124.2	134.0	138.2
Chicago, IL	158.9	166.8	171.2
Cincinnati, OH-KY-IN	110.5	116.3	119.9
Cleveland, OH	116.8	121.8	125.1
Colorado Springs, CO	130.5	138.5	144.9
Columbus, OH	117.6	121.7	125.0
Denver, CO	140.6	152.2	171.3
Detroit, MI	119.6	132.6	140.0
Eugene-Springfield, OR	119.4	124.4	129.5
Ft. Lauderdale-Hollywood-Pompano Beach, FL	123.7	128.6	136.1
Greensboro-Winston-Salem-High Point, NC	117.3	123.5	124.8
Hartford, CT	138.1	142.8	150.7
Honolulu, HI	307.0	297.0	290.0
Kansas City, MO-KS	106.8	114.0	120.7
Lake County, IL	153.5	159.4	164.0
Las Vegas, NV	123.2	128.2	130.8
Los Angeles Area, CA	176.5	192.6	205.3
Madison, WI	126.8	131.8	136.5
Miami-Hialeah, FL	117.7	121.5	134.6

Metropolitan area	1997	1998	1999
Milwaukee, WI	125.3	132.9	135.3
Minneapolis-St. Paul, MN-WI	118.4	128.0	138.7
New Haven-Meriden, CT	134.1	137.8	145.7
New York-N. Jersey-Long Island, NHY-NJ-CT	177.9	188.1	203.2
NY: Bergen-Passaic, NJ	205.4	213.5	221.8
NY: Middlesex-Somerset-Hunterdon, NJ	176.7	184.2	196.8
NY: Monmouth-Ocean, NJ	147.7	152.6	164.4
NY: Nassau-Suffolk, NY	164.0	175.4	190.4
NY: Newark, NJ	193.0	199.2	212.0
Orange Cnty. (Anaheim-Santa Ana) CA	229.8	261.7	281.5
Philadelphia, PA-NJ	126.3	129.7	124.8
Phoenix, AZ	113.7	120.2	126.4
Portland, OR	152.4	158.1	165.0
Providence, RI	119.6	124.4	128.8
Raleigh-Durham, NC	152.8	159.8	165.0
Reno, NV	143.4	147.2	150.6
Richmond-Petersburg, VA	114.2	122.0	128.5
Riverside-San Bernardino, CA	114.3	121.5	128.7
Sacramento, CA	116.1	125.6	133.8
Salt Lake City-Ogden, UT	128.6	133.5	137.9
San Diego, CA	185.2	207.1	231.6
San Francisco Bay Area, CA	286.2	321.7	365.3
Sarasota, FL	114.1	123.1	134.8
Tallahassee, FL	111.7	114.6	117.8
Trenton, NJ	137.7	139.5	144.2
Tucson, AZ	106.8	112.6	117.7
Washington, DC-MD-VA	166.3	172.1	176.5
Wilmington, DE-NJ-MD	123.7	123.9	120.6
Worcester, MA	(NA)	(NA)	117.0
W. Palm Beach-Boca Raton-Delray Beach, FL	133.4	126.6	131.0

NA: Not available.

Fig. 8.   Median sales price of existing single-family homes (National Association of Realtors). ($000).

- put them into a UK boarding school
- enrol them in a school in the United States
- enrol them in a school in America which offers a British style curriculum.

Schools in the last category, which prepare pupils for British examinations or the International Baccalaureate, tend to be few and far between, and generally only in those centres where there is a sizeable British community (see also Chapter 5).

THE FINANCIAL AND OTHER REWARDS

Will I earn more money in the United States? Will my salary go as far as it would at home? These are the questions that are often uppermost in people's minds when they consider taking up a posting in the United States. Unfortunately, there is no simple answer.

If you are recruited in the UK for a short-term contract you may well earn more than the average for a particular job. The same will doubtless be true if you are sent to the United States by your firm when all the perks and other inducements are taken into account. Others may not be so lucky; resident aliens, for instance, may have to settle for pay rates that are closer to the local norms.

When it comes to the actual cost of living, one can only generalise. Household goods are generally cheaper than in the UK. So are cars and houses. In 1999 Dresdner Kleinwort Benson found the price of the average urban dwelling was 8.3 times the average disposable income per head compared with 13.2 times in the UK.

The cost of accommodation can vary considerably from city to city and from state to state. New York City is expensive to live in, but probably no more so than London; and renting an apartment in Manhattan could well set you back the same amount as its equivalent in Mayfair. However, if you are living in Manhattan the chances are that your employer is paying your rent anyway.

There are, of course, cheaper areas where you can live reasonably well, just as there are in Greater London and if you have to pay your own rent, you will doubtless head for these. Boston, Los Angeles, San Francisco and Washington DC are other cities where accommodation tends to be on the expensive side, as the table in Figure 8 shows, but elsewhere housing is relatively cheap.

For instance, in Houston it is possible to find a modest, three-bedroomed house for around $60,000, or an apartment to rent for $600 per month or less. (To calculate annual rents approximately, divide the figures for house prices in the table by ten.)

However, you should not count your chickens before they are hatched, since there are various obstacles to be negotiated. One of the most difficult is the immigration hurdle. The next chapter is devoted to this.

2

Getting Into the United States: The Red Tape

This book is primarily about getting a job in the United States, not about the United States immigration laws. However, an understanding of these laws is vital in order to ensure a trouble free entry into the United States. Your working intentions will determine and be determined by the type of visa you apply for.

A few myths need to be dispelled first:

- You don't need a visa in order to take up casual work in the United States.
  Wrong. If you are employed in the United States in any capacity you need a work visa; anybody without one is classified as an illegal immigrant and is breaking the law. Nonetheless, there are plenty of people who are willing to take the risk regardless of the consequences.

- In order to work in the United States you need first to obtain a 'green card'.
  Wrong. The **Alien Registration Receipt Card**, to give it its official title, is for people with permanent resident status, and not everybody needs this. Most newcomers to the United States enter on non-immigrant (temporary) visas which permit them to work and can often be extended or adjusted.

- It is essential to use a lawyer to obtain a work permit.
  Wrong. United States immigration laws may be complicated, but many people and employers manage quite happily without a legal adviser. Besides if you do not qualify for a visa, using a lawyer will not change anything. However, if your situation is complicated or you have doubts about your eligibility it is prudent to seek advice.

THE NEED FOR A VISA

As you saw in the first chapter, the United States no longer has an open door policy with respect to immigration. The country's population has grown enormously, so partly to protect the interests of its workforce it now imposes limits on immigrants. For instance, a maximum of 675,000 immigrants are allowed in annually. Whether you seek temporary employment or permanent residence you have to apply for a visa before you go.

The only exceptions to the rule are citizens of certain countries (including Britain) who are making a holiday or business trip of 90 days or less, and are in possession of a return ticket. People who can claim American citizenship by reason of birth or parentage are also exempt. Anybody else needs to get an appropriate visa, whether they are involved in an exchange or a course of study, or whether they are planning to settle permanently.

Be warned. If you enter the country without an appropriate visa and take up employment, you and your employer are breaking the law. While you may manage to get away with it for a time – and quite a lot of people do – you are running a considerable risk. You will be regarded as an illegal immigrant, and if you are found out you could be deported and prohibited from entering the United States again. The longer you stay, the greater the danger of being found out.

There are ways out of the dilemma.

- You may be able to legalise your status with the Immigration and Naturalisation Service. But if you have been unlawfully present for over six months you will be barred from legalising your status for three years. For anyone who has outstayed his welcome in this way for over a year the bar is for ten years. There are few exceptions to this rule.

- You can marry a United States citizen, and file a petition for a green card.

- The Federal Government has offered an amnesty to illegal immigrants in the past, but you cannot count on it happening in the future.

If you are hoping to enter the United States job market by the back door, you had better forget it. Immigration officials (particularly those at major ports of entry, such as New York and

Los Angeles) can be very strict. If they suspect you are a job seeker posing as a tourist, they have powers to search you and your luggage. Should they find a job offer or job advertisements among your belongings, or discover that you have not enough cash to finance your visit, they could well refuse you entry.

That is why I recommend you try to get things right from the start. By wading through this chapter you should gain an insight into US immigration practices and what type of visa you should aim for.

THE 1990 IMMIGRATION LAW (IMMACT 90)

United States immigration law underwent a complete overhaul in 1990. You therefore need to make sure that any advice or information you get is completely up to date, otherwise you may find yourself setting off on completely the wrong track.

The information given below should serve as a guide, but do not regard it as the last word. If your position is a complicated one, you or any firm that wants to employ you will need to obtain advice from the nearest United States consulate (for applicants outside the United States), or the nearest Immigration and Naturalization Service (INS) office (for applicants within the United States). Alternatively, you could refer to manuals such as *Applying for a United States Visa* or call on the services of an immigration lawyer or consultant.

If you decide to use a lawyer, the US Embassy can supply you with a list of American immigration lawyers operating in the UK and you will find several listed in Appendix F. *Obtaining Visas and Work Permits*; (How To Books) has a more extensive list covering several countries. I would recommend you deal with specialists who practise within your own country, and whose reputation you can check up on. Also, be prepared to shop around.

First, though, you need to decide how long you intend to be in the United States. If you do not intend to stay in the country permanently, but just for a matter of months or years, you will need a non-immigrant (temporary) visa of some kind, which in many cases can be extended.

Even if your long-term aim is permanent residence, there is no reason why you should not start off with a non-immigrant visa. For one thing, these are normally easier to obtain. There is nothing to prevent you from petitioning for adjustment of status to that of permanent resident at a later date once you are in the country.

NON-IMMIGRANT (TEMPORARY) VISAS

To determine what kind of visa you require you should ask yourself the following questions:

- Are you going purely for a holiday or for a business trip?
  Under the Visa Waiver Pilot Programme (VWPP) citizens of Western Europe, Japan and New Zealand do not need a visa, if their visit is for less than 90 days and they are in possession of a return ticket. However, it is impossible to extend your stay or change your immigrant status.

  If you plan to stay longer, travel by a non-participating carrier or if you are a citizen of another country, you will need to obtain a business visitor visa (**B-1**) or a tourist visa (**B-2**).

- Are you planning to undertake temporary vacation employment?
  or
  Do you want to undertake a paid traineeship (internship) or academic exchange?
  or
  Do you want to work as an au pair for a year?
  You will probably be eligible for exchange visitor status which is a fairly quick and straightforward process. It involves approaching a sponsoring organisation, such as BUNAC, Camp America, CIEE and certain au pair agencies, which are authorised to issue you with Form IAP-66. This enables you to obtain a category **J-1 visa**. Chapter 3 deals with exchanges in detail.

- Are you involved in an approved cultural exchange programme?
  If you are at least 18 years old and providing practical training, employment and the sharing of the history, culture and traditions of your home country you should apply for a **Q** visa which enables you to take paid employment. Normally the

prospective employer or agent will submit the application to INS.

- Do you plan to work in the United States on a temporary basis but do not qualify for an exchange visitor visa?
  You will need an **H-2 temporary worker visa**. However, first of all your prospective employer will need to apply to the state department of labor for labor certification and demonstrate that he has not been able to recruit a US resident for the post. In the case of non-graduates this can take time as the employer may be required to advertise the post locally first.
  If the job requires a graduate, and you have a degree or equivalent, you might be eligible for an **H-1B visa**. A professional nurse qualifies for an **H-1A visa.**

- Are you planning to do a traineeship not covered by the exchange visitor visa?
  Your employer has to submit an application for an **H-3 industrial trainee visa** to the local office of the Immigration and Naturalization Service (INS).

- Are you planning to study in the United States and work during the vacation?
  If you enter the United States on an **F visa** you are not normally entitled to take a job in your first year, though on-campus employment is permitted provided it does not displace a United States resident. If you want to undertake employment off-campus (for instance, during the vacation), you will need to apply to the Immigration and Naturalization Service (INS) for permission.

- Do you have specialist knowledge to first degree level or beyond, equivalent experience, or a licence to practise and does the job require these qualifications?
  You are eligible to apply for a **H-1B visa** which will allow you to stay up to six years (with renewals). There is a quota of 115,000 H-1B visas annually, and once the quota is used up no further visas can be issued until the start of the next fiscal year (in October). In response to pressure from employers the quota could eventually be raised to as many as 200,000 visas.
  First your prospective employer has to submit an attestation to the United States Department of Labor documenting the

PLEASE TYPE OR PRINT YOUR ANSWERS IN THE SPACE PROVIDED BELOW EACH ITEM

	DO NOT WRITE IN THIS SPACE

1. SURNAMES OR FAMILY NAMES (Exactly as in Passport)

B-1/B-2 MAX   B-1 MAX   B-2 MAX

2. FIRST NAME AND MIDDLE NAME (Exactly as in Passport)

OTHER _____MAX
Visa Classification

3. OTHER NAMES (Maiden, Religious, Professional, Aliases)

MULT OR_____
Number Applications

4. DATE OF BIRTH (Day, Month, Year)   8. PASSPORT NUMBER

MONTHS_____
Validity

L.O. CHECKED _____

5. PLACE OF BIRTH
City   Province   Country   DATE PASSPORT ISSUED (Day, Month, Year)

ISSUED/REFUSED
ON _____BY_____

Under SEC. 214b 221g_____INA

6. NATIONALITY   7. SEX ☐ Male ☐ Female   DATE PASSPORT EXPIRES (Day, Month, Year)

Refusal Reviewed by _____

9. HOME ADDRESS (include apartment no., street, city, province and postal zone)

10. NAME AND STREET ADDRESS OF PRESENT EMPLOYER OR SCHOOL (Postal Box number unacceptable)

11. HOME TELEPHONE NO.   12. BUSINESS TELEPHONE NO.

13. COLOR OF HAIR   14. COLOR OF EYES   15. COMPLEXION

16. HEIGHT   17. MARKS OF IDENTIFICATION

24. PRESENT OCCUPATION (if retired state past occupation)

18. MARITAL STATUS
☐ Married ☐ Single ☐ Widowed ☐ Divorced ☐ Separated
If married give name and nationality of spouse

25. WHO WILL FURNISH FINANCIAL SUPPORT INCLUDING TICKETS?

19. NAMES AND RELATIONSHIPS OF PERSONS TRAVELING WITH YOU (NOTE: A separate application must be made for each visa traveler, regardless of age.)

26. AT WHAT ADDRESS WILL YOU STAY IN THE USA?

20. HAVE YOU EVER APPLIED FOR A U.S. VISA BEFORE, WHETHER IMMIGRANT OR NON-IMMIGRANT?
☐ No
☐ Yes   Where _____
When?_____Type of Visa?_____
☐ Visa was issued   ☐ Visa was refused

27. WHAT IS THE PURPOSE OF YOUR TRIP?

21. HAS YOUR U.S. VISA EVER BEEN CANCELED?
☐ No
☐ Yes   Where? _____
When? _____By Whom? _____

28. WHEN DO YOU INTEND TO ARRIVE IN THE USA?

22. Bearers of visitors visas may generally not work or study in the U.S.
DO YOU INTEND TO WORK IN THE U.S. ? ☐ No   ☐ Yes
If YES, explain

29. HOW LONG DO YOU PLAN TO STAY IN THE USA?

23. DO YOU INTEND TO STUDY IN THE U.S   ☐ No   ☐ Yes
If YES, write name and address of school as it appears on form I-20.

30. HAVE YOU EVER BEEN IN THE USA?
☐ No
☐ Yes   When?_____
For How long? _____

NONIMMIGRATION VISA APPLICATION   COMPLETE ALL QUESTIONS ON REVERSE OF FORM

OPTIONAL FORM 156 (Rev-6-93) PAGE1 50156-108
Department of State

NSN 7540-00-139-0053

Fig. 9. Non-immigrant visa application.

31. **(a)** HAVE YOU OR ANYONE ACTING FOR YOU EVER INDICATED TO A U.S. CONSULAR OR IMMIGRATION EMPLOYEE A DESIRE TO IMMIGRATE TO THE U.S.? **(b)** HAS ANYONE EVER FILED AN IMMIGRANT VISA PETITION ON YOUR BEHALF? **(c)** HAS LABOR CERTIFICATION FOR EMPLOYMENT IN THE U.S. EVER BEEN REQUESTED BY YOU OR ON YOUR BEHALF?

(a) ☐ No ☐ Yes **(b)** ☐ No ☐ Yes **(c)** ☐ No ☐ Yes

32. ARE ANY OF THE FOLLOWING IN THE U.S.? (If YES, circle appropriate relationship and indicate that person's status in the U.S., i.e. studying, working, U.S. permanent resident, U.S. citizen, etc.)

HUSBAND/WIFE_____ FIANCE/FIANCEE_____ BROTHER/SISTER_____
FATHER/MOTHER _____ SON/DAUGHTER _____

33. PLEASE LIST THE COUNTRIES WHERE YOU HAVE LIVED FOR MORE THAN 6 MONTHS DURING THE PAST 5 YEARS. BEGIN WITH YOUR PRESENT RESIDENCE

Countries	Cities	Approximate Dates

34. **IMPORTANT:** ALL APPLICANTS MUST READ AND CHECK THE APPROPRIATE BOX FOR EACH ITEM:

A visa may not be issued to persons who are within specific categories defined by law as inadmissible to the United States (except when a waiver is obtained in advance). Are any of the following applicable to you?

- Have you ever been afflicted with a communicable disease of public health significance, a dangerous physical or mental disorder, or been a drug abuser or addict? .... ☐ Yes ☐ No

- Have you ever been arrested or convicted for any offense or crime, even though subject of a pardon, amnesty, or other such legal action? .... ☐ Yes ☐ No

- Have you ever been a controlled substance (drug) trafficker, or a prostitute or procurer? .... ☐ Yes ☐ No

- Have you ever sought to obtain, or assist others to obtain a visa, entry into the U.S., or any U.S. immigration benefit by fraud or willful misrepresentation? .... ☐ Yes ☐ No

- Were you deported from the U.S.A. within the last 5 years? .... ☐ Yes ☐ No

- Do you seek to enter the United States to engage in export control violations, subversive or terrorist activities or any unlawful purpose? .... ☐ Yes ☐ No

- Are you a member or representative of a terrorist organization? .... ☐ Yes ☐ No

- Have you ever ordered, incited, assisted, or otherwise participated in the persecution of any person because of race, religion, national origin, or political opinion under the control, direct or indirect, of the Nazi Government of Germany, or of the government of any area occupied by, or allied with the Nazi Government of Germany, or have you ever participated in genocide? .... ☐ Yes ☐ No

A **YES** answer does not automatically signify ineligibility for a visa, but if you answered **YES** to any of the above or if you have any question in this regard, personal appearance at this office is recommended. If appearance is not possible at this time, attach a statement of facts in your case to this application.

35. I certify that I have read and understood all the questions set forth in this application and the answers I have furnished on this form are true and correct to the best of my knowledge and belief. I understand that any false or misleading statement may result in the permanent refusal of a visa or denial of entry into the United States. I understand that possession of a visa does not entitle the bearer to enter the United States of America upon arrival at port of entry if he or she is found inadmissible.

DATE OF APPLICATION _____ APPLICANT'S SIGNATURE_____

If this application has been prepared by a travel agency or another person on your behalf, the agent should indicate name and address of agency or person with appropriate signature of individual preparing the form.

SIGNATURE OF PERSON PREPARING FORM_____
if other than applicant)

DO NOT WRITE IN THIS SPACE

> STAPLE EMBASSY'S COPY
> OF APPLICATION
> FEE RECEIPT HERE

1½ inch square

PHOTO

Optional Form 156 (Rev. 6-93) PAGE 2
Department of State THIS FORM IS SUPPLIED GRATIS

Staple photo here

Fig. 9. – continued.

salary, working conditions and absence of a strike or lockout, and this process can take a little time. In the case of nurses and other professionals in great demand some of the red tape may be waived.

- Are you a person considered outstanding in your particular field (*eg* as a scientist, artist or entertainer)?
  You are eligible for an **O-1** for which labor certification is not required.

- Are you a recognised athlete, entertainer or artist going to compete or perform in the US?
  You should apply for a **P-1** visa.

- Are you being sent to the United States by your company?
  You should be eligible for an **L-1 Intra Company Transferee visa**, provided you have worked for the company for one year during the three years preceding your application for a visa. The stay is limited to seven years for executives and managers and five years for individuals with specialist knowledge. There are usually few, if any, problems in obtaining visas for high-ranking executives.

- Are you seeking temporary admission to the United States to manage substantial trade between the United States and your own country?
  If so, you are eligible to apply for an **E-1 Treaty Trader visa**. However, you must be an individual trader or an executive or be performing services that are essential to the company's operation in the United States. The company must also show that it is engaged in continuous trade of a substantial nature between the United States and a country with which the United States has a Treaty of Commerce and Navigation. (See also Chapter 9.)

- Are you seeking temporary admission in order to develop and/or direct a substantial investment in the United States?
  You are eligible to apply for **E-2 Treaty Investor** status based on the following criteria:
  —investment of substantial funds
  —the enterprise is up and running
  —the investment is more than marginal

—you are in a position to develop and direct the enterprise.

Employees of a Treaty Investor are also eligible if they are executives, highly trained staff or essential to the operation by reason of their qualifications.

For anyone in the E category the initial period of a stay is one year, but this can be extended almost indefinitely. (See also Chapter 9.)

Other types of visa

There are various other categories of non-immigrant visa, such as for diplomats and for the staff of international organisations, but in most cases the employer is responsible for getting the visa, and this procedure presents no real problems. A person working for a religious organisation, for instance, would just need a letter from the employing organisation certifying his credentials to support his application.

If you intend to study in the United States it is also necessary to obtain a visa, and the institution where you plan to study will provide you with the appropriate form (I-20A). However, bear in mind that a study visa does not automatically grant you the right to work on a part-time or seasonal basis. If you wish to do so, you should apply for permission to accept employment on Form I-538. This form also needs to be completed if you want to extend your stay or transfer to another academic institution.

Applying for a non-immigrant (temporary) visa

1. The first step

This will normally be to get in touch with the nearest United States consulate or INS office to find out which procedures you must go through.

- Exchange visitors must complete **Form OF-156** obtainable from the nearest US Consulate. J-1 applicants must also submit **Form IAP-66** and Q-1 applicants **Form I-129** prepared by the sponsoring organisation (*eg* CIEE, BUNAC).

- For H, L, O and P visas, your prospective employer or agent must first submit **Form I-129** (Petition for a Nonimmigrant Worker) to the INS.

- For E-1 and E-2 visas you may need to complete a supplemental form in addition to **Form OF-156** and submit it to the nearest US consular office.

2. Approval of the application
If the application is approved the INS issues the **Notice of Approval of Non-Immigrant Visa** petition **(Form I-797)** to the consulate that is dealing with your application.

Should you have not yet submitted Form **OF-156** (application form), this is the time to do so together with your passport, a passport sized photograph and any other documentation you are asked for.

If your application is turned down, you may appeal to the regional commissioner in control of the INS or the consulate to which you have applied.

3. Immigration procedures on arrival in the United States
On arrival at the port of entry make sure you look reasonably presentable. Immigration officers have been known to refuse entry to people whose appearance is bohemian or unkempt, as well as those with the wrong kind of visa. If entry is refused unjustly, you have no right of appeal, unless you are seeking asylum.

The length of time you are permitted to stay in the United States is entered on your **INS Arrival/Departure Record (Form I-94)**. This is an important document which will play a part in any subsequent immigration procedures and you should take good care of it.

4. Extension or change of status
Once in the United States you can apply for an adjustment of non-immigrant status or for an extension to your stay. With **Form I-539** this will normally be done through the regional office of the Immigration and Naturalization Service – the addresses of which are in Appendix G.

If your application is not granted you can ask for a review – a 'motion to reopen and reconsider' in officialese.

The main types of Non-Immigrant (Temporary) Visa
(with numerical limits where applicable)
B-1   Business visitor
B-2   Tourist

F-1	Student taking academic course
E-1	Treaty Trader
E-2	Treaty Investor
L-1	Intra-Company transferee
H-1A	Professional nurse
H-1B	Specialist occupation (115,000)
H-2A	Agricultural worker (temporary or seasonal)
H-2B	Other worker category
H-3	Trainee (not medical or academic) (50)
J-1	Exchange visitor
M-1	Full-time vocational student
O-1	Person with extraordinary ability in the sciences, arts, education, business and athletics
P-1	Recognised athlete, entertainer or artist (25,000)
Q	Cultural programme participant
R-1	Person in religious occupation

IMMIGRANT VISAS

The chances are that you will be able to skip the second half of this chapter. Immigrant visas are generally more difficult to obtain, and in any case the majority of people from the UK who go to work in the United States do so on non-immigrant (temporary) visas, which have already been dealt with.

However, if at some time in the future you decide to settle permanently in the United States you will need to apply for immigrant status and an Alien Registration Receipt Card (the 'green card'). (Later on you may decide to go the whole hog and become a naturalised United States citizen, but that will not be discussed in this book.)

Full immigrant status can be granted on the basis of:

- family relationships

- your trade or profession (employment based preferences)

- other criteria (*eg* the Diversity Immigrants Scheme).

Family relationships
If you have close relatives living in the United States this can generally facilitate matters. The level of family sponsored immigration is currently set at 480,000.

Immediate relatives

- Are you the spouse or child of a United States citizen?

- Are you the parents of United States citizens who are 21 years old or more?

   In both the above cases numerical limits do not apply and you should therefore experience no difficulty in getting an immigrant visa.

Family sponsored preferences
Here you have to stand in the queue to take up places that have not been taken up by immediate relatives. The annual numerical limit is determined by subtracting the previous year's immediate relative total from the specified world-wide level of family sponsored immigrants (*ie* 480,000). The following questions will help you work out whether you qualify:

- Are you the unmarried son or daughter of a United States citizen?
  You come under **FSP 1** for which there is a quota of 23,400.

- Are you the spouse or child of a permanent resident?
  You come under **FSP 2A** for which there is a minimum quota of 87,394.

- Are you the unmarried son or daughter of a permanent resident and over 21?
  You come under **FSP 2B** for which there is a minimum quota of 26,266.

- Are you the married son or daughter of a citizen?
  You come under **FSP 3** for which there is a quota of 23,400.

- Are you the brother or sister of a citizen aged 21 years or over?
  You come under **FSP 4** for which there is a quota of 65,000 a year.

Employment Based Preferences
If you have no family connections in the United States you may be able to enter the country on the strength of your

employment or entrepreneurial skills. Under the new Immigration Act the number of employment based immigrants has been increased substantially from 54,000 to 140,000. Work out whether you qualify by asking:

- Are you an individual with extraordinary ability in the arts, sciences, education, business or athletics?

- Are you a professor or researcher recognised internationally as outstanding in your field and with three years' experience, entering the United States for a tenured or tenure track position?

- Are you a multinational executive or manager employed with the sponsoring employer or affiliate for at least one year in the three years preceding your application for residence in or entry to the United States?

- Are you working in a religious occupation?

Anyone who fits the above criteria is regarded as a **Priority Worker** and falls into **Employment-Based Preference Category One** (E1) for which the annual quota is 40,000. No labour certification is required, but for people in the last three categories the prospective employer must provide a job offer and apply to the INS.

- Do you possess advanced qualifications in a professional field?

- Are you a person of exceptional ability in the arts, sciences or business?

If so, you could be considered for **Employment-Based Preference Category Two** (E2), **Members of the Professions**, for which the quota is 40,000 plus any unused visas from Category One. Labor certification is required **or** Schedule A designation (nurses and physiotherapists, *etc*) **or** you have to be in a shortage occupation defined in the Labor Market Information Pilot Program. This means that employers need to obtain a certificate from the Department of Labor demonstrating that there are not sufficient United States workers who are able, willing, qualified and available for the position in which they are seeking to recruit an alien.

- Are you a skilled worker with a minimum of two years' training or experience?
- Are you a professional with a Bachelor's degree?
- Do you have less than two years' training and experience?

You may fall into **Employment-Based Preference Category Three (E3)**, **Professionals, Skilled and Unskilled Workers**, for which the quota is 40,000 plus any unused visas from Categories One and Two. However, no more than 10,000 visas are available to Unskilled Workers. You are subject to the same restrictions (labor certification, *etc*) as Category Two.

- Are you employed in a professional capacity by a religious organisation?
- Are you an overseas employee of the US Government?
- Are you a retired employee of an international organisation?
- Are you a current or former employee of the United States Armed Forces?

You fall into **Employment-Based Preference Category Four – Special Immigrants** (E4), which also includes Panama Canal employees and others. The quota is 10,000.

- Are you an investor in a new commercial enterprise that will create full-time employment for at least ten persons who are not members of your immediate family?

Employment Based Preference Category Five (E5) sets aside 10,000 visas for foreign investors, of which not less than 3,000 are reserved for investors in rural or high unemployment areas. The minimum investment is normally $1 million but $500,000 in a targeted area of high employment or a rural area.

Other categories of immigrant visa

Diversity Immigrants
In October 1994 a new category of visa came into effect under which applicants from certain countries are selected in random order. Applicants are required to have either a high

school education or at least two years' work experience in an occupation that requires two years' training or experience. Only one petition may be submitted each year and there is a quota of 55,000 visas.

Currently people born in Ireland (Eire and Ulster) and various other countries are eligible to participate in the Diversity Immigrant Visa Lottery. However, if you were born elsewhere in the UK you are not eligible for this scheme unless your spouse or a parent was born in a qualifying country. (Natives of Canada, China, Mexico, the Philippines, Taiwan, Vietnam, *etc* are not eligible either.) To participate, send your name, date and place of birth to the DV Programme in Kentucky. See www.travel.state.gov for details.

Fiancé(e)s of American citizens
A person who plans to get married to a US citizen needs a K visa to enter the United States, and the US citizen needs to file a petition (Form I-129K) with the appropriate regional office of the INS. The marriage has to take place within 90 days of entry, and a petition then has to be lodged with the INS for adjustment of status to legal permanent residence.

Refugees and asylum seekers
Registration for classification as a refugee requires the completion of Form I-590, and for an asylum seeker Form I-589.

Immigrant visas: how to apply

1. The first step

- For a family sponsored immigrant visa your relative should normally file a petition (Form I-130) with the regional office of the Immigration and Naturalization Service (INS) in the United States.

- For an employment based immigrant visa, Form I-140 must be filed with the INS.

- Where labor certification is necessary the applicant must complete Department of Labor Form ETA-750B (Statement of Qualifications) and send it to the prospective employer who completes Form ETA-750A (Application for Certification) and forward it to the local office of the State Employment

Service. For Schedule A the employer submits a completed, uncertified Form ETA-750 and I-140 petition to the INS. For current information on the Labor Market Information Pilot Program you should contact INS.

- Special immigrants (E4) must file a Form I-360 petition with an INS office.

- Investors (E5) should file a Form I-360 petition with the INS.

- Information regarding the Diversity Immigrant Visa Lottery can be obtained from US Embassies and Consulates and the application has to be sent to the National Visa Centre, Portsmouth, New Hampshire.

2. Preliminary application
In most cases the consulate will send you two forms: the **Preliminary Questionnaire for Residence (OF-169)** and the **Biographic Data for Visa Purposes Form (OF-179)**.

3. Interview
Eventually you will be called for an interview and need to submit an **Application of Immigrant Visa and Alien Registration (Form 230)**. The consular officer will inform visa applicants of the documents required to support the application (*eg* passport, birth certificate, police certificates).

4. Medical examination
You will need to undergo a medical examination conducted by a doctor designated by the consular officer, and for which a fee is payable.

5. Visa fees
A fee is payable for the visa which is not refundable.

6. Issue of a visa
Immigrant visas are issued in the chronological order in which the petitions were filed, and you should not rely on being issued with a visa very promptly. If you fall into a category which is over-subscribed there may be a waiting period of some years. A visa is valid for four months from the date of issue.

7. Arrival in the United States
On arrival the immigration authorities will stamp a temporary 'green card' stamp in your passport. Your alien registration receipt card will be sent to you in the post several months later.

Applying for immigrant status in the United States

If you decide to apply for permanent residence once you are in the country, you will normally need to contact the INS office closest to your place of residence. Applications are usually sent by post, but some offices can deal with you in person.

Note that it is not a case of 'once an immigrant always an immigrant'. If you leave the United States you could lose your immigrant status. To avoid this, you should obtain a re-entry permit if you plan to stay outside the United States for more than a year. This involves completing **Form I-130 Application for Issuance or Extension of Permit to Re-enter the United States**. If you take out citizenship, this formality is no longer necessary.

PEOPLE NOT ELIGIBLE FOR VISAS

Certain visa applicants are considered statutorily ineligible. The main categories are:

- sufferers of communicable diseases (*eg* tuberculosis)
- people with a dangerous physical or mental disorder
- people who have committed serious criminal acts
- terrorists, subversives, members of a totalitarian party
- people likely to become public charges in the United States
- anyone who has used fraud or other illegal means to enter the United States
- anyone with convictions for domestic violence and stalking
- anyone without proof of vaccination against certain diseases (including measles, polio, hepatitis B).

It may however be possible to get a waiver of ineligibility, which would permit a visa to be issued.

If you have been an exchange visitor in the past you may have to live outside the United States for two years before you can apply for another visa, while physicians who plan to practise medicine must pass a qualifying exam before they can get a work visa.

You need to bear in mind that immigration policy and procedures are subject to modification and some of the information in this chapter may be rendered invalid by future legislation.

The monthly newspaper *Going USA* publishes details of the latest immigration rules and there are a number of websites on the Internet which answer frequently asked questions (FAQs) regarding immigration (*e.g.* www.uslawyer.com). The US Embassy Visa Office in London operates a general information line.

3

Vacation Jobs and Exchanges

This book draws a distinction between people who are interested in spending a substantial part of their careers or lives in the United States and those whose aims are short-term. Young people, for instance, want to experience the country at first hand and are prepared to undertake a variety of vacation jobs in order to finance their trip. Others, both young and old, are keen to go to America in order to develop skills in their particular fields.

While anyone wishing to undertake employment needs to obtain a visa, if you are participating in a recognised exchange programme this process is usually little more than a formality. There are a number of agencies based in Britain and Ireland which are authorised by the US Government to issue the necessary documentation (the IAP-66 form) for obtaining the **J-1 Exchange Visitor Visa**, though for some programmes different arrangements may be necessary. The most significant of these are listed towards the end of the chapter.

You must bear in mind that you may only work under the terms of the exchange programme and are not eligible to seek other employment while you are in the United States. Nor will you normally be allowed to take up employment there within two years of the exchange. On the brighter side you are automatically exempt from paying US social security and income tax, and the visa is issued free.

Unfortunately for most of these exchange programmes a limit is placed on numbers of participants and eligibility criteria are often restrictive. If you find that you do not qualify for any of the programmes mentioned in this chapter, you will have to look into the possibility of obtaining a different kind of visa, and this can take time. For an **H-2 Temporary Worker Visa** or an **H-3 Industrial Trainee Worker** the prospective employer has to obtain the necessary labor certification first, and you will be subject to social security tax.

THE OPPORTUNITIES AVAILABLE

Working in children's camps

A great many American youngsters – some seven million – spend their summer holidays in camps run by organisations such as the YMCA, the scouting organisations, religious or philanthropic agencies as well as by private individuals. There are over 12,000 camps in all; some are fully residential and in areas of natural beauty, while others are in effect day centres providing recreational facilities during the hours of daylight.

There are broadly two types of post available.

Camp counsellors

These are camp leaders or organisers who put together a programme of activities and encourage their protegees to participate. This can be challenging work, since American youngsters can be lively and precocious, and you may well be expected to demonstrate that you have experience of dealing with children.

As the ICCP brochure points out:

> 'Spending a summer as a camp counsellor in an American camp may not be for everyone; it can mean long days, hard work and little privacy and spare time. Working as a camp counsellor can also mean a lot of adjustments while living in a simple and often isolated setting. Participation in ICCP is not a low-cost ticket to "see the USA" or a money-making summer job.'

Ancillary staff

These are the backroom boys and girls – the cooks, the cleaners, the people who maintain the campsite. This can turn out to be tiring work involving long hours, especially at the beginning of the camp season when there can be much to prepare. Flexibility and a capacity for hard work are essential.

The *Parents' Guide to Accredited Camps* published by the American Camping Association lists around 2,500 summer camps and includes a section on the camp job market. See also BUNAC, Camp America, Camp Counsellors USA and YMCA entries in this chapter.

Other vacation jobs in the United States

There are a number of seasonal jobs available, especially during

For counsellors

0700	Wake up call
0745	Flag raising
0800–0830	Breakfast
0830–0900	Clean-up
0900–1200	Activities
1200–1230	Lunch
1230–1330	Rest hour
1330–1700	Activities
1730–1800	Dinner service
1800–1830	Dinner
1900–2100	Evening activities
2100–2200	Lights out
2400–0100	Curfew – All staff back in cabins

For ancillary staff

0630	Kitchen duties begin
0730–0800	Breakfast service and auxiliary duties begin
0800–0830	Office duties begin
0830–1200	General duties
1130–1230	Lunch service duties (1–2 hours off midday)
1230–1700	Resume duties
1800–2030	Resume auxiliary duties (Evenings usually off duty)
2400–0100	Curfew – All staff back in cabins

Fig. 10. A typical Camp America schedule.

the summer in resorts around the country. If you are still a student it may well be possible to enter the US on an Exchange Visitor visa provided you set about things the right way. The jobs do not have to be related to your course subjects or your intended profession, and may well pay better than jobs in summer camps.

The current *Summer Employment Directory of the United States* will give you an idea of the types of jobs available. Many of the jobs are seasonal ones in summer resorts, notably in the hotel and catering industry. The National Park Service has openings virtually everywhere, and in states such as Colorado guiding jobs are available.

There are also behind the scenes jobs with summer theatres, in amusement and theme parks and on ranches. In the bigger conurbations temporary office work may be available. If you are particularly enterprising and lucky, you may find more unusual employment. BUNAC reports that three participants on its programmes have worked as a masseuse, an oyster digger and a private detective!

There are two ways of setting about getting a job under the exchange visitor scheme:

- You arrange your job in advance and apply to an agency such as BUNAC or Camp America that can issue an **IAP-66** form. Many people do this through personal contacts in the United States or by applying to organisations mentioned in handbooks such as the *Summer Employment Directory of the United States.*

- You try your luck at getting a job on arrival. However, in order to qualify for an Exchange Visitor Visa, you may need to find a private sponsor in the United States who is acceptable to the authorities. You can either contact employers direct or try an employment agency specialising in temporary work. **The National Association of Temporary Services** is the trade body for these. (See also Chapter 6.)

Au pair work
It is now possible, if you are aged between 18 and 26, to spend a year working as an au pair on an Exchange Visitor Visa. For jobs in the United States you will normally be expected to have some experience of looking after children, and also to be a car driver and a non-smoker. You will be required to look after the children and undertake light household duties for around 40 hours a week. In return you receive:

- pocket money of around $125 a week

- your board and lodging

- your travel expenses

- up to six hours a week of classes in a subject of your choosing

- two weeks' paid vacation
- the chance to travel during the 13th month of your visa.

Since September 1997 au pairs hoping to work in the USA have been required to provide evidence that they have:

- had 200 hours' experience with infants
- undertaken 24 hours' training in child development
- undertaken eight hours' training in child safety
- taken a psychometric test.

A number of people enter America as tourists in order to take up positions as au pairs and nannies, but this is a risky business these days. For instance, you could be turned back by immigration officials at your port of entry; or your employers could be fined for illegally employing an alien.

An excellent reference book for would-be au pairs is *The Au Pair and Nanny's Guide* by Susan Griffith and Sharon Legg (Vacation Work).

Internships
An internship is not a prison sentence but an opportunity to gain work experience, normally in one's chosen career field. Students on vocationally based courses in Britain tend to get placements in the British Isles, but if you wish to gain international experience, why not try for a placement in the United States? Among the organisations that can facilitate such a move are **AIESEC** (business sector), **IAESTE** (technical and scientific placements), the **Mountbatten Internship Programme** and **CIEE** (most sectors). If your college or employer can arrange an internship for a US national in the UK on a reciprocal basis, so much the better.

While an internship may last up to 18 months, many are much shorter, and are confined to vacations. To get an idea of the range of internships available, you should browse through a copy of the directory *Internships* (Writers' Digest). A significant proportion of internships in the directory are open to non-Americans, provided they have the necessary documentation, including federal government jobs in Washington. Some offer salaries; others do not.

Professional exchanges

These exchanges should be seen not so much as a chance to earn money, but as a form of professional development. Sometimes these exchanges are organised by professional organisations. Teachers and academics need to look to either the Central Bureau or the Fulbright Commission.

Post-to-post exchanges are available for teachers and lecturers with at least five years' experience. Although posts can be exchanged for a term, it is more usual for people to spend a complete academic year abroad. Under the Central Bureau scheme, teachers from the UK are seconded on full salary and receive a grant to offset the increased cost of living and travel expenses.

The British American Chamber of Commerce also has schemes for the employees of its member organisations.

THE PRINCIPAL AGENCIES

AgriVenture/IAEA
YFC Centre
National Agricultural Centre
Stoneleigh Park
Kenilworth
Warwickshire CV8 2LG
Tel: (0124) 7669 6584
Fax: (0124) 7669 6684
E-mail: uk@agriventure.com
Website: www.agriventure.com

This exchange programme administered by the International Agricultural Exchange Association offers programmes to the USA and other countries for UK, Irish and some European passport holders for 5½ months to 9 months. Applicants must be aged 18–30, have no dependants, possess a full driving licence and have approximately one year's experience in their chosen category of agriculture/horticulture. Current costs start around £1,800.

AIESEC UK
2nd Floor
29–31 Cowper Street
London EC2A 4AT

Tel: (020) 7549 1800
Fax: (020) 7336 7971
E-mail: workabroad@uk.aiesec.org
Website: www.uk.aiesec.org

AIESEC, which stands for Association Internationale des Etudiants en Sciences Economiques et Commerciales, is the world's largest student-run educational charity. It specialises in providing paid placements lasting from 8 weeks to 78 weeks for graduates and undergraduates in countries other than the UK. Most placements are in business-related disciplines (accounting, marketing, economics, information systems, finance, etc) and engineering. AIESEC offers only a few placements in the USA. Information for applicants can be gained through the website.

Aupaircare
1565 Stratford Road
Hall Green
Birmingham B28 9JA
Tel: (0121) 733 6444
Fax: (0121) 733 6555
Website: www.100s-aupairs.co.uk

An agency which places au pairs with American families for a year. It provides orientation sessions on arrival and support from local co-ordinators. Age range: 18–26. Both males and females are eligible. Also recruits for Camp USA (www.campusa.com).

Au Pair in America
37 Queen's Gate
London SW7 5HR
Tel: (020) 7581 7311
Fax: (020) 7581 7355
E-mail: info@aupairamerica.co.uk
Website: www.aupairamerica.co.uk

This American Institute for Foreign Study (AIFS) programme places over 4,000 young people annually with American host families for 12 months. It arranges an orientation course in New York on arrival, accomodation and free air travel to one's destination, a weekly allowance of approximately $140 plus a study allowance. Support is provided by a network of community counsellors. A $400 deposit is payable which is refunded on the successful completion of the contract.

British Universities North America Club (BUNAC)
16 Bowling Green Lane
London EC1R 0BD
Tel: (020) 7251 3472
Fax: (020)7251 0215
E-mail: enquiries@bunac.org.uk
Website: www.bunac.org

This is a non-profit, non-political educational student club with branches on many university campuses throughout the UK. Since 1962 BUNAC has operated general student work exchange programmes and is recognised by the appropriate government agencies in Britain and the United States. It runs similar schemes in Canada, Australia, New Zealand, Ghana, Jamaica, South Africa and Argentina and works in conjunction with the travel bureau of:

The Union of Students in Ireland (USIT)
19 Aston Quay, Dublin 2
Tel: Dublin 778117

In a normal year it handles up to 10,000 placements.

For participants who register for its programmes BUNAC deals with the paperwork and arranges orientations, insurance and cheap flights to the United States. The programmes are:

Summer Camp USA
This involves working as a camp counsellor (leader) in a children's holiday camp for up to 4 months. To be eligible for this programme you need to be aged 18 to 35, but not necessarily a student. You need to have experience of working with children. Interviewing starts in November and carries on until early May, but it is a case of the early bird catching the worm: the sooner you apply, the better your chance of getting a placement.

Kitchen and Maintenance Programme (KAMP)
This programme also involves working at children's summer camps for up to 4 months in an ancillary capacity doing a variety of jobs, such as cooking, doing the laundry, cleaning, site mainte-nance and driving. You need to be a full-time student and a

member of BUNAC, and are expected to attend an orientation session during the Easter vacation.

Work America
This is a more flexible programme which allows you to take almost any job anywhere in the USA for the summer (June to October) enabling you to sample the real America. You must be a full-time student studying for a degree or HND. Gap Year students are also eligible.

Many people find their jobs through the *Work America Job Directory* obtainable from BUNAC, but there is no reason why you should not make your own employment arrangements. If you can find a private sponsor, you will be able to go to the United States on spec.

OPT USA
This is an internship programme enabling people to do a course-related or career-related placement with an American host organisation in conjunction with the American YMCA's Internal Program Service.

Camp America
37A Queen's Gate
London SW7 5HR
Tel: (020) 7581 7373
Fax: (020) 7581 7377
E-mail: brochure@campamerica.co.uk

Camp America (part of AIFS) organises two programmes:

Camp America Camp Counsellor Programme
This programme has been in operation since 1969 and places around 7,000 people a year in over 1,000 camps. It is open to suitable people aged between 18 and 35. The commitment is for 9 to 10 weeks and participants must be able to start in June.

Camp America Campower Programme
This is for younger, less experienced people who do not qualify for counsellor positions, though in this case participants have to be full-time students. Many of the jobs are kitchen jobs, but people with secretarial and technical skills are also needed as are janitors, groundsmen and nightwatchmen.

Camp Counselors USA
6 Richmond Hill
Richmond on Thames
Surrey TW10 9QX
Tel: (020) 8332 2952
E-mail: 100744.1754@compuserve.com
Website: www.campcounselors.com

27 Woodside Gardens
Musselburgh
Edinburgh EH21 7LJ
Tel: (0131) 665 5843
Website: www.campcounselors.com

The organisation has two programmes:

Summer Camp Work
This programme operates along similar lines to BUNACAMP and Camp America and is for people between the ages of 18 and 30 (including teachers and nurses). Applications are accepted between October and March for the coming summer. The organisation arranges orientations in Britain and in New York and provides free insurance and air fares. The minimum commitment is for nine weeks. International headquarters is at 698 Emerson Street, Palo Alto, CA94301.

Work Experience USA
An opportunity for full-time students aged 19–28 to gain work experience for up to 4 months between June and September in a job tailored to individual needs. The package includes a job offer, return air fare, insurance, 2 days' orientation and accommodation on arrival.

Central Bureau for International Education and Training
The British Council
10 Spring Gardens
London SW1A 2BN
Tel: (020) 7389 4004
Fax: (020) 7389 4426
E-mail: centralbureau@britishcouncil.org
Website: www.centralbureau.org.uk

3 Bruntsfield Crescent
Edinburgh EH10 4HD
Tel: (0131) 447 8024

16 Malone Road
Belfast BT9 5BN
Tel: (02890) 664418

The Bureau organises post to post exchanges for teachers and lecturers. More than a hundred British educators exchange their jobs with American partners each year. The American side of the exchange is handled by the United States Information Agency (USIA).

Council on International Educational Exchange (CIEE)
52 Poland Street London W1V 4JQ
Tel: (020) 7478 2020 and 2000
Fax: (020) 7734 7322
Website: www.councilexchanges.org.uk
Council Exchanges, as it is usually known, is the UK affiliate of a private, non-profit making organisation in the United States which promotes educational exchanges between countries. It offers two work-related programmes:

Internship Programme
Under this scheme students and recent graduates can undertake a period of course-related practical training in the USA lasting up to 18 months. Participants are responsible for finding their own work placements, but Council Exchanges handles all the paperwork, offers insurance cover and provides various support services in the USA including an orientation day.

Work and Travel USA
This scheme is open to students in full-time higher education in the UK, including Gap Year students with an unconditional offer. Participants are able to work during the summer anywhere in the USA, and do not need to arrange their job in advance.

The Fulbright Commission
Fulbright House
62 Doughty Street
London WC1N 2LS

Tel: (020) 7404 6994
Fax: (020) 7404 6874
E-mail: education@fulbright.co.uk
Website: www.fulbright.co.uk

The Commission promotes educational exchange between the United Kingdom and the United States through its US Educational Advisory Service and the US-UK Fulbright Awards Programme which provides scholarships for postgraduate study and fellowships and scholarships for lecturing or research in the USA.

The US Educational Advisory Service has a reference library which holds several directories of internships in the USA, copies of the *Chronicle of Higher Education* which lists positions available at US colleges and universities, and information on US education institutions at all levels. Its educational advisers can answer queries regarding any aspect of studying in the USA.

International Association for the Exchange of Students for Technical Experience (IAESTE)
Central Bureau
The British Council
10 Spring Gardens
London SW1A 2BN
Tel: (020) 7389 4774
Fax: (020) 7389 4426
Website: www.iaeste.org.uk

Founded at Imperial College London in 1948 this is a world-wide organisation represented in over 50 countries. It offers short-term course-related work experience in three broad categories: scientific (e.g. in a company laboratory or research institute), professional (work designed to improve your professional capabilities) and manual (with little technical content but offering an insight into foreign work patterns and conditions).

The scheme is open to full-time students between 19 and 30 who must normally be nominated by an educational institution or sponsored by a company in the UK. IAESTE welcomes reciprocal placements for incoming foreign trainees. Placements in the United States tend to be of several months' duration. The organisation works closely with AIPT in the US.

Mountbatten Internship Programme
13 Moffats Lane
Brookman's Park
Hatfield
Herts AL6 7RX
Tel: (01707) 661870
Fax: (01707) 660083

This is a personal development programme started in 1984 which offers work experience in New York City to young people aged 19 upwards (including graduates) with qualifications in bookkeeping, secretarial studies, management and business studies. A year's internship can lead to an award of the Certificate in International Business (Oxford University Local Examinations Syndicate). A monthly living allowance is payable.

The National Centre for Work Experience
344–354 Grays Inn Road
London WC1X 8BP
Tel: (020) 7833 5520
Fax: (020) 7833 9710
E-mail: ncwe@ncwe.com
Website: www.ncwe.com

US/UK Career Development Programme
This scheme (formerly administered by CIEE) enables young professionals aged 18 and over to undertake up to 18 months' career-related employment in the USA. Normally relevant qualifications and at least one year's full-time work experience are required, but hospitality and tourism students in higher or further education are also eligible.

Participants may arrange their own placements through the Centre's on-line matching service: www.pinpointtraining.org. The programme is administered in the US by the Association for International Practical Training which acts as one's legal sponsor and provides on-going support on arrival. AIPT is based at Park View Building, Suite 320, 10400 Little Patuxent Parkway, Columbia, MD 21044. Tel: (001) 301 997 2200.

The Richmond Fellowship International
16 Europoint
5–11 Lavington Street

London SE1 0NZ
Tel: (020) 7945 6187
Fax: (020) 7945 6190
E-mail: rif.uk@virgin.net

This voluntary organisation offers people aged 23 and over with qualifications or experience in social work, nursing and teaching to work with the mentally ill, abused children and drug addicts in Florida. Candidates also need a current driving licence.

Winant-Clayton Volunteer Association
Davenant Centre
179 Whitechapel Road
London E1 1DU
Tel: (020) 7375 0547

The Association offers opportunities for up to 20 volunteers a year to undertake work on various community projects in New York City or on the East Coast for around two months. The projects include residential and day centres for the physically and mentally handicapped psychiatric rehabilitation centres, play schemes for inner city children and luncheon clubs for the elderly.

Volunteers receive board, lodging and pocket money during their placement, and are normally expected to pay the air fare. However, a few bursaries are available. Applications need to be submitted by early January.

John Winant, incidentally, was the US Ambassador to Britain during the Second World War who brought groups of Americans over to Britain to carry out voluntary social work in association with Revd 'Tubby' Clayton, the founder of Toc H.

YMCA International Camp Counsellor Programme (ICCP)
71 W 23rd Street
Suite 1904
New York
NY 10010
Tel: (001) 212 727 8800 ext 122
Fax: (001) 212 727 8814
Website: www.ymca.net

This is a programme which recruits staff for more than 400 children's summer camps, organised not only by the YMCA itself, but also by scouting organisations and individuals. Some camps cater for disadvantaged and handicapped people or concentrate on teaching special skills.

The age range for applicants is between 20 and 30, though camp staff usually range in age from 18–23. Camps vary in size and some may have as many as 100 staff working in different capacities. The main need is for:

General counsellors who live with and supervise groups of 6–10 campers, care for camper health and safety, organise camp activities and assist in specific programme areas.

Skill specialists who organise and teach specific activities, such as swimming, sports or crafts.

YMAK participants – ancillary staff involved in cooking, office work and general maintenance.

In some camps staff may perform a number of different roles.

A placement lasts 9–10 weeks, and you will be provided with air fares, medical insurance, pocket money and support services.

OTHER ORGANISATIONS:

ATD Fourth World
48 Addington Square
London SE5 7LB
Tel: (020) 7703 3231
Fax: (020) 7252 4276
Website: www.ukonline.co.uk/atd.uk/

British Trust for Conservation Volunteers
36 St Mary's Street
Wallingford
Oxon OX10 0EU
Tel: (01491) 839766
Fax: (01491) 839646
Website: www.btcv.org.uk

International Voluntary Service
Old Hall
East Bergholt
Colchester
Essex CO7 6TQ
Tel: (01206) 298215

Fax: (01206) 299043
Website: www.ivsgbsouth.demon.co.uk

These organisations organise placements of up to one month's duration often at international workcamps in the United States.

FURTHER READING

Summer Employment Directory of the United States (Writer's Digest Books).

Internships (Writer's Digest Books). *Volunteer Work* (Central Bureau).

Directory of International Internships (Office of Overseas Study, Michigan State University, East Lansing, MI 48824).

Advisory List of International Travel & Exchange Programs (Council on Standards for International Education Travel, 1906 Association Drive, Reston, VA 22091).

Peterson's Summer Jobs USA (Peterson's Guides, Princeton, NJ).

4

Arranging a Job Before You Leave

Much of the rest of this book concentrates on the needs of people who are planning to work in the United States for a period of years rather than months. Chapter 6 will be of more interest to people who are already in possession of a work permit, stand a good chance of getting one or qualify for permanent residence because of close family ties. If you do not fall into this category, your search starts here.

As stressed before in this book, unless you are a full-time student, you normally need an offer of employment before you can obtain a visa entitling you to work in the United States. Unfortunately, even if you are offered a position you cannot always count on a visa being forthcoming. You stand a good chance, however, if you possess good qualifications and you have skills that are in short supply in the locality of the employer.

This, though, is putting the cart before the horse. Finding a job is the initial step, so first take a look at ways and means of accomplishing it.

REPLYING TO ADVERTISEMENTS

If you see a job advertised, it is reasonable to assume that there is a genuine vacancy to be filled. Sometimes the advertiser is the employer himself; but many employers use intermediaries (recruitment consultants and employment agencies) to find their staff.

Advertisements in British or Irish publications

If the advertisement appears in a publication or on a website in a country outside the United States it means that the job is open to non-Americans and that the employer is reasonably confident that he can obtain the necessary authorisation for the issue of a work permit.

Many job advertisements tend to be placed not by the companies or organisations themselves but by intermediaries working on their behalf based in the UK or Ireland. These intermediaries will be familiar with British procedures and terminology, and you will normally need to send your application with a British style CV to an address in the British Isles. No fee should be charged.

If you have to apply to an address in the United States, you should not assume that the recipient is completely *au fait* with British qualifications and working practice. If you are a member of a professional association, write out your designation in full and explain what it means; the same goes for qualifications such as A-Level and City and Guilds. You may also need to draft an American style résumé in preference to a British style CV in order to comply with local labour laws. This might involve omitting reference to your age or date of birth, your religion or your sex. (See Appendix E.)

Virtually every national daily or Sunday newspaper carries advertisements for jobs in America from time to time. You should also peruse professional journals for vacancies, such as *Computer Weekly* in the case of IT experts, and *Nursing Times* for nurses.

Advertisements in international job papers

The overwhelming number of advertisements in British newspapers and journals tend to be for posts within the UK (or Eire, in the case of Irish publications), but there are a number of publications that concentrate on the would-be expatriate.

Publications which may include jobs in the United States are: *Overseas Jobs Express, Nexus, Going USA* and *Home and Away*. Their addresses are listed in Appendix D. There are also job listings which reproduce advertisements from other periodicals, but these may not be completely up to date. Do not overlook websites specialising in overseas jobs, such as www.overseas.jobs.com.

Advertisements in the American press

While some American employers may welcome applications from overseas, the majority will be looking for someone who is already resident in the country. Working on the principle that a bird in the hand is always worth two in a bush, employers will prefer to hire someone who is on the spot, not several thousand miles away.

Unless the employer is recruiting for a senior or highly specialised post, or has a number of vacancies, it will probably not be worth the time, effort and cost to set up an interview abroad and go through a lot of red tape with the Immigration and

Naturalization Service (INS). Only if the organisation cannot find the candidates it wants will its personnel department look further afield.

This is not to say that there is no point at all in looking through the adverts in US journals and magazines or on the Internet. These may not lead you to a specific position, but they will give you an idea of the opportunities available and the salary you could expect. Such information will come in extremely useful if you decide to try speculative approaches to find a job. But on the whole you would need to be very lucky to land a position this way.

The disadvantages

Advertisements, of course, have one major disadvantage: they often elicit a large number of applicants, the majority of whom never reach the shortlist.

In order to avoid being screened out in the early stages of the sifting process, you need to make a special effort and tailor your application to fit the specifications laid down in the advertisement, either by adapting your CV accordingly or by writing a carefully worded letter. Appendix E should give you a few ideas.

There is a school of thought that advises would-be candidates to get ahead of the competition. This means adopting a speculative approach to finding a job, seeking out vacancies before they are advertised. How does one do it?

SPECULATIVE APPLICATIONS

Recruitment consultants in the UK

The role of intermediaries in the recruitment process has already been mentioned. Firms in the United States, like those in the UK, very often delegate their recruitment. So rather than send off applications to individual firms it is more sensible to contact an agency which recruits for positions in your field for a range of companies.

You need, however, to do your homework carefully before putting pen to paper. The majority of recruitment consultants recruit only for positions within the British Isles; and those that do undertake international recruitment are more likely to recruit for the Middle East, Europe or the Far East. Even if you track down an agency that recruits for the United States, it may not offer jobs in your particular field. Many international consultancies specialise in particular job sectors.

Don't overlook the services of your local Job Centre which can do a search for you of international vacancies currently held on the International Placing Agency's database.

How do you find out who does what?
You get an idea by referring to the Recruitment and Employment Confederation website, The Expat Network Contact Directory, or *The Executive Grapevine's* directories. Alternatively, you can turn to Appendix B in this book which lists a select group of consultancies and agencies that recruit for the United States to a greater or lesser extent. The list is by no means complete but includes organisations that supplied details of their current needs when this book was in progress.

Alas, circumstances change and no reference book can claim to be completely up-to-date. Employment markets tend to be volatile and recruitment requirements can change over a period of just a few months. The best plan is to peruse the advertisement columns of newspapers, international job lists and trade journals, and take note of the agencies recruiting for the United States which seem to handle your type of job. Send them your CV with a covering letter and ask them to put your details on file.

Do not necessarily expect an acknowledgement of your speculative letter; some organisations are inundated with speculative applications – often from people who have not done their homework properly and have applied to a firm that is not remotely interested in their skills. If you have selected the agency with care, you are more likely to get noticed.

Recruitment consultants in the United States
The chances of landing an appointment through a speculative approach to a recruitment consultant in the United States from abroad are slim, unless you are an exceptionally well-qualified person with much sought after expertise. As Intercristo, the Christian Placement Agency, explains:

'. . . Communication between the potential employer and applicant is time-consuming and cumbersome. This places the applicant at a severe disadvantage compared to candidates who are more accessible to potential employers.'

On the other hand, if you happen to be visiting America there is no harm in knocking on the doors of recruitment agencies to find out what kinds of jobs are on offer and leaving your particulars. Remember, though, that no job can be yours unless you can secure the required work visa. Note that you may have to pay a fee if the agency succeeds in placing you; more of this in Chapter 6.

Since a number of US consultancies have branches in the UK, it may be more sensible to contact these first of all to find out if there is any point in your applying to their office in, say, New York or San Francisco. If you have skills that are much in demand, the branch over here might be prepared to forward your details to their transatlantic colleagues.

Personal contacts

Have you a cousin three times removed living in Wyoming? Does your brother-in-law have connections with a firm in Omaha? Is your uncle on the board of a British plc with a subsidiary in Des Moines? Does a pal of yours know a chap who runs an engineering outfit in San Diego?

If you do not know the answers, perhaps it is time to remedy the situation by asking around. Networking, or what used to be called 'the old boy network', continues to flourish today. I would be surprised if at least half the people in the UK and Ireland did not know someone who lives in the United States, possibly a relative. If you have no acquaintances across the Atlantic, then you could try contacting the relevant user group on the Internet.

Do not expect your American contacts (once you have tracked them down) to find you a job from out of the blue. However, they might be able to give you an idea of the lie of the land, and suggest employers in their immediate area that might be worth trying. They might also be willing to keep an eye open for job openings in your particular field.

Transfer or secondment

If you are in employment, have you explored the possibility of going to the United States with your firm or organisation? Some multi-nationals like to second key staff to overseas affiliates, while smaller organisations may exchange employees for short periods with companies abroad.

If you make it known that you are keen to work in the United

States, you may well find that opportunities do arise. Your very keenness could be a point in your favour. You may find it surprising, but some key employees do not relish the prospect of a posting abroad, particularly if they have family commitments, and your employer may prefer to send someone who is enthusiastic and committed rather than a reluctant expatriate who needs various inducements before he will budge.

If you are sent abroad by your employer you will enjoy the best of all worlds including a generous relocation allowance, continuity of employment and possibly an enhanced salary.

Companies in the UK
There are numerous companies and organisations which function on both sides of the Atlantic, and if you join one of these and prove your worth, there is a possibility that you might be posted to the United States in the course of time.

Two categories of company are worth considering:

- British, Irish or other European companies with business interests in the United States

- American companies with subsidiaries in UK and Ireland.

The first category is more likely to offer you the opportunity of a US posting, particularly if you have prior experience or special knowledge of the country. Careful research will pay dividends; and in order to be in the right place at the right time you should watch out for companies that are aiming to expand their operations in the United States. Some British hotel companies, for instance, have acquired US hotel chains in recent years. A good business reference library will have information on the leading firms in both the UK and the United States. You need to go and search out books such as the *Directory of US Subsidiaries of British Companies, Dun and Bradstreet's Million Dollar Directory, Dun and Bradstreet's Regional Business Directory* and *Thomas Register of American Manufacturers*. The business, trade and professional press is also required reading. (See Bibliography.)

Firms in the United States
Speculative applications from afar are unlikely to yield positive results; you may not even receive an acknowledgement. There

are, of course, exceptions. If you are an acknowledged expert in your particular field or have skills that are in short supply, you could be successful in landing a position. However, do not count on it.

If you are planning a trip to America, the position is different. You can send off a copy of your résumé with a covering letter that mentions you will be passing through the city where the employer is based on such-and-such a date, and you would welcome an opportunity to visit him. While there is no guarantee that this approach will open doors, you may arouse the recipient's curiosity sufficiently to gain an invitation to an interview.

This approach could prove expensive, since your fare across the Atlantic is unlikely to be reimbursed by the people you see. However, if you target a number of companies and organisations effectively, your chances of gaining a hearing – and ultimately a position – will be enhanced.

Many leading companies are now on the Internet and have their own websites which describe their activities and outline their recruitment needs. For further details see Appendix I.

A useful reference book for people planning direct applications is Dun & Bradstreet's *Employment Opportunities Directory (The Career Guide)* which lists 5,000 employers and their employment needs. Unhappily, few, if any, reference libraries in this country seem to have it on their shelves and the tome is extremely expensive. There are plenty of reference books (see Bibliography) which list American companies, and you would be able to consult some of them in a large public reference library, such as:

The City Business Library
1 Brewers Hall Garden
London Wall
London EC2V 5BY.
Tel: (020) 7638 8215.

You could try ordering a specific book at your local public library through the Interlibrary Loans System.

'Situation wanted' advertisements

Invididuals sometimes advertise their availability in British publications that circulate in the United States (*eg The Economist*), but you could also try American newspapers and journals or the Internet. Some of the main newspapers are listed in Appendix G and a few, but by no means all, have UK agents who can handle your advertisement.

It is difficult to judge how successful self-advertising really is. You are more likely to achieve success if you include an e-mail address or fax number for replies, mention that you will be visiting America in the near future and indicate that you either have, or are able to obtain, the necessary permits.

Miscellaneous organisations

Migration organisations, such as Four Corners Emigration and Workpermit.com, maybe able to offer advice and assistance to people planning to work in the United States, including:

- lists of companies employing your particular trade or pro-fession together with all employment bureaux and consultants in any area of your choice

- help in assessing employability

- advice on all your approaches to personnel officers and employers

- interviews in the UK on behalf of US companies

- CV preparation.

Expat Network operates Joblink which forwards its members' CVs to overseas employers.

Publications such as *Going USA, Overseas Jobs Express* and *Nexus* publish articles on finding work and may suggest contacts.

WHAT ARE THE POTENTIAL PROBLEMS?

One problem you encounter when applying for a job in the United States from another country is that the process takes time even if you use e-mail. In most cases your details have to be sent across the Atlantic, and before the employer can take you on he has to obtain permission to employ you (labor certification) from the authorities. Once this comes through your nearest US consulate has to be informed, and even then some time may elapse before you are granted the appropriate visa. You may, for instance, have to be interviewed by the US consul or undergo a medical, so it could take months before you get the go-ahead. On the other hand, all the formalities might be completed in a matter of weeks.

Another major problem with applying for a job from the UK is that more often than not you do not get a chance to visit your prospective employer and see the working environment for yourself at first hand. Normally only senior (and well-paid) executives of some years' standing with their company are given the chance to see their workplace in advance. If you do not like what you see on arrival, it is too late to do anything about it.

This is less of a problem for people who already know the United States as a result of having visited the country or, better still, lived there. If you have not, you need to be given a thorough briefing before you commit yourself irrevocably. Do not rely on Hollywood films to give you sufficient insight into everyday American life.

Most organisations brief their staff as a matter of course or enlist the help of outside agencies, such as the Centre for International Briefing at Farnham Castle. (Others are listed in Appendix F.) If no orientation is mentioned you could contact organisations such as Corona International, which can put you in touch with people who have returned from the US, or ECA International which produces a self-assessment package *Planning to work abroad.*

Even with the best of briefings you have to take certain things on trust and rely on the impressions of other people whose tastes and inclinations may diverge quite markedly from your own. What may seem like the next best thing to a holiday for some people can turn out to be a damp squib for others.

In order to avoid disappointment, you must make every effort to understand what you are letting yourself in for. Talk to people who have lived and worked in the US; make sure that you understand the differences in working practice and life style that you will encounter. Read up about the place where you will be staying.

US Tourism Information may have useful free information on the place you are making for, albeit with something of a tourist gloss, and the US Information Service (at the US Embassy) can provide an information pack and answer specific questions on the US. *The Economist Business Travel Guide: US* is worth consulting.

The monthly journal *Going USA* contains useful reports on

living in the US. Expat Network publishes *Location Reports* and ECA *Country Profiles for Expatriates.*

YOUR CONTRACT

Before you leave the country you should be asked to sign a contract. If you are being sent abroad by your company a contract may not be deemed necessary, but you should have a memorandum which details your responsibilities and entitlements.

A contract is just as much for your benefit as that of your employer, and you should read it through carefully and query matters which are unclear. It is also sensible to ask a solicitor or an expatriate service organisation to read it through and offer their comments.

These are some of the details you need to look out for:

- the name and address of your employer
- your job title and responsibilities
- staff member you are answerable to
- the location of your employment
- your net salary and dates of payment
- the commencement date and duration of your employment
- working hours.

Some items may need to be gone into in greater detail, such as:

- Paid leave. Don't take this for granted, particularly if you are employed on contract terms. In any case, leave entitlements in the US are far from generous – often only one or two weeks per year.
- Sick leave. Often there is no open-ended entitlement but a fixed number of days when sickness pay can be claimed. (See Chapter 7.)
- Medical insurance. Make sure this is provided and will be adequate for your needs. (See also Chapters 5 and 7.)
- Accommodation. Contract workers may get a daily allowance

to cover accommodation costs, which will be similar to those enjoyed by American employees working outside their home states. Sometimes accommodation is provided, particularly a hotel on arrival.

- Hardship allowance. This may be payable if you take up employment in Alaska.

- Married allowance. Normally contract employees would not be eligible for extra allowances if accompanied by their spouse and family. If you are being transferred to the United States by your employer such a perk is more likely to be forthcoming.

- Pension. Contract posts, particularly short-term ones, do not always have a pension provision. Some employers, however, may offer a 401K transferable pension scheme. (See also Chapter 5.)

- Termination bonus. This is not usually offered with US postings.

- Fares to and from your destination. With company transfers it is normal for fares to be paid for the employee and his dependants. If you are a contract employee, the chances are that only your fare will be paid. Only in very exceptional circumstances should you pay your own fare.

- Baggage allowance. Transferees are likely to have more generous entitlements than a contract employee.

- Premature termination of contract. There should be a clause that covers procedures in such an eventuality.

- Restrictions. There may be restrictions on your working for other organisations.

No contract will be able to deal with every eventuality, and you need to familiarise yourself with working conditions in the US before you leave. (See Chapter 7.) Adequate preparation is, of course, vital and you should read the following chapter with care.

5

Preparations Before Departure

Any trip abroad, even just a week's holiday, involves a certain amount of preparation. If you are planning to be away for an extended period – whether months, years or forever – preparing for the move needs to be done thoroughly and systematically.

CHECKLIST

This chapter is a checklist of things that you need to think about. Not all the items will be of concern to you – particularly if your stay will be a short one or you are single and unencumbered – but the longer you are planning to stay in the United States the more matters there will be to attend to. I therefore suggest you look through the list and note down what is of importance to you.

The topics covered in this chapter in alphabetical order are:

- arrival arrangements
- banking
- car
- credit and charge cards
- customs and prohibited articles
- doctor and dentist
- driving licence
- educational arrangements (for your children)
- financial advice
- your flat or house
- health
- insurance
- investments

- journals
- kin
- library
- luggage and personal effects
- moving
- National Insurance
- orientation
- passports
- pension
- pets
- professional advisers
- qualification certificates
- redirection of mail
- rental agreements
- subscriptions
- tax
- travel
- utilities – electricity, gas, telephone, water
- visas
- voting rights.

Arrival arrangements

It is sensible to inform your prospective employer when you plan to arrive. The chances are you will be travelling to the United States by air, in which case you should state the flight number in addition to the estimated arrival time. Long haul flights are some-times delayed.

Find out what arrangements have been made for meeting you and accommodating you on arrival; and make sure you have one or two contact telephone numbers in case arrangements go awry.

Banking

You need to inform your UK bank of your imminent change of address and discuss arrangements for the administration of your account during your absence (*eg* how you plan to top up your account to service regular payments). Since the bank may not have a branch at your destination (some British and Irish banks have affiliates or representatives in the United States), you could also ask if it can recommend a bank in the locality and provide a letter of introduction. This will facilitate opening a bank account in the United States in case your employer has no procedures to help you in this respect.

Even if you are planning to leave the UK for good, it is sensible to keep your account open and topped up – for the time being at least – as there may be occasions in the future when it is more convenient to make or receive payments in sterling.

You will also need to arrange for money to tide you over the first month or so in the United States. This involves purchasing foreign exchange in the form of dollars and dollar travellers cheques (other denominations are not readily accepted) and perhaps arranging for a bank transfer. Note that you will also be able to withdraw cash with a credit or charge card.

Car

In many parts of the United States public transport is fairly rudimentary, and you will find that some means of private transport is essential. There is, however, little point in shipping your car to the country – unless it happens to be a very distinguished one – since automobiles are much cheaper over there. In any case, it will probably not meet US safety, bumper and emission standards, which are very tough; modification can work out prohibitively expensive.

For more information on emission standards contact:

The US Environmental Protection Agency
Manufacturer Operations Division (EN-340F)
Investigation/Imports Section
401 M Street SW
Washington DC 20460
USA
Website: www.epa.gov

Note that in order to import a car you will need prior written approval from the EPA or a manufacturer's label affixed to the vehicle stating it meets all US emission requirements.

For information on bumper and safety requirements you should get in touch with:

The US Department of Transportation
National Highway Traffic Safety Administration
Director of the Office of Vehicle Safety Compliance (NEF-32)
400 Seventh Street SW
Washington DC 20590
USA
Website: www.nhtsa.dot.gov

As a non-resident you may import a vehicle duty-free into the United States, but duty is payable if the car is sold within a year of importation. Employees of foreign governments and international organisations on assignment in the United States may be exempt from the compliance regulations; and the same is true for non-residents who import the car for one year and then export it.

If you are going to America for a number of years it will make sense to sell your vehicle and rely on car hire for visits to the UK. Do not forget to inform the Driver and Vehicle Licensing Agency and your insurance company when the car is sold and claim a refund on your insurance if appropriate.

If your stay in the United States is for a shortish period, you could put your vehicle in storage or entrust it to a friend or relation. Whatever you do, make sure you inform your insurance company of your plans.

The US Customs Service publishes a useful leaflet entitled *Importing A Car* which is obtainable either from:

The US Customs Service
Department of the Treasury
Washington DC 20229
USA
Website: www.customs.ustreas.gov

or the Customs Attaché of the US Embassy.

Credit and charge cards
Before you leave, you ought to inform your card company of your new address for statements. Credit and charge cards are

used widely in America, and are a most convenient method of payment and obtaining cash. If you need to hire a car, for instance, the deposit is often waived if you produce a credit or charge card.

In view of the widespread use of these cards in the United States, you might find yourself at a disadvantage if you do not own one. It is therefore worth looking into the possibility of obtaining either type of card, ideally by approaching a bank or building society that does not charge for their issue.

If your credit limit is fairly low, this might be a good time to have it raised, to enable you to cope with the extra expenses you will incur in settling in. Note that you will continue to be billed in sterling.

Ultimately you may well decide to open a credit card account in the United States which will bill you in dollars. However, as in the UK, it may take a little time before the account is operational.

Customs and prohibited articles

You will normally be allowed to import personal and household effects free of duty. One litre of alcohol may be brought in duty free provided this does not conflict with the laws of the state in which you arrive. Two hundred cigarettes or the equivalent can also be imported free of duty. The leaflet *US Customs Hints*, available from the Customs Attaché of the US Embassy, offers further information.

Restrictions are imposed on the import of firearms, narcotics and certain foodstuffs, notably meat. For further information on the import of foodstuffs contact:

The Import/Export and Emergency Planning Staff
US Department of Agriculture
Animal Plant & Health Inspection Service
VS 6505
Belcrest Road
Hyattsville MD 20782
USA.
Website: www. aphis.usda.gov

The Customs Attaché at the US Embassy may also be able to advise.

During your flight or voyage to the United States you will be given a customs declaration (Form 6059B) to fill in, which is designed to expedite customs clearance on arrival. Failure to declare a prohibited item can lead to an on-the-spot fine.

Doctor and dentist
Visit your dentist before you leave and ask him to make sure your teeth are in good shape, since dental care in the United States can be extremely expensive and is not always covered by medical insurance.

A visit to your doctor is also in order to tell him of your plans and perhaps have a check-up. You may in any case have to have a medical examination prior to confirmation of your appointment or in order to satisfy immigration requirements. If you have a particular medical condition that requires you to take prescription drugs, you should ask the doctor for a letter that you can take to a medical practitioner in the United States. You may also need to show the letter to customs officials at your port of entry.

If you are likely to be out of the country for a lengthy period of time you should surrender your NHS card to the local Family Practitioner Committee, or hand it to the immigration officer at your point of departure.

Driving licence
You could acquire an International Driving Licence from the AA or RAC but it is really not necessary to do so, since you will be able to drive on your own licence for a year. When the year is up you will need to take a US driving test. The ability to drive is a great asset in the United States since public transport is not available everywhere. If you do not drive already, sooner or later you will probably need to learn, simply in order to survive. Although US driving tests are reckoned to be easier than UK ones, you may prefer to pass your test in more familiar home surroundings.

The rules of the road in the United States differ in some respects from the British Highway Code, and you should take steps to familiarise yourself with them.

Educational arrangements
If your children are of secondary school age, you need to decide whether they are likely to re-enter the British educational system later in their lives. If so, they really need to be enrolled at a school which adheres to the British system or prepares them for the

International Baccalaureate (IB) – a highly regarded qualification which is recognised by all universities.

There are various options:

- A boarding school in Britain. Private schools can be costly, unless your employer can be persuaded to meet most or part of the bill, but a number of local authorities also run schools for children whose parents are abroad. They are listed in the Directory of Maintained Boarding Schools (DFES). Further information is available from the Independent Schools Information Service (ISIS), Gabbitas Educational Consultants, SFIA and the State Boarding Information Service (STABIS).

- A school offering a British style or IB curriculum in the USA, such as:

  Anglo-American School
  18 West 89 Street
  New York NY 10024.

  Armand Hammer United World College of the American
    West
  PO Box 248
  Montezuma NM 87731.

  United Nations International School
  24-50 East River Drive
  New York NY 10010.

  Washington International School
  3100 Macomb Street NW
  Washington DC 20008.

  There are also French schools in Los Angeles, San Francisco and Houston. If you wish to enrol your children in one of the above mentioned schools, do not leave it until the last moment, otherwise you will find there are no places available.

- A correspondence course. Mercer's College provides a complete tuition service by correspondence for children living abroad with their parents up to the age of 18, while the Worldwide Educational Service Home School offers an educational programme for the under-13s which enables parents with no teaching experience to educate their children.

Bear in mind that the residential status of your children could be crucial when the authorities in the UK come to deciding whether they are to be treated as British students or foreign students with respect to fees. It would be wise to explore the financial implications of moving your children to the United States if they are approaching college age.

If, on the other hand, you are likely to be living in the United States indefinitely, there is everything to be said for enrolling your child(ren) in an American school. If you opt for **public** (*ie* **state**) **education** (which is free), you can find out about local schools by contacting the Department of Education of the state in which you will be living (addresses in Appendix G) or the School Board of the district where you plan to reside. Alternatively, you may decide to opt for a **parochial school** (run by a religious denomination) or a **private (independent) school**. *The Handbook of Private Schools* or *Independent and Boarding Schools World Yearbook* can provide details of the latter.

Ultimately your offspring may well want to attend a college in the United States, though this can prove an expensive business since interest-free loans are not as readily available as they are in the UK. For more information on higher education I suggest one of the following:

- *Lovejoy's College Guide*, C.E. Lovejoy (Simon & Schuster).

- *Comparative Guide to American Colleges* J. Cass and M. Birnbaum (Harper & Row).

- *Profiles of American Colleges* (Barron's Educational Series).

- *Study in the USA* (Study in the USA Inc, 119 S Main St, Suite 220, Seattle, WA 98104).

Financial advice

If you are planning to be in the United States for some time it will pay you to find a reputable adviser who can help you understand the tax and other financial implications of the move and give you advice on such matters as insurance, pensions, *etc.* Your bank may be able to offer advice through one of its specialist branches, or you could turn to one of the specialist advisers that advertise in

expatriate journals. Some of these are included under Useful
Addresses (Appendix F).

Your flat or house in the UK

If you own a house or flat there are various options open to you,
depending on how long you will be away.

Leave the accommodation empty

This is fine provided you live in a part of the country that is
reasonably secure, your absence is likely to be short and there
is no risk of squatters moving in. However, your insurance company may increase the premium, and if you have a mortgage, your
bank or building society might have qualms. In any case, both
organisations should be informed.

Ask someone to look after it for you

This is quite a sensible option provided the person lives quite
close. If you are unable to find a neighbour, friend or relative who
will take on the responsibility, you could contact an organisation
that offers houseminding services, such as Animal Aunts or
Homesitters Ltd. People participating on exchange programmes
often allow their exchange partners use of the house.

Let it

This is a way of paying for the upkeep of the property and helps
pay off the mortgage, if you have one, but you need to check first
whether the lender approves. It is always best if you can find a
tenant whom you know and trust, as not every tenant turns out to
be reliable. Failing that, you can either advertise for a tenant
yourself or appoint a letting agent to do the work for you. Whatever course you take you must ensure that the tenant signs a
properly drawn up legal contract which enables you to repossess
the house on your return, i.e. an assured shorthold tenancy.
   A good agent will:

- advertise for tenants
- interview prospective tenants
- take up references
- draw up a leasing agreement and serve relevant notices
- draw up inventories

- visit properties and attend to any complaints or queries
- collect rent
- serve notice to quit and attend court
- attend to building repairs and any major building work
- account to clients by way of statements and payment of rents
- pay water rates and other charges
- negotiate rent increases
- deal with insurance claims.

If you plan to return during your vacations, contact the accommodation office of local colleges and universities to see if they have staff or students who need to rent accommodation during term time only.

Sell it
This is a sensible option if you are planning to stay in the US for several years, but you will need to set the process in train some time before you leave. In recent years houses have taken a long time to sell.

There is no need to deal with such matters here, since there are several excellent books on buying and selling houses and flats, *eg*: *Which? Way to Buy, Sell and Move House* (Consumers' Association).

You may well decide to use some of the proceeds to finance the purchase of property in the US. Initially you should find a safe and profitable haven for your cash.

And if your accommodation is rented . . .
Make sure that you give your landlord plenty of notice.

Health
There are no special vaccinations that you need to have before going to the United States, since you are unlikely to encounter any particular health hazards there. However, in view of the costs of health care in America it makes sense to ensure you are in the best of health before you go. Visits to your doctor and dentist have already been suggested; it would also be a good idea to go to the optician for an eye test or for a spare pair of spectacles.

The Department of Health produces a booklet *Health Advice for Travellers*, which is obtainable from many post offices and pharmacies. See also the note on medical insurance.

Insurance

Medical and accident insurance
The United States does not have the equivalent of the British National Health Service, and what government health provision there is tends to be limited to only a small sector of the population, particularly the destitute and the elderly.

It is therefore up to individuals to ensure that they are properly insured against illness. Many employers assume this responsibility, and if you are fortunate you may well find that medical insurance is one of the perks of the job. If this is not the case, you will need to make your own arrangements, though this could work out expensive.

None of the medical expenses you incur in the United States can be refunded by the NHS, but you will continue to be eligible for free treatment in Britain when you return or when visiting, provided you have not taken up permanent residence in the United States.

There are a number of insurance companies and brokers in the UK that will insure you for a short visit to America, including BUPA, Expat Network and PPP. Not all will be prepared to do so for the longer term, and you may find it is easier to insure yourself with an American insurer, such as Blue Cross, when you arrive.

The Health Insurance Association of America will be able to answer any queries. The organisation produces a number of useful leaflets, such as: *What You Should Know About Health Insurance* and *How to Use Private Health Insurance with Medicare.*

When looking at a health plan, whether it is to be provided by your employer or financed by yourself, it is vital to make sure you have adequate cover. Here are a few of the questions you need to ask.

- What percentage of the cost of treatment do I have to pay, if any?
- What kinds of treatment (*eg* dental, psychiatric) are excluded?
- How soon do benefits start?

- Am I covered for existing medical conditions?

- Does the policy cover prescription drugs?

- Is there a ceiling on the amount I can claim each year?

Life insurance
You need to notify your insurance company of your impending move. This might be a good time to review your needs.

Insurance of personal effects
This is a matter that you should look into. If you employ removers they should be able to advise you; otherwise you may be able to arrange an insurance package which includes medical, accident, loss and damage provisions.

Investments
If you have any investments, you need to inform the organisations concerned (*eg* unit trust managers, the Premium Bond office, your stockbroker) of your change of address. You may also wish to appoint someone to look after them in your absence (*eg* your bank or solicitor).

This may be a timely moment, if you are planning to be away an appreciable length of time, to review your investment strategy in the light of your new circumstances, in order to make your investments as tax efficient as possible. Bear in mind that if you become a permanent US resident, the Internal Revenue Service will tax you on your total worldwide income.

In the past many expatriates have found it profitable to move their investments into an offshore haven such as the Channel Islands or the Isle of Man, but you could run into legal difficulties if you try to do this with any US earnings. So you would be wise to take advice from a financial expert who is *au fait* with expatriate financial matters.

Journals and newspapers
If you subscribe to journals you need to weigh up whether to continue your subscription or not. If not, you need to cancel; if you wish to continue, you should notify the publisher of your change of address.

If you are going to a part of the United States where British publications are hard to come by, you might consider taking out a subscription to a publication such as *The Guardian Weekly* or

The Economist in order to keep abreast of developments in the UK and elsewhere. Only a minority of US newspapers provide extensive coverage of international news. There are, incidentally, some British newspapers in the United States: the *British Weekly* serves the British community in California, the *Florida Brit* circulates in Florida, while the monthly *Union Jack* has a national circulation. (See under California, Appendix G.)

Another way of keeping in touch is to listen in to the BBC World Service, in which case you may wish to take out a subscription to its monthly programme bulletin *On Air*. The BBC also broadcasts on the Internet, has an international TV service and is extending its satellite TV coverage. (See Appendix F.)

There are a number of journals which cater especially for expatriates to which you might consider subscribing, *eg: The Independent International, Resident Abroad*. (See Appendix D for details.)

Kin (next of)
Make sure that your employers and professional advisers know the name and address of your next of kin in case of accidents. Details of your next of kin should also be noted in your diary and passport.

Library
Your local public library will probably have some useful books on the United States, and you should endeavour to read or, at least, browse through some of them before you go, in order to familiarise yourself with the prospect before you. The **Centre for International Briefing** has an excellent library, geared to expatriate needs, which can be used for a fee.

Do not forget to return any library books you have borrowed otherwise you could incur a steep fine in the future.

Luggage and personal effects
If you are only planning to be in America for a matter of months, the best plan is to travel light. If you are planning to be there for some years you will want to take a lot of your possessions with you, if at all possible. However, due to cost constraints you will not be able to take everything, so you need to work out what you really need and what you can do without.

For instance, if you are going to be in furnished accommodation there is clearly no need to take much furniture with you, except perhaps for a few choice items. It can either stay in your home or, if you are selling the house, you could put it in storage. Bulky electrical goods are best left behind since they are relatively cheap in the United States. Besides, the current in the US is different (110V 60Hz against 240V 50Hz in the UK), the TV transmission system is different, and you would need transformers and adaptors for two-pin sockets.

Household items (such as cutlery, sheets, blankets, kitchen utensils) are quite sensible items to take along; curtains are not, since you won't know the size of your windows. Books are weighty items, and you will need to think twice about shipping out your whole library, unless it happens to be very valuable.

There is little point in indulging in a shopping spree before you leave, since items are often available more cheaply in the United States. Instead save your cash until you arrive and discover exactly what you need.

Airlines are more generous these days than they used to be with regard to accompanied luggage, with dimensions a more important consideration than weight. Check whether your employer is prepared to pay for a modest amount of extra accompanied luggage, and whether there are allowances for items sent by sea or unaccompanied air freight.

Moving
If you have a large number of items to ship, the best plan is to enlist the aid of an experienced and reputable international removal contractor and leave him to do the packing, make all the transport arrangements and sort out the paperwork. Normally, if your employer is paying for the move, he will expect you to get a number of quotes before giving the go-ahead.

There are a number of removal firms that can handle international removals, a few of which are listed in Appendix F. If no firm near you is mentioned contact the British Association of Removers (Overseas Group) or the Institute of Freight Forwarders Ltd.

National Insurance
There is a **Social Security Agreement** between the UK and the United States to ensure that you do not have liability for contributions in both countries at the same time.

If you work in America for a UK employer for not more than five years you will remain insured under the UK National

Insurance scheme and normal Class 1 contributions will be paid. Contributions will not be payable to the US scheme. Self employed people ordinarily resident in the UK also remain insured in the UK when working in the United States.

On the other hand, if you go to America to work for a US or other non-UK employer you may have to contribute to the US social security scheme. It is sensible to contact the US authorities on arrival to find out about your obligations.

You should let your local social security office know of your date of departure and address in the US. Further information is available from:

Benefits Agency Overseas Branch
Tyneview Park
Whitley Road
Benton
Newcastle upon Tyne NE98 1BA
Tel: (0191) 228 7777
Website: www.dwp.gov.uk

National Insurance Contributions Office
Inland Revenue
International Services
Longbenton
Newcastle upon Tyne NE98 1ZZ
Tel: (0845) 915 4811 or (0191) 225 4811
Website: www.inlandrevenue.gov.uk

Residents of Northern Ireland should contact:

Operational Support Division
Overseas Benefit Unit
Block 2
Castle Buildings
Stormont
Belfast BT4 3SP

National Insurance Contributions Office
International Services
Inland Revenue
24–42 Corporation Street
Belfast BT1 3DP

For information on the US social security scheme contact:

Federal Benefits Unit
United States Embassy
24 Grosvenor Square
London W1A 2LQ.

The relevant authorities in the United States are:

Social Security Administration Office of International Policy
PO Box 17741
Baltimore MD 21235
(contribution enquiries).
Website: www.saa.gov

Social Security Administration Office of International Policy
PO Box 17049
Baltimore MD 21303
(other enquiries).
Website: www.saa.gov

Orientation
In order to get off to a good start it is vital to be briefed
thoroughly not only about the job, but also about living conditions. There are subtle differences between the way of life in the
United States and life on this side of the Atlantic which could
catch you unawares, so you need to be aware of these differences
and prepare for them.

A number of organisations conduct their own orientation
programmes; others use the expertise of briefing centres, such as
the Centre for International Briefing at Farnham Castle, Culture
Shock Consulting and Employment Conditions Abroad. Another
organisation which may be able to brief you is Corona International which publishes a useful series of booklets entitled *Notes
for Newcomers*. There are a number of useful publications you
could consult, such as *Living and Working in America, Living in
the USA, Long Stays in America, Culture Shock: USA* and *Culture
Shock: USA South*. (See Bibliography.) However, a person-to-
person briefing is infinitely preferable, since you have the
opportunity to ask your own questions.

Passports

You will need to obtain a full passport from the passport agency and can get a passport application form from your Post Office. If your passport is about to expire, you would be wise to renew it. For further information telephone (0870) 521 0410.

UK Passport Office addresses

Globe House
89 Eccleston Square
London SW1V 1PN
Website: www.passport.gov.uk

Olympia House
Upper Dock Street
Newport
Gwent NP1 1XA
(for Wales and the West of England).

Aragon Court
Northminster Road
Peterborough PE1 1QG
(for the Midlands and Eastern England).

5th Floor
India Buildings
Water Street
Liverpool L2 0QZ
(for the North of England and North Wales).

3 Northgate
96 Milton Street
Cowcaddens
Glasgow G4 0BT
(Scotland, London and Middlesex).

Hampton House
47–53 High Street
Belfast BT1 2QS
(Northern Ireland).

Milburngate House
Durham DH1 5ZL

Pension

If you are taking up a contract appointment, the chances are that you will not be covered by any pension scheme, and it would be worth your while to explore the possibility of contributing to a personal pension scheme. If you are already working for a company based in the UK or Ireland, you need to clarify whether the company pension scheme covers postings abroad. The Society of Pensions Consultants or Company Pensions Information Centre, both in London, may be able to advise or put you in touch with someone who can.

Pets

It is normally possible to take your pets with you to the United States, but you need to be aware of certain restrictions, such as quarantine periods in certain states. The leaflet *Pets, Wildlife, US Customs* gives full details of the restrictions. A health certificate from a vet will be needed, and bear in mind that certain states impose quarantine periods. You will need to enlist the services of an animal transport service which will deal with all the necessary documentation. Some addresses are listed in Appendix F.

However, you ought to consider whether your pet will necessarily relish the change. Vets or animal charities can advise, and you should contact the DEFRA PETS helpline for information on the Pet Passport scheme which is now extended to the USA.

If you are off on a short-term assignment it may be more convenient to find your pet a home with friends or relations during your absence; or you could enlist the aid of a pet-minding service, such as Animal Aunts. (See Useful Addresses.)

Professional advisers

It is important to inform professional advisers, such as solicitors and accountants, of your new address. In addition, you may have to make arrangements with at least one of them for the day to day management of your affairs while you are away. By granting him power of attorney, for instance, he will be able to sign documents on your behalf. If you have not yet made a will, this could be a good time to do so.

On the other hand, you may feel you are quite able to handle your affairs yourself from the other side of the Atlantic.

Qualification certificates
It is advisable to take all your diplomas and certificates – and those of your dependants – with you, as prospective employers and the authorities may need to inspect them. Photocopies alone may not suffice.

Redirection of mail
While you may make a Herculean effort to inform all and sundry of your move, you will inevitably miss out someone or some organisation, such as a long-lost aunt in Australia who decides to get in touch after 20 years. You therefore need to arrange to have your mail redirected. If you have tenants, you may be able to prevail on them to do the honours; or the Post Office will redirect your mail – for a fee. Forms are available at any Post Office.

Rental agreements
If you have rental agreements remember to cancel them in good time. If buying on credit or hire purchase, you should inform the finance company in question of your movements.

Subscriptions
Subscriptions to associations should either be cancelled or the organisation concerned be informed of your new address. See also under Journals.

Tax
You need to inform both the Inland Revenue and the Treasurer of your local district or borough council so that they can assess your liability to income tax and local taxes (*ie* council charge, community charge or rates). You might even get a rebate! If you are self-employed and subject to VAT, you will have to tell the local VAT inspector as well.

The Inland Revenue produces a number of booklets that will guide you, including IR 25 which sets out the rules governing the taxation of income from overseas. As a rule of thumb, if the Inland Revenue regards you as non-resident in the UK for tax purposes you will not be liable for UK income tax, though you may well have to pay it to the United States authorities. However, the rules changed in 1998 and you will need to be resident outside the UK for a complete tax year (6 April to 5 April) in order to qualify for non-residential status. You should not, however, have to pay income tax twice over since there is a double taxation agreement between the UK and the United States. US taxation is dealt with in the next chapter but you can obtain advance information from the Internal Revenue Service c/o the US Embassy.

There are a number of expatriate tax advisers (some of them listed in Appendix F) and if your tax affairs are complicated you may wish to seek advice in order to minimise tax liability both in the UK and United States. Books such as the *Allied Dunbar Expatriate Tax Guide* and *Working Abroad* are also worth dipping into.

Travel arrangements
It is normal for your employer to pay your fares, and if not, you should enquire why not. Expect to travel by air rather than on the QE2, and if you are on contract do not rely on getting free air travel for your dependants. Allow yourself plenty of time to get to the airport.

Utilities – electricity, gas, telephone, water
Inform the respective companies of the date of your departure and arrange for the payment of outstanding bills and disconnection, if appropriate. Also cancel milk and newspaper deliveries.

Visas
The different visa categories are explained in Chapter 2. If you have any doubts or your situation is complicated, you may need to seek help from a lawyer or consultant specialising in US immigration law. The US Embassy can supply you with a list of these, or you can refer to Appendix F.

Voting rights
British people who live abroad now have the right to vote in elections, thanks to the **Representation of the People Act 1989**, and you can receive information on this from the Electoral Registration Officer of the district in which you reside.

If you wish to receive election literature you should inform the offices of the different parties in the constituency in which you reside, since this is the place where you have your vote. On arrival in the United States you need to contact the nearest British Consulate for the appropriate voting registration forms and an explanatory leaflet.

6

Looking for a Job on Arrival

Making contact with potential employers who are thousands of miles away is not always an easy matter. Conducting your job search from within the United States itself can work out more satisfactory. You then have a chance to see what conditions are like, assess job prospects and employers, and understand what you are letting yourself in for.

However – and I cannot stress this point too much – in order to be able to work in the United States you need to be in possession of the appropriate kind of visa. If you are not, before you take up a position you must seek to regularise your status with the Immigration and Naturalization Service. (The local offices are listed in Appendix G.) This is no mere formality, and there is no guarantee that you will be granted the necessary permission.

If you possess an **Alien Registration Receipt Card** (the 'green card') there is no problem. This document indicates that you have been granted permanent residence, and allows you to get a job anywhere without restriction. In most other situations, the employer will have to obtain permission to employ you, and since it can take months to get the necessary go-ahead, many firms will think twice before taking you on. The subject of visas has been dealt with in Chapter 2.

This chapter is aimed mainly at people who have the necessary permission to work in the United States. However, it will also be of interest to anyone who decides to visit America for a holiday or business trip and carry out a job reconnaissance at the same time. You may be fortunate enough to come across an employer who offers you a job on the spot, but it is just as valuable to glean information about the jobs market that will be useful to you in the future.

As in the UK there is no one certain way of finding a job, and you will achieve success sooner if you try a variety of approaches. Where you base yourself is also crucial. Generally speaking, you need to position yourself in an area where there are plenty of opportunities in your particular field. This will normally mean in or near a large and expanding commercial or industrial centre. In this respect California, New York and parts of Texas are better bets than Wyoming or South Dakota.

SHOULD I APPROACH AN EMPLOYER DIRECT?

The direct approach can be very productive, especially if you research the jobs market thoroughly beforehand. You need to identify employers who could make use of your expertise, and in particular ones that appear to be expanding and taking on extra staff. Among the useful sources of information are:

- Commercial and professional directories (see Bibliography). Dun & Bradstreet's *Employment Opportunities Directory* is particularly useful because it gives details of the recruitment practices and requirements of different companies.

- Reports and articles in newspapers and journals, on radio and TV, particularly the business news.

- Professional associations, careers counsellors, friends and acquaintances.

- The Internet. Many companies have their own websites.

You then need to see if you can identify individuals within the organisation who might be interested in your expertise and have the authority to recruit personnel. In small outfits this could well turn out to be the managing director himself. Otherwise, contact the personnel officer, who in larger firms is likely to have the title Vice President of Human Resources.

This step involves one of the following procedures:

A personal visit
If the organisation is in the locality where you are staying, you could call in and ask about current and future recruitment needs. If things look promising, see if you can make an appointment with the relevant person and leave a copy of your résumé (American style CV). If the firm is a small one you may be lucky enough to see someone straight away, but normally you will have to make an appointment for a later date.

Be prepared to ask questions about the organisation itself and how a person with your experience and qualifications would fit in. Before leaving, see if you can pick up brochures about the organisation. Such information could prove useful at some future meeting.

A letter or e-mail message
On the whole speculative letters are less effective than personal visits, but unless you are prepared to spend an enormous amount on your job hunting it is not feasible to visit organisations throughout the United States purely 'on spec'. Distances are greater than you think: for instance, Istanbul is much closer to London than Los Angeles is to Boston.

If the organisation is within a few hundred miles of your base, you could increase the effectiveness of your application by indicating that you will be in the vicinity during the course of the next few weeks and asking for an appointment. For positions further afield you should consider targeting a number of employers in just a few, well-chosen states. Then, if some interest is shown, you can back the application up with a visit in which you kill several birds with one stone.

In the case of more distant employers you need to stress your mobility and willingness to relocate. Your initial base in the United States, after all, is (or should be) essentially a temporary one.

(For a sample of a speculative application letter turn to Appendix E.)

A telephone call
If you have a confident telephone manner, you could try canvassing for job leads by telephone. In this way you can cover a lot of ground in a short period of time. John Truitt's book *Telesearch: Direct Dial the Best Job of Your Life* describes this technique in some detail.

Do not expect every phone call to result in a job interview. Some organisations may dislike this type of approach and will ask you to apply in writing; others will give you details of their needs and send you an application form; others will state that they have no recruitment plans. But if you do get an encouraging reaction, be prepared to describe briefly your skills and job objectives.

You may achieve greater success if you adopt a more subtle approach. Instead of asking for a job, why not mention that you are visiting the area and would like to have a look at the company or organisation? Americans are usually very welcoming to foreign visitors and might be flattered by your interest. You may not land a job as a result of your enquiry, but you will doubtless pick up useful information and possibly some job leads.

PRIVATE RECRUITMENT AGENCIES

As in the UK there are many recruitment organisations that find staff for their clients, some of which are household names on this side of the Atlantic, too. The main difference is that firms operating in the United States have the right to charge job seekers a fee – normally a percentage of the first month's or year's salary – if they achieve a placement. Not all do so, and generally speaking the more reputable agencies don't. In some states there are laws that place a limit on how much an agency can charge.

Just as in the UK, too, there are agencies which cover the whole range of jobs and others that specialise in certain sectors. Catering for the top of the market are the executive search firms (sometimes known as 'headhunters') which recruit for high level positions. The vacancies they handle are not always advertised, and the firms approach candidates they deem suitable for the positions. There is no harm at all in sending your résumé to a consultancy with a good track record in your particular field and asking to be put on their files.

There is often an overlap between executive search firms and those that deal with jobs at middle management and other levels. Some firms operate under one roof, using a number of different names according to job level and specialisation.

One very good way of finding an employment agency is by personal recommendation. There are, alas, cowboy outfits that are more intent on earning a fast buck than on making satisfactory placements, and these are to be avoided. Otherwise you can find the names by looking through the job advertisement columns of newspapers and journals or in telephone directories (*Yellow Pages*). Appendix C lists a number of leading firms. In some directories employment agencies are classified according to their specialisation.

Many recruitment consultancies belong to one of the following organisations that publish directories of their members: Association of Executive Search Consultants, National Association of Personnel Services and the National Association of Temporary and Staffing services. (Addresses: see Appendix G.)

Temporary help agencies

There are some 3,500 national, regional and independent companies operating in this field, including some names familiar in UK high streets (*eg* Manpower). Normally such companies recruit their own employees and assign them to clients for limited periods as needed.

The breakdown of jobs in the industry is as follows:

63 per cent office/clerical positions

15 per cent industrial work; *eg* assembly line workers and janitors

11 per cent technical and professional jobs; *eg* engineers, accountants, lawyers, computer programmers, draughtsmen, managers

10 per cent medical; *eg* nurses, therapists, nursing orderlies, lab technicians

(Source: National Association of Temporary & Staffing Services)

Temporary employment is a growth area, and the technical and medical sectors appear to be growing faster than the others. This trend is expected to continue. It is particularly attractive to people in search of flexible working hours, additional income or a way back into the job market. In some cases a temporary job can lead to a permanent engagement.

This is probably only an option for people in possession of a 'green card', since non-immigrant visas are not normally issued to people engaged by a temporary help agency. If you are a student with permission to work or have exchange visitor status (see Chapter 3) you might well contact such a firm in your quest for vacation employment.

The National Association of Temporary & Staffing Services is the national trade organisation for the temporary help industry and publishes a directory of its members. (See also Appendix C.)

JOB ADVERTISEMENTS

In the United States there is no national press as we know it. Virtually all newspapers serve a particular locality, and even a national newspaper such as the *Wall Street Journal* appears in regional editions.

This means that when looking for a job you will need to look in the newspapers published in the region where you plan to work. If you are living in New York and want to work in San Francisco, there is little point in looking through the classified ads of the *New York Times*. You need to get hold of a San Francisco paper.

In Appendix D and Appendix G the names and addresses of the leading newspapers are listed state by state. If you are living outside the state concerned you may have to arrange for copies to be sent to you. However, nowadays, some have excellent websites which include job advertisements. Find out which are the best days for job advertisements; the Sunday editions are usually a good bet.

Professional and trade journals normally have national distribution, and would therefore include job advertisements for all areas in the United States. *The National Business Employment Weekly* – a weekly supplement of the *Wall Street Journal* – and other more specialised job listings are also worth looking at. (See Appendix D.)

The Internet is growing in popularity as a medium for advertising vacancies, and you can make contact with an extensive number of agencies and employers by accessing websites such as www.cweb.com, www.careermosaic.com and www.adamson-line.com.

As you saw in Chapter 4, the trouble with job advertisements is that they normally generate a lot of replies. You are probably up against stiff competition and therefore need to prepare your application as expertly as possible. (See Appendix E for ideas on how to do this.) Furthermore, it is no use replying to just one or two job ads; you need to reply to several in order to increase your chances of success.

PUBLIC SECTOR AND OTHER EMPLOYMENT SERVICES

The state employment services, sometimes called **Job Service**, operate in conjunction with the US Department of Labor Employment Service and have some 2000 local offices, which are listed on the Internet under www.jobcenter.com. They are similar to Job Centres in the UK, do not charge a placement fee, and recruit for both white collar and blue collar positions, though not usually for senior and middle ranking ones.

Most states have computerised job banks which provide daily

listings of job openings in the area of public and private sector vacancies. In addition there is a network of **Federal Job Information Centres** throughout the country. The addresses of the departments handling the employment service are listed state by state in Appendix G. The website for Jobbank is www.ajb.dni.us.

There are various other non-commercial recruitment organisations operated by voluntary organisations. **Intercristo,** for instance, is a Christian placement network which finds personnel for Christian organisations within the United States. For the older job seeker there are **40+ Clubs.**

College placement offices are another source of information about jobs, more specifically for graduates. Of course, their main preoccupation is finding jobs for their own graduates, but if you are lucky, you may find a placement officer who can spend a little time with you. For addresses you should consult the *Directory of Career Planning & Placement Officers* obtainable from:

College Placement Council Inc.
Box 2263
Bethlehem PA 18001
USA.

NETWORKING

Making use of one's contacts is one of the most successful methods of landing a job in the United States – for US residents, at least – but as a newcomer you may feel at a disadvantage. You arrive knowing virtually nobody and need time to build up a network of contacts in a strange land.

How can you overcome this difficulty? The best solution is to begin to develop your network before your departure for the New World. You should have plenty of contacts at home – relatives, business colleagues, people you socialise with, professional contacts, *etc* – so why not ask them to suggest people whom you might look up on your visit? There is also scope for making contacts on the Internet.

Do not overlook the services of organisations to which you belong – your trade union, professional association, local church, the local Rotary Club, for instance. Many such associations have counterparts in the United States, and some of the professional ones are listed in the appropriate job sector of Appendix A. Find out the names and addresses of local representatives in the area(s) where you will be staying and either get a letter of introduction or drop them a line to announce your visit. Chambers of Commerce in the United States are also worth approaching.

WHAT ARE THE PROS AND CONS OF JOB HUNTING FROM A US BASE?

There are obvious advantages to conducting your job search within the United States. You have a chance to meet potential employers and their staff face to face and to see working conditions in different companies at first hand. You also have access to much more information on job opportunities in the form of press advertisements, reference books, job guides and advisers.

On the other hand, if you do not have residential status (and most visitors to the United States do not) you may find companies reluctant to employ you, even if you possess exceptionally good qualifications and experience. This could be because there are plenty of skilled people in the area and so there is no need to call on expertise from abroad. However, a more plausible reason is that the employer (like most American employers) has no experience of recruiting 'aliens' and is therefore unfamiliar with the procedures for obtaining a work visa.

To overcome this reluctance the onus is on you to explain the immigration rules: how the employer must apply to the US Department of Labor for labor certification and that when this comes through you will need to contact the Immigration and Naturalization Service (INS). (For addresses, please see Appendix G.) While immigration attorneys can be used, they are not always necessary if the employer has good grounds for offering you the job.

Visits 'on spec' cost money, of course, and there is no guarantee that in the end you will find a job. You therefore need to make sure that you have adequate financial support to proceed with your job search, since you will not qualify for government hand-outs if you have never worked in America before.

Another consideration is that if you are recruited outside the United States, you will normally get extra perks, notably free travel to your post and back together with some help in moving your belongings. There is also a better chance that you will be dealing with people who know the ropes about work visas for aliens and are able to make all the necessary arrangements speedily.

A final point: make sure that you sign a contract, which sets out the terms and conditions of your employment in detail. Then, in the event of a dispute between your employer and yourself you have some form of legal protection.

7

Working Conditions and Financial Obligations

One golden rule for a person planning to work overseas is: take nothing for granted. This applies just as much to the United States as it does to some country in the Third World; for while superficially things may look the same as they do back home, they seldom are.

This is certainly true with respect to the world of work. US employment laws and working practices may be different from those you are used to. Contracts, for instance, are less likely to be open-ended; in fact, many people are on short-term contracts and new agreements have to be negotiated every two or three years. Moreover, American employers are in a position to terminate a job at any time without justification.

In some respects employees in the United States receive less protection than workers in Europe. That is not to say that America has no labour laws; in fact, there is plenty of legislation both at the federal and state levels, some of it extremely detailed. It is designed to prevent unfair employment practices and discrimination, and to regulate the health and safety of employees.

Your best protection, however, is the contract that you sign. It should spell out the terms and conditions of your employment clearly, so that if your employer should renege on any parts of the agreement you can take him to court. As Americans are somewhat litigious by nature, legal disputes with employers are not uncommon.

YOUR CONTRACT

At the end of Chapter 4 you saw what conditions you should look for in a contract signed in the UK or Ireland.

What should I look for in a USA contract?
A contract signed in the United States should include:

- the name and address of your employer
- your job title and responsibilities
- the staff member you are answerable to
- the location of your employment
- your net salary and dates of payment
- the commencement date and duration of your employment
- the working hours.

Statutory benefits

In addition to pay there are three benefits that the employer is required to provide by law:

Social security payment

He has to make a contribution to your Social Security account (the equivalent to National Insurance in the UK) with the Federal Government.

Unemployment compensation

Your employer must pay into the Government insurance programme that pays unemployment benefit to employees who lose their jobs. The employee does not have to contribute to the scheme.

Workmen's compensation

The employer also has to bear the full cost of contributions to this scheme which provides benefits to employees injured or disabled at work.

Discretionary benefits

The other benefits are discretionary (*ie* employers are not required by law to provide them, though most of them offer at least some). When negotiating your contract you need to pay attention to these points.

Vacation

Vacation entitlements are modest by European standards: seldom more than two weeks per annum except for senior employees, while a new employee might only get one week off.

In addition there are various public holidays: New Year's Day, Memorial Day (last Monday in May), Independence Day (4 July),

Labor Day (first Monday in September), Thanksgiving (fourth Thursday in November) and Christmas Day. Note that a lengthy break at Christmas is unusual.

Sick leave
Employees are allowed to take a specific number of days each year for sickness or compassionate leave – typically six days in all. Note that visits to the dentist or doctor during the working day may be deducted from your sick leave entitlement.

Life insurance
Many employers offer low-cost or free life insurance, normally based on the employee's salary.

Medical insurance
Traditionally businesses have provided health care insurance for their staff, but as the cost of health care rockets some have started to cut back on benefits. When negotiating your contract you should make sure that the provision offered will be adequate for your needs. (See below.)

Pension plans
As in the UK there are company pension plans, some of them funded entirely by the employer, others requiring contributions from both employer and employee. If you are working on a short-term contract, you may be ineligible for such a scheme.

Other benefits
These would include profit sharing schemes (normally restricted to long-term employees), training allowances, social and sports facilities, counselling, low-cost loans. Company cars and luncheon vouchers are not very common.

MEDICAL MATTERS

In the United States there is no government funded health service catering for everybody on the lines of the National Health Service in the UK. True, government spending on healthcare amounts to $1 trillion (6.3% per cent of GDP, compared with 5.8% per cent in the UK) but this tends to be limited to the over-65s and the long-term disabled. Over 40 million Americans have no health insurance at all.

Medical costs in America are high, and you must expect to spend eight times more on healthcare than you would in the UK. Even a routine visit to the dentist can set you back a tidy sum. That is why you ought to make sure that you and any dependants you have in the United States have adequate medical insurance cover.

Fortunately, many employers have company medical plans for their staff, and around 90 per cent of employees with private health insurance are covered by such plans. However, a number of these plans cover only a proportion of the expenses incurred (normally between 70 and 90 per cent), and may exclude dental care. So you may need to explore the possibility of topping up your employer's scheme with an individual policy.

Sickness benefit is provided by:

- the federal government in the case of disabilities that are total and permanent

- certain states for short periods of illness or disability

- private insurance plans in other states. These are often funded by employers.

The Health Insurance Association of America publishes some useful consumer guides, including *The Consumer's Guide to Health Insurance, The Consumer's Guide to Medicare Supplement Insurance* and *The Consumer's Guide to Disability Insurance*.

WORKING PRACTICES

The working day is normally from 8am to 4.30pm in factories, 8.30am to 5pm for offices and the 40-hour week tends to be the norm. Americans tend to be sticklers for timekeeping, and you will be expected to arrive punctually and not slink off before the end of the working day. It is quite normal even for executives to clock in.

Employees are expected to pull their weight, and if you want to succeed in your job you must be prepared to work long hours; firms are quite ready to dismiss backsliders with no reasons given. There is no specific federal government regulation regarding termination of employment, but the normal practice is to give two weeks' notice or severance pay. If you are laid off you may be able to collect unemployment insurance, but not for an open-ended period.

By contrast, equal opportunity legislation tends to work in the employee's favour. The Equal Employment Opportunity Commission of the Federal Department of Labor prohibits discrimination on the basis of race, religion, colour, sex, national origin, handicap, age and virtually everything else. Americans are much more prone to taking employers to court than employees on this side of the Atlantic.

Many states have additional laws designed to counter discrimination in employment, sexual harassment and smoking in public places, and one needs to be aware of these. State laws can affect the way you apply for a job: in some states you should not enclose a photograph with your application. One clearly has to be circumspect in one's relationships towards subordinates of the opposite sex, while chain smokers are in danger of being ostracised.

Working practices often reflect the values of the society in which they operate. In the United States individualism, enterprise and financial success are highly regarded, especially in the urban areas. While British people share many of these attitudes, people from other cultures may find the American way of work perplexing because their societies have a different system of values.

If you come into this category, Geert Hofstede's *Culture's Consequences* is required reading. The Institute for Training in Intercultural Management in the Hague offers courses in understanding and working with other nationalities, as does its UK affiliate, Howell & Associates. Other organisations involved in preparing people for working in the United States are: the Centre for International Briefing and Culture Shock Consulting.

TAXATION

'In this world nothing can be said to be certain, except death and taxes', wrote Benjamin Franklin over 200 years ago. In the United States the tax system, like death, has the habit of catching up with you in the end, so you need to be aware of some of its features.

Federal Income Tax

If you take up employment in America, you are liable to be taxed unless you fall into one of the exempt categories, such as diplomats, students and exchange visitors.

Many Americans live in awe of the Internal Revenue Service (the US equivalent of the Inland Revenue) whose tentacles seem to be everywhere. Departing aliens, for instance, may not be permitted to leave the country unless they can produce a certificate of compliance (sometimes known as the sailing permit or departure permit) at the port of departure.

To obtain this certificate, if you have earnings in the United States you must first file Form 1040C to the IRS office in your district; if you have received no income from US sources you need to submit Form 2063. Mercifully, tourists, students and the staff of foreign governments and international organisations are exempt.

The 'ins' and 'outs' of US taxation are long and complex, and beyond the scope of this book. You can, though, get various guides free of charge from the Internal Revenue Service itself. The relevant ones are *US Tax Guide for Aliens* and *Your Federal Income Tax* (which is at least three times as long as this book!).

The first thing the IRS will want to establish is whether you are a non-resident alien or resident alien for tax purposes. Green card holders are automatically regarded as residents by the IRS, and people on non-immigrant visas who have been present in the United States for a substantial part of the year also fall into this category. The chart in Figure 11 will help you decide. Complications occur in the case of people who commute between the UK and America, and if you have been both a non-resident alien and a resident alien during the course of one tax year.

The US tax year coincides with the calendar year. If you are a non-resident alien in the eyes of the IRS, and engaged in a trade or business, you will need to apply for a **taxpayer identification number** at the local office of the Social Security Administration and file your income tax return on Form 1040NR. Resident aliens file Form 1040EZ, 1040A or 1040 and must apply for a taxpayer identification number too, as soon as they start earning income subject to US tax.

A US income tax form is a complex document, since there are several allowances you may be able to claim (including certain medical and dental expenses). Many Americans employ a certified public accountant (CPA) to complete their tax return for them – at a cost of a few hundred dollars – but if you work diligently through the tax guides mentioned above, you should be able to do it yourself.

For employees a system similar to Pay As You Earn operates in the United States, though it is not obligatory. You must let your employer know whether you are a resident or non-resident alien and agree with him how much tax you expect to pay so that the correct amount of tax can be withheld. If you are a resident alien you need to let him have a **Certificate of Alien Claiming Residence in the United States** (Form 1078).

When you come to fill in your tax form at the end of the tax year, you may find you are due for a refund or additional payment if there is a discrepancy between what has been withheld and what you should have paid on your tax form. Note that there are deadlines for the submission.

State and local taxes

Most of the states also levy taxes on individuals (though until now Texas has been an exception). This takes the form of income tax, and the rates can vary considerably from state to state. To find out what proportion of your income you have to pay, you should contact the tax department of the state in which you intend to live and work. (Addresses in Appendix G.) The table in Figure 14 will also give some indication.

You may also need to pay local taxes to the city or county in which you live, and these often take the form of a sales tax or a property tax. Residents of Metropolitan Atlanta, for instance, pay:

- federal tax

- state income tax

- property taxes (rates)

- a sales and use tax (currently four per cent).

Social Security

The federal government also deducts social security tax, which is similar to our National Insurance and goes towards your pension and Medicare. However, bear in mind that Medicare benefits are only available to certain groups. Because of reciprocal agreements between the United States and other countries, including the UK, as a non-resident alien you may well be able to pay UK National Insurance contributions instead. You may also have to contribute to a disability insurance scheme in certain states.

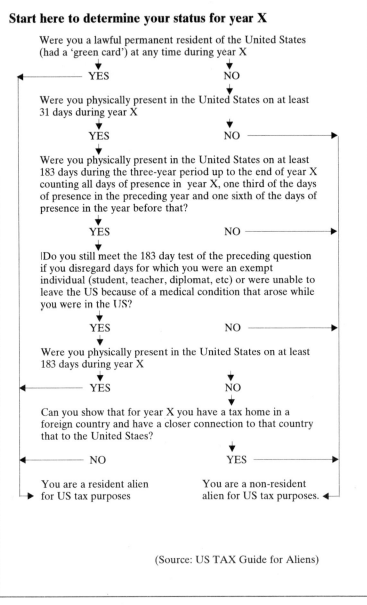

Fig. 11. Determining your tax status.

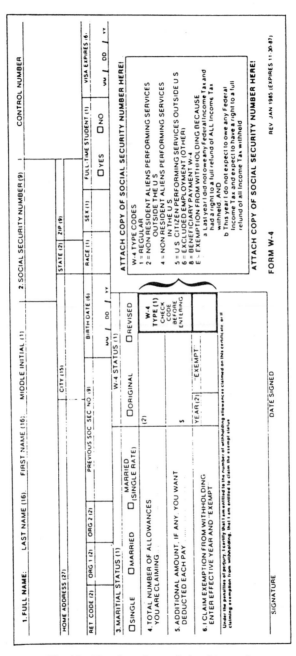

Fig. 12. Employer's tax deduction card.

EMPLOYEE'S PAY STATEMENT

C.G. Nickerson Supply Co.
4567 Melrose
Miami, FL. 33199

HOURS		WAGES				DEDUCTIONS				
REGULAR	OVERTIME	REGULAR	OVERTIME	OTHER	GROSS PAY	FICA	WITHHOLDING TAX	HEALTH INSURANCE	CREDIT UNION	NET PAY

Fig. 13.   Example of an employee's pay statement showing basic and overtime pay, tax and other deductions.

US State and Local Taxes

(Data based on average family of four (two wage earners and two school age children) owning their own home and living in a city where taxes apply. Comprises State and local sales, income, auto, and real estate taxes.)

City	Total taxes paid, by gross family income level (dollars)				Total taxes paid as percent of income			
	$25,000	$50,000	$75,000	$100,000	$25,000	$50,000	$75,000	$100,000
Alburquerque, NM	1,684	3,794	6,529	9,171	6.7	7.6	8.7	9.2
Atlanta, GA	1,951	4,444	7,466	10,253	7.8	8.9	10.0	10.3
Baltimore, MD	2,037	5,490	8,597	11,381	8.1	11.0	11.5	11.4
Boston, MA	2,181	5,004	8,075	10,816	8.7	10.0	10.8	10.8
Charlotte, NC	1,869	4,180	6,930	9,704	7.5	8.4	9.2	8.7
Chicago, IL	2,124	4,177	6,565	8,625	8.5	8.4	8.8	8.6
Columbus, OH	2,154	4,571	7,472	10,333	8.6	9.1	10.0	10.3
Denver, CO	1,647	3,591	5,698	7,675	6.6	7.2	7.6	7.7
Detroit, MI	2,551	5,278	8,215	10,907	10.2	10.6	11.0	10.9
Honolulu, HI	2,168	4,778	7,905	10,805	8.7	9.6	10.5	10.8
Houston, TX	1,325	2,433	3,808	4,869	5.3	4.9	5.1	4.9
Indianapolis, IN	1,945	3,716	5,717	7,528	7.8	7.4	7.6	7.5
Jacksonville, FL	982	1,769	2,841	3,664	3.9	3.5	3.8	3.7
Kansas City, MO	2,175	4,231	6,704	9,160	8.7	8.5	8.9	9.2
Las Vegas, NV	1,450	2,296	3,520	4,461	5.8	4.6	4.7	4.5
Los Angeles, CA	1,970	4,222	7,526	11,004	7.9	8.4	10.0	11.0
Memphis, TN	1,519	2,467	3,999	5,208	6.1	4.9	5.3	5.2
Milwaukee, WI	2,371	5,421	8,574	11,420	9.5	10.8	11.4	11.4
Minneapolis, MN	1,679	4,584	8,167	11,349	6.7	9.2	10.9	11.3
New Orleans, LA	1,449	3,335	5,747	7,798	5.8	6.7	7.7	7.8
New York City, NY	2,123	5,707	9,872	13,878	8.5	11.4	13.2	13.9
Oklahoma City, OK	2,095	4,167	6,855	9,318	8.4	8.3	9.1	9.3
Omaha, NE	2,081	4,321	7,284	10,050	8.3	8.6	9.7	10.0
Philadelphia, PA	3,241	6,098	9,136	11,882	13.0	12.2	12.2	11.9
Phoenix, AZ	2,051	3,889	6,123	8,292	8.2	7.8	8.2	8.3
Portland, ME	2,705	6,094	10,139	13,752	10.8	12.2	13.5	13.8
Seattle, WA	1,871	3,188	4,823	6,135	7.5	6.4	6.4	6.1
Virginia Beach, VA	2,214	4,297	6,892	9,296	8.9	8.6	9.2	9.3
Washington, DC	2,203	4,660	7,933	10,984	8.8	9.3	10.6	11.0
Wichita, KS	1,894	3,661	6,251	8,697	7.6	7.3	8.3	8.7
Average[1]	2,027	4,221	6,885	9,318	8.1	8.4	9.2	9.3
Median[1]	1,970	4,180	6,870	9,318	7.9	8.4	9.2	9.3

[1]Based on selected cities and District of Columbia.

Fig. 14. Estimated state and local taxes paid by a family of four in selected cities: 1997.

Form **W-7**
(Rev. February 1996)

Department of the Treasury
Internal Revenue Service

Application for IRS Individual Taxpayer Identification Number

▶ See instructions. ▶ Please type or print.

▶ For use by individuals who are NOT U.S. citizens, nationals, or permanent residents.

OMB No. 1545-1483

FOR IRS USE ONLY

Please note the following when completing this form:

● *This number is for tax purposes only.* **Do not submit** *this form if you have, or are eligible to obtain, a U.S. social security number (SSN).*

● *Receipt of an ITIN creates no inference regarding your immigration status or your right to work in the United States.*

● *Receipt of an ITIN does not make you eligible to claim the earned income credit (EIC).*

Reason you are submitting Form W-7. (Check only one box. See instructions.)

a ☐ Nonresident alien required to obtain ITIN to claim tax treaty benefit

b ☐ Nonresident alien filing a U.S. tax return and not eligible for an SSN

c ☐ U.S. resident alien (based on days present in the United States) filing a U.S. tax return and not eligible for an SSN

d ☐ Dependent of U.S. person ⎱ Enter name and SSN of U.S. person (see instructions) ▶ ....

e ☐ Spouse of U.S. person ⎰

f ☐ Other (specify) ....

		First name	Middle name
1 Name (see instructions)	1a Last name (surname or family name)	First name	Middle name
Name at birth if different . ▶	1b Last name (surname or family name)	First name	Middle name
2 Permanent residence address, if any (see instructions)	Street address, apartment number, or rural route number. **Do not use a P.O. box number.**		
	City or town, state or province, and country. Include ZIP code or postal code where appropriate.		
3 Mailing address (if different from above)	Street address, apartment number, P.O. box number, or rural route number.		
	City or town, state or province, and country. Include ZIP code or postal code where appropriate.		

Fig. 15. Application form for IRS individual taxpayer identification number.

4 Birth information	Date of birth (month, day, year) / /	Country of birth	City and state or province (optional)	5 ☐ Male ☐ Female

6 Family information (see instructions)	Father's last name (surname)		First name	Middle name
	Mother's maiden name (surname)		First name	Middle name

7 Other information	7a Country(ies) of citizenship	7b Foreign tax identification number	7c Type of U.S. visa (if any) and expiration date

7d Describe identification document(s) submitted (see instructions).
☐ Passport ☐ Driver's license/State I.D. ☐ INS documentation ☐ Other................
Issued by: Number:

7e Have you previously received a U.S. temporary Taxpayer Identification Number (TIN) or Employer Identification Number (EIN)?
☐ No/Do not know. Skip line 7f.
☐ Yes. Complete line 7f. If you need more space, list on a sheet and attach to this form. (See instructions.)

7f TIN ☐☐☐ - ☐☐ - ☐☐☐☐   EIN ☐☐ - ☐☐☐☐☐☐☐
Enter the name under which the TIN was issued.   Enter the name under which the EIN was issued.

Sign Here

Under penalties of perjury, I (applicant/delegate/acceptance agent) declare that I have examined this application, including accompanying documentation and statements, and to the best of my knowledge and belief, it is true, correct, and complete. I authorize the IRS to disclose to my acceptance agent returns or return information necessary to resolve matters regarding the assignment of my IRS individual taxpayer identification number (ITIN).

► Signature of applicant (if delegate, see instructions)	Date (month, day, year) / /	Phone number
► Name of delegate, if applicable (type or print)	Delegate's relationship to applicant ☐ Parent ☐ Guardian	

Keep a copy of this form for your records.

Acceptance Agent's Use ONLY	► Signature	Date (month, day, year) / /	Phone: ( )
	► Name and title (type or print)	Name of company	FAX: ( )
			EIN
			....

For Paperwork Reduction Act Notice, see page 4.   Cat. No. 10229L   Form **W-7** (Rev. 2-98)

Fig. 15. – continued.

Form **1040**

Department of the Treasury—Internal Revenue Service
U.S. Individual Income Tax Return 1999 (7) IRS Use Only—Do not write or staple in this space.

For the year Jan. 1–Dec. 31, 1999, or other tax year beginning , 1999, ending

OMB No. 1545-0074

Label

(See instructions on page 18.)

Use the IRS label. Otherwise, please print or type.

L A B E L

H E R E

Your first name and initial | Last name | Your social security number

If a joint return, spouse's first name and initial | Last name | Spouse's social security number

Home address (number and street). If you have a P.O. box, see page 18. | Apt. no.

City, town or post office, state, and ZIP code. If you have a foreign address, see page 18.

▲ **IMPORTANT!** ▲
You must enter your SSN(s) above.

Presidential Election Campaign (See page 18.)

Do you want $3 to go to this fund? . . . .
If a joint return, does your spouse want $3 to go to this fund?

| | Yes | No | Note. Checking "Yes" will not change your tax or reduce your refund. |

Filing Status

Check only one box.

1 | Single
2 | Married filing joint return (even if only one had income)
3 | Married filing separate return. Enter spouse's social security no. above and full name here. ▶
4 | Head of household (with qualifying person). (See page 18.) If the qualifying person is a child but not your dependent, enter this child's name here. ▶
5 | Qualifying widow(er) with dependent child (year spouse died ▶ 19). (See page 18.)

Exemptions

6a | | Yourself. If your parent (or someone else) can claim you as a dependent on his or her tax return, do not check box 6a.

b | | Spouse

c | Dependents:

(1) First name Last name	(2) Dependent's social security number	(3) Dependent's relationship to you	(4) ✓ If qualifying child for child tax credit (see page 19)

If more than six dependents, see page 19.

d | Total number of exemptions claimed

No. of boxes checked on 6a and 6b

No. of your children on 6c who:
• lived with you
• did not live with you due to divorce or separation (see page 19)

Dependents on 6c not entered above

Add numbers entered on lines above ▶

Fig. 16. US Income tax form.

Income

Attach Copy B of your Forms W-2 and W-2G here. Also attach Form(s) 1099-R if tax was withheld.

If you did not get a W-2, see page 20.

Enclose, but do not staple, any payment. Also, please use Form 1040-V.

7	Wages, salaries, tips, etc. Attach Form(s) W-2	7
8a	Taxable interest. Attach Schedule B if required	8a
b	Tax-exempt interest. DO NOT include on line 8a	8b
9	Ordinary dividends. Attach Schedule B if required	9
10	Taxable refunds, credits, or offsets of state and local income taxes (see page 21)	10
11	Alimony received	11
12	Business income or (loss). Attach Schedule C or C-EZ	12
13	Capital gain or (loss). Attach Schedule D if required. If not required, check here ▶ ☐	13
14	Other gains or (losses). Attach Form 4797	14
15a	Total IRA distributions . 15a b Taxable amount (see page 22)	15b
16a	Total pensions and annuities 16a b Taxable amount (see page 22)	16b
17	Rental real estate, royalties, partnerships, S corporations, trusts, etc. Attach Schedule E	17
18	Farm income or (loss). Attach Schedule F	18
19	Unemployment compensation	19
20a	Social security benefits . 20a b Taxable amount (see page 24)	20b
21	Other income. List type and amount (see page 24)	21
22	Add the amounts in the far right column for lines 7 through 21. This is your total income ▶	22

Adjusted Gross Income

23	IRA deduction (see page 26)	23
24	Student loan interest deduction (see page 26)	24
25	Medical savings account deduction. Attach Form 8853	25
26	Moving expenses. Attach Form 3903	26
27	One-half of self-employment tax. Attach Schedule SE	27
28	Self-employed health insurance deduction (see page 28)	28
29	Keogh and self-employed SEP and SIMPLE plans	29
30	Penalty on early withdrawal of savings	30
31a	Alimony paid b Recipient's SSN ▶	31a
32	Add lines 23 through 31a	32
33	Subtract line 32 from line 22. This is your adjusted gross income	33

For Disclosure, Privacy Act, and Paperwork Reduction Act Notice, see page 54. Cat. No. 11320B Form **1040** (1999)

Fig. 16. – continued.

Form 1040 (1999)   Page 2

Tax and Credits	34	Amount from line 33 (adjusted gross income)	34
	35a	Check if: ☐ **You** were 65 or older, ☐ Blind; ☐ **Spouse** was 65 or older, ☐ Blind. ▶ 35a	
	b	Add the number of boxes checked above and enter the total here .	
		If you are married filing separately and your spouse itemizes deductions or you were a dual-status alien, see page 30 and check here . . . . . . ▶ 35b ☐	
Standard Deduction for Most People	36	Enter your **itemized deductions** from Schedule A, line 28, **OR standard deduction** shown on the left. **But see page 30** to find your standard deduction if you checked any box on line 35a or 35b **or** if someone can claim you as a dependent	36
Single: $4,300	37	Subtract line 36 from line 34	37
Head of household: $6,350	38	If line 34 is $94,975 or less, multiply $2,750 by the total number of exemptions claimed on line 6d. If line 34 is over $94,975, see the worksheet on page 31 for the amount to enter .	38
Married filing jointly or Qualifying widow(er): $7,200	39	**Taxable income.** Subtract line 38 from line 37. If line 38 is more than line 37, enter -0- .	39
	40	**Tax** (see page 31). Check if any tax is from a ☐ Form(s) 8814 b ☐ Form 4972 ▶	40
Married filing separately: $3,600	41	Credit for child and dependent care expenses. Attach Form 2441	41	
	42	Credit for the elderly or the disabled. Attach Schedule R.	42	
	43	Child tax credit (see page 33)	43	
	44	Education credits. Attach Form 8863	44	
	45	Adoption credit. Attach Form 8839	45	
	46	Foreign tax credit. Attach Form 1116 if required . . .	46	
	47	Other. Check if from a ☐ Form 3800 b ☐ Form 8396 c ☐ Form 8801 d ☐ Form (specify)	47	
	48	Add lines 41 through 47. These are your **total credits** . . . . ▶	48
	49	Subtract line 48 from line 40. If line 48 is more than line 40, enter -0- . . . . ▶	49
Other Taxes	50	Self-employment tax. Attach Schedule SE	50
	51	Alternative minimum tax. Attach Form 6251	51
	52	Social security and Medicare tax on tip income not reported to employer. Attach Form 4137	52
	53	Tax on IRAs, other retirement plans, and MSAs. Attach Form 5329 if required . . .	53
	54	Advance earned income credit payments from Form(s) W-2	54
	55	Household employment taxes. Attach Schedule H.	55
	56	Add lines 49 through 55. This is your **total tax** . . . . ▶	56

Fig. 16. – continued.

Payments

57	Federal income tax withheld from Forms W-2 and 1099 . .	57
58	1999 estimated tax payments and amount applied from 1998 return .	58
59a	Earned income credit. Attach Sch. EIC if you have a qualifying child	59a
b	Nontaxable earned income: amount ▲	
	and type ▲	
60	Additional child tax credit. Attach Form 8812	60
61	Amount paid with request for extension to file (see page 48)	61
62	Excess social security and RRTA tax withheld (see page 48)	62
63	Other payments. Check if from a ☐ Form 2439 b ☐ Form 4136	63
64	Add lines 57, 58, 59a, and 60 through 63. These are your **total payments** . . ▲	64

Refund

Have it
directly
deposited!
See page 48
and fill in 66b,
66c, and 66d.

65	If line 64 is more than line 56, subtract line 56 from line 64. This is the amount you **OVERPAID**	65
66a	Amount of line 65 you want **REFUNDED TO YOU.** . . . . ▲	66a
▲ b	Routing number	▲ c Type: ☐ Checking ☐ Savings
▲ d	Account number	
67	Amount of line 65 you want **APPLIED TO YOUR 2000 ESTIMATED TAX** ▲	67	

Amount You Owe

68	If line 56 is more than line 64, subtract line 64 from line 56. This is the **AMOUNT YOU OWE.**	68
	For details on how to pay, see page 49 . . . . ▲	
69	Estimated tax penalty. Also include on line 68 . . .	69	

Sign Here

Joint return?
See page 18.
Keep a copy
for your
records.

Under penalties of perjury, I declare that I have examined this return and accompanying schedules and statements, and to the best of my knowledge and belief, they are true, correct, and complete. Declaration of preparer (other than taxpayer) is based on all information of which preparer has any knowledge.

Your signature	Date	Your occupation	Daytime telephone number (optional) ( )
Spouse's signature. If a joint return, BOTH must sign.	Date	Spouse's occupation	

Paid Preparer's Use Only

Preparer's signature	Date	Check if self-employed ☐	Preparer's SSN or PTIN
Firm's name (or yours if self-employed) and address		EIN	
		ZIP code	

Form **1040** (1999)

Fig. 16. – continued.

8

Working for Yourself

So far in this book you have looked at ways of finding an employer in the United States. This chapter looks at another option worth consideration: working for yourself.

Self-employment is admittedly not an easy option, but for anyone who has experience of running his own business, setting up in the United States will not be so very different. Immigrants from all over the world have done this: and the many ethnic shops, restaurants and factories you find in the country prove that success often favours the bold.

If you plan to invest $1 million ($500,000 in certain designated areas) in the creation of a new business, the purchase of an existing business or the infusion of capital into an existing business, you will probably qualify for full immigrant status. Investors with lesser amounts of capital will have to settle for a non-immigrant visa (see Chapter 2).

- **L-1 Intra-company transfer visa:** This applies where you are setting up a company as a branch, subsidiary or affiliate of a foreign operation. Once it has been established for a year you may qualify for a permanent visa. Some foreign nationals purchase a business and title the purchase in the name of the US subsidiary.

- **E-1 Trade visa:** This applies where you establish a company that trades between the USA and your home country. Fifty-one per cent of trade must be between these two countries. There is no limit on the number of visa extensions.

- **E-2 Treaty investor visa:** This is the most common way for foreign investors to live and work in the US, and it is available to investors, managers, and employees with specialist knowledge. The investment has to be substantial and depends on the nature of the business. The smaller the cost of establishing the business the higher the percentage of investment required.

WHAT'S MY FIRST STEP?

How does one set up on one's own account in the United States? There are basically four approaches you could consider:

- buy a business
- open a branch of your UK business in the United States
- set up a joint venture with an American company
- set up your own business from scratch.

Before you take the plunge it is vital to do some market research. To do this properly will involve one or more visits to the United States to find out the lie of the land.

If you are thinking of **acquiring a business** you need to ask around to see if the asking price is reasonable and the business has a bright future. This is not a time for throwing caution to the wind, and you should bear in mind that even some leading companies based in the UK have made disastrous acquisitions in America over the past decade.

A **branch office** is an excellent plan for anyone seeking to distribute or service his company's products in the United States. However, there is plenty of scope for the small business-man outside manufacturing; for example, as an international recruitment consultant, estate agent, relocation expert or business consultant servicing clients on both sides of the Atlantic.

A **joint venture** is also worth considering, not least because of the benefit in terms of market experience and local know-how an American partner can offer. However, you will need to proceed with caution and consider a number of possible partners before coming to any decision.

Starting from scratch is a risky activity, and you need to be confident of the viability of your project before embarking on it. New businesses wherever they are started tend to have a high casualty rate, with only a small proportion surviving until their fifth birthday.

UK sources of advice and assistance
Anyone planning to start a business in their own country requires advice and assistance. If you are planning to start a business – however large or small – in a foreign country your need is even greater.

If you are a UK citizen there are a number of British organisations you can call on:

- Department of Trade and Industry, British Overseas Trade Board, Exports to North America Branch, which publishes the *UK Businessman's Guide to American Law, Business Practices and Taxation.*

- British Trade and Investment Office, British Consulate General, New York, which publishes a booklet entitled *Setting Up Your Own Business in the USA* and can provide a list of recommended lawyers.

- Other British missions in the United States – the Commercial Office of the Embassy in Washington and the various Consulates-General.

- The British-American Chamber of Commerce, in London, New York and California, and the British-Florida Chamber of Commerce.

US sources of advice and assistance
There are also plenty of organisations in the United States that may be able to provide you with advice. The larger you are, and the more likely you are to employ US residents and contribute to the US economy, the greater the range of financial incentives available to you.

The Department of Commerce
The International Trade Administration publishes *Investment in the USA*. The Industrial Development Section publishes the *Site Selection Handbook*, which has details of the financial assistance, tax incentives and special services for industrial development. The Bureau of Economic Analysis produces the *Survey of Current Business* and other publications. The Commercial Attaché at the US Embassy may be able to provide you with the information you need.

The state governments
Generally speaking, the individual states of the Union have a very positive attitude to foreigners wishing to set up in business, even if the business is relatively small. Different states compete with one another to attract newcomers, often offering tax and

other incentives, and many produce detailed brochures on the advantages they offer to investors. Their economic development departments (listed in Appendix G) should be able to offer you advice. Many of them have offices in Europe and a few, notably California, Florida, New Jersey and New York, are represented in London.

Local chambers of commerce and trade or professional associations
City and state chambers of commerce are a useful source of local business intelligence, and should be able to suggest useful professional contacts. (Chambers of commerce are listed in Appendix G; a number of trade and professional associations appear in Appendix A.)

US Small Business Administration
Although created to assist US residents to set up their own businesses, the Administration produces a wide range of publications and videos of interest to any small scale entrepreneur, which cover all elements of business from financial management to marketing and crime prevention. In addition, Small Business Development Centres provide training, counselling and research; Small Business Institutes provide free management studies; SCORE (Service Corps of Retired Executives) provides free training and one-to-one counselling; and specialised financing is available. While you as a newcomer may not be eligible for all of these benefits, there is no harm in asking about them.

Other sources of advice
These include banks, lawyers, accountants and business consultants; in the larger centres you may find the affiliates of UK or Irish firms. There are also several excellent handbooks on starting businesses.

MATTERS FOR CONSIDERATION

American law can be baffling to a newcomer, and if you are setting up in business you will have to take care not to put a foot wrong. It is therefore advisable to engage the services of a reputable lawyer who can not only deal with the legal requirements of your business, but also ensure that you do not fall foul of the Immigration and Naturalisation Service.

As in the UK there are basically three types of business organisation:

- the sole proprietor
- the partnership
- the corporation.

It is up to you and your adviser to decide which of the three is most suitable for you. There are, incidentally, four other types of companies – the limited partnership, the statutory partnership association, the unincorporated association and the business trust, but these are rarely used these days.

All entities doing business in the United States are subject to laws enacted at three levels of government – federal, state and local. While there may be considerable similarity between the laws, there are also significant differences. If you are planning to employ people, you need to be conversant with the labour regulations of the state in which you operate.

The economic development office of the state may help to steer you through some of the red tape. Its officials can advise you about any licences you need to operate your business and of the regulations that apply to your activities. The relevant chamber of commerce or local branch of the Small Business Administration should also be able to help.

From the city, town or county in which you intend to operate you may well have to obtain a business licence and make sure that you are not contravening planning laws, building codes and other regulations. You will also have to register with the state tax office and the federal Internal Revenue Service, which can provide you with a *Going Into Business* Tax Kit.

If you start to employ people, the IRS will provide you with an employer's identification number, and you will need to contact the state labor department and various arms of the federal Department of Labor, notably:

- The Occupational Safety and Health Administration, which sets standards for health and safety at work

- Unemployment Insurance Service, which levies a contribution from employers to provide dole to the unemployed

- Employment Standards Administration, which regulates working hours, the employment of minors, minimum wages, *etc.*

WHAT BUSINESS?

The details mentioned above should indicate that people starting up on their own in the United States, as indeed anywhere, need to have their wits about them. Americans are not averse to driving hard bargains, and make no allowances for enterprises that are just finding their feet. All the more reason for doing a thorough investigation into the market in advance.

Many people prefer to make use of their professional skills, and this is very sensible. If you are qualified in some branch of the health care field, for instance, you could set up your own practice, though care needs to be taken to choose the right locality. Bear in mind that you will need to make sure your qualifications are recognised, and you may be required to take an examination.

Computer consultants and electronic systems designers should also be able to make a good living. There could also be scope for self-employed plumbers, electricians and gardeners, particularly in such states as Florida where there are large numbers of elderly people and a booming construction industry. However, you will need to make out a good case for yourself in order to get the necessary work visa.

You may find there is no real demand for the skills you deployed back home, in which case you will need to investigate alternatives. You could look into the possibility of buying a small business, such as a shop, a rest home or a restaurant. There is something of a vogue for British style pubs in California and Florida, and if you see yourself in the role of 'mine host' this could be an option for you.

Taking on a franchise is another possibility. A franchisor provides you with the knowhow (and sometimes equipment, marketing and supplies) in return for a fee and a percentage of the profits. However, not all franchises are as profitable and trouble-free as they may sound, and you should take appropriate advice (legal and financial) before you enter into any agreement.

The International Franchise Association may be able to advise you of the standing of a particular franchisor.

You should, however, guard against jumping on a bandwagon, since such vehicles have a nasty habit of coming to an abrupt halt. Ideally, you need to be in a sector with good prospects for expansion. The final chapter will attempt to suggest which sectors these are.

9

Looking Ahead

Most of this book has concentrated on the here and now, but if you have long-term aspirations you have to look ahead. In the words of John Galsworthy: 'If you do not think about the future you cannot have one.'

This chapter looks into the future. It speculates about future job prospects in the United States, and in particular, the most promising job sectors and areas for employment. If, however, you are interested in exploring other options – returning home, or perhaps moving on to some other country – these questions are also dealt with briefly.

WHAT ARE THE FUTURE JOB PROSPECTS?

During the Clinton administration the American economy went from strength to strength while others, especially in the Far East, faltered. This meant more jobs and better prospects in many regions, though some states were untouched by the newly found prosperity.

More recently the economy has been in a fragile state and companies have cut back on staff, including recruitment from overseas. But America has been here before and eventually confidence will return.

Certain industries will require fewer staff, either because they are in decline or because of increases in productivity; the automobile and textile industries are cases in point. Others will require more staff, because they are expanding. The outstanding examples here are the health care and home care sectors.

Clearly it makes sense to look for jobs where there is going to be a growth in demand. Fortunately we have some useful forecasts to go by; every two years the Bureau of Labor Statistics of the US Department of Labor produces employment projections for each occupation. The latest projections to hand relate to the period 1996–2006.

Figure 17 shows the occupations that are expected to grow the fastest with the IT sector topping the bill. Indeed, the number of IT jobs looks set to double. Health care occupations are also likely to undergo a rapid expansion – partly, one suspects, in response to the growing health care needs of an ageing population.

Other sectors which will require many more staff in the future are pre-school education and special education. Prospects also look good for legal assistants (paralegals) and people working in the financial sector. There will also be more opportunities for restaurant managers and musicians.

By contrast numerous manufacturing occupations are likely to decline, especially in the textile, electronics and plastics industries, as a result of automation. Fewer bookkeepers, accounting and auditing clerks will be needed in offices, and the number of typists is likely to fall as well. Telecommunications is also going to lose jobs. However, these are not sectors where much recruitment was done from abroad anyway.

To return to the expanding occupational sectors, while many of the extra jobs mentioned will be taken up by Americans, not all of them will be. Reviewing data showing the mathematical proficiency of pupils in the twelfth grade, an American labour expert noted that 'a very small pool of young people today appear educationally prepared for many of the occupations projected to grow most rapidly in the 1990–2005 period'.[1]

However, predictions need to be taken with a pinch of salt as they may be based on inaccurate data. In the 1980s the National Science Foundation predicted a shortfall of trained engineers and scientists by 2005, yet at present there is a glut of PhD graduates in engineering (electrical, civil and chemical), maths, bioscience and economics.

THE MOST PROMISING AREAS

Americans are much more mobile than Europeans, and far more prepared to move to where the action is. Consequently during the 1970s and 1980s there was a migration from the north and east of the country to the booming Sunbelt region stretching from southern California to Virginia. The Rocky Mountain states also experienced growth during this period, while the Great Plains experienced decline.

[1]Ronald Kutscher in his article *New BLS Projections: Findings and Implications* (Monthly Labor Review, November 1991).

Occupation	Employment (1,000)		Change		Quartile rank by 1997 median hourly earnings	Education and training category
	1998	2008	Number (1,000)	Percent		
Computer engineers	299	622	323	108	1	Bachelor's degree
Computer support specialists	429	869	439	102	1	Associate degree
Systems analysts	617	1194	577	94	1	Bachelor's degree
Database administrators	87	155	67	77	1	Bachelor's degree
Desktop publishing specialists	26	44	19	73	2	Long-term on-the-job training
Paralegals and legal assistants	136	220	84	62	2	Associate degree
Personal care and home health aides	746	1179	433	58	4	Short-term on-the-job training
Medical assistants	252	398	146	58	3	Moderate-term on-the-job training
Social and human services assistants	268	410	141	53	3	Moderate-term on-the-job training
Physician assistants	66	98	32	48	1	Bachelor's degree
Data processing equipment repairers	79	117	37	47	2	Postsecondary vocational training
Residential counsellors	190	278	88	46	3	Bachelor's degree
Electronic semiconductor processors	63	92	29	45	2	Moderate-term on-the-job training
Medical records and health information technicians	92	133	41	44	3	Associate degree
Physical therapy assistants and aides	82	118	36	44	3	Associate degree
Engineering, natural science, and computer and information systems managers	326	468	142	43	1	Work experience plus bachelor's or higher degree
Respiratory therapists	86	123	37	43	2	Associate degree
Dental assistants	229	325	97	42	3	Moderate-term on-the-job training
Surgical technologists	54	77	23	42	2	Postsecondary vocational training
Securities, commodities, and financial services sales agents	303	427	124	41	1	Bachelor's degree
Dental hygienists	143	201	58	41	1	Associate degree
Occupational therapy assistants and aides	19	26	7	40	2	Associate degree
Cardiovascular technologists and technicians	21	29	8	39	2	Associate degree
Correctional officers	383	532	148	39	2	Long-term on-the-job training
Speech-language pathologists and audiologists	105	145	40	38	1	Masters degree
Social workers	604	822	218	36	2	Bachelor's degree
Bill and account collectors	311	420	110	35	3	Short-term on-the-job training

Fig. 17. Fastest growing occupations. (US Bureau of Labor Statistics)

Occupation	Employment 1996	% Change 1996–2006	Numerical change
Telephone installers and repairers	37,000	–74	–27,000
Computer operators	291,000	–32	–94,000
Fishers, hunters, trappers	47,000	–21	–9,600
Shoe and leather workers	21,000	–20	–4,300
Electrical home entertainment equipment repairers	33,000	–19	–6,200
Prepress workers (printing)	155,000	–17	–27,000
Apparel workers	835,000	–16	–133,000
Farm equipment mechanics	44,000	–16	–7,000
Private household workers	802,000	–15	–121,000
Textile machinery operators	272,000	–14	–38,000
Petroleum engineers	13,000	–14	–1,900
Mining engineers	3,100	–13	–400
Farmers and farm managers	1,290,000	–9	–118,000
Telephone operators	319,000	–9	–30,000
Typists, word processors and data entry clerks	1,088,000	–7	–74,000
Tool and die makers	134,000	–7	–9,400

Fig. 18. Fastest declining occupations: 1996–2006.
(US Bureau of Labor Statistics).

These areas continue to look promising. The value of exports from Arizona, Utah, Idaho, Colorado and Oregon doubled between 1990 and 1995 thanks to proximity to fast growing markets in Asia and Latin America, and a 1996 DRI/McGraw Hill survey estimated that two thirds of the job growth of the next five years would come in the south and west (which includes Alaska and New Mexico). States in the south east such as Maryland, Delaware, Kentucky, West Virginia, Oklahoma and the District of Columbia will see 10 per cent job growth.

As far as one can predict, the need for oil is going to continue, so 'the oil patch', as it is sometimes known, will continue to prosper, apart from a few blips now and then. One would expect the high-tech industries that have sprung up in the region to have a bright future. Defence-related industries, however, look less secure.

Although the Mid West has experienced difficulties in the agricultural sector, many of its cities are flourishing. Minneapolis-St Paul is just one of the centres which is keen to attract outsiders, and so is Nebraska which currently boasts the lowest unemployment rate in the US. The North East offers the worst prospects for employment and growth because of its high costs and downsizing in financial services, utilities and defence. However, New York City has always been the leading centre for finance, publishing, fashion and entertainment, and is likely to remain so into the distant future.

RETURNING HOME TO AN ESTABLISHED POSITION

If you are on the permanent staff of a company you can expect a transfer home sooner or later. This can be a relief to some; but more often than not it will be a wrench, particularly if you have come to enjoy the American life style.

'Re-entry', as the return home is sometimes described, is not always a smooth process, and you will need to call on your capacity for adaptation once more. The International Committee of the Chartered Institute of Personnel and Development offers sound advice:

• Take time to wind down properly.

• Assess and review the change in yourself and those at home.

- Gradually re-establish relations with friends, relatives and professional contacts.

- Plan long- and short-term goals along with strategies for achieving them.

- Accept that you will probably suffer some reverse culture shock, particularly of an organisational, financial and psychological nature.

MOVING ON

If you are on a contract, you may have the option of renewing it; but on the other hand you may well feel it is time to get up and go. Americans believe that if you want to get on you move on rather than stay with the same company for years on end.

There are five main options to consider:

Get another job in the United States

You are well placed to find yourself a better position with another employer. This is easy if you are a resident alien with a 'green card'; but if you are on a temporary visa your new employer will have to be informed and told about the business of obtaining labour certification. This can, of course, take time, so you need to plan ahead.

Start your own business in the United States

It is relatively easy to buy a small business or to set up your own, but if you are not a permanent resident you will need to obtain the appropriate visa. (See also Chapter 8.)

Find a job back home

If you are on an exchange visitor visa you will be expected to return home, as your stay in America has been in the nature of an educational visit designed to develop your career in your own country rather than in the United States.

People who have been overseas for a number of years often need time to readjust, and would be wise to take note of the CIPD advice to permanent employees given above. It is also advisable to set about the process of finding yourself a job in the UK well before your departure. Keep your eye on the job columns in UK publications and send off speculative applications.

Seek an overseas posting elsewhere

It is a good idea to approach contacts who know you first of all. Your present employer, for instance, may have operations overseas, and if you have been recruited through an agency, they may have other overseas postings that might be suitable.

The United States is a good place for overseas job hunting, particularly for South America and the Pacific Rim. American companies often recruit non-Americans for overseas assignments, partly because they are more adaptable but also because there are usually fewer visa problems. There are a number of manuals that will set you off in the right direction. For instance, *Getting a Job Abroad* or *Teaching Abroad* (if you are a teacher). (See Appendix H.)

Sign up for a study course

The international jobs market is a very competitive place, and if you want to stay in it you need to keep abreast of modern developments in your field. If you do not, you will soon cease to be an attractive proposition to employers. No company is going to employ a has-been – especially a foreign has-been – when they can pick someone more recently qualified who may well be cheaper to employ.

You may be lucky enough to be with an employer who offers training facilities, though if you are employed on contract terms the chances are that you will not benefit from them. Otherwise, why not look into the possibility of home study courses, part-time tuition at night school, or consider taking a sabbatical?

If you plan to stay in the United States, take a look at handbooks such as the *NHSC Directory of Home Study Schools*, the *Handbook of Trade and Technical Careers and Training* or one of the guides to higher education mentioned in the Educational Arrangements section in Chapter 5.

GETTING ADVICE

At some stage in your career you may decide that you need advice, particularly if you are contemplating changing direction.

Where can I find advice in the USA?

In the United States you will find a range of facilities at your disposal.

College career services

Most colleges, universities and community colleges have career counselling centres offering workshops, individual counselling and other programmes, and you should be able to use these services even if you are not following a course at the institution. Several can be contacted on the Internet via www.career.com.

Libraries

Many public libraries have career information centres which bring together a wide range of materials relating to careers and job finding. Some of them also provide courses or lectures on career choice.

Adult education centres

Some of these provide career guidance in the form of courses, seminars or individual counselling sessions.

Public voluntary organisations

A number of voluntary organisations exist to help job seekers, often those from minority groups. State and City governments may also offer employment advice services.

Employers

A number of the larger firms now have career development officers, usually within the personnel and training departments, who can help you plan ahead. They also bring in outplacement agencies to counsel staff who are made redundant.

Private careers counsellors

Richard N Bolles' *What Color is your Parachute?* lists selected job counsellors. You might also contact the National Employment Counsellors Association.

If you return to the UK and require some form of counselling, the British Association of Counselling can suggest qualified people you can turn to or you might approach the careers service of a local education authority. *How to Manage Your Career*, Roger Jones, contains some useful addresses.

THE KEY TO SUCCESS

Hopefully by this stage no reader has any illusions that finding a job in America is an easy task, especially for a non-American. No job is going to come looking for you; instead you need to put in considerable effort to search out suitable opportunities, more so than if you are seeking a job in your own country.

Persistence, however, is not sufficient; you also need to be well informed. An expatriate jobs magazine boasts, 'The *Nexus* commitment is research, research and more research', and this is precisely the attitude you need to adopt if you are serious about working in the United States.

The remainder of this book is devoted to helping you with your research into job opportunities. Follow up the various leads, offer a good account of yourself, and one day you may well surmount the odds and attain your objective: a worthwhile and interesting job in the USA. Good luck!

Appendix A
JOB SECTORS

This section looks at various job disciplines and provides suggestions and contacts (professional associations, trade unions, publications, major employers) which may be able to assist you in finding a job in your particular specialism. Where recruitment organisations are mentioned, they are normally UK-based and their full details can be found in Appendix B.

Accountancy

One plan is to join a large international accountancy firm such as PriceWaterhouseCoopers and see if it is possible to transfer to the US. Otherwise you could approach a specialist recruitment agency or a US accountancy firm. Opportunities arise from time to time for recently qualified ACAs in mainstream auditing.

Certified public accountants (CPAs) need a licence and are regulated by the accountancy board of the state in which they practise. This could entail taking a four part exam prepared by the American Institute of Chartered Public Accountants. Registered public accountants are subject to less stringent criteria, but this designation is being phased out in most states. Accounting practitioners are licensed in four states. The National Association of Accountants offers a certificate in management accounting and the Institute of Internal Auditors also offers a certificate.

To find out more about the requirements you should contact either your own professional institute in the UK, the accountancy board of the state where you wish to work, or one of the American professional associations.

Useful addresses
American Institute of Certified Public Accountants, 1211 Ave of the Americas, New York, NY 10036. Website: www.aicpa.org.
Association of Chartered Accountants, 666 5th Avenue, Suite 350, New York NY 10103.

Institute of Certified Management Accountants, 10 Paragon Drive, Montvale, NJ 07645.

National Society of Certified Accountants, 1010 N Fairfax Street, Alexandria, VA 22314. Website: www.nsacct.org

Institute of Internal Auditors, 249 Maitland Ave, Altamonte Springs, FL 32701-4201. Website: www.rutgers.edu/accounting/raw/iia

Recruitment consultants
HW Group, Financial Recruitment Int'l, TRC.

Advertising, public relations, marketing and retail

This is a very competitive but expanding business, and you might do best to gain an entry to one of the British firms operating in this area.

Useful addresses and publications
Public Relations Society of America, Inc, 33 Irving Place, New York, NY 10003. Website: www.prso.org

American Association of Advertising Agencies, 405 Lexington Avenue, New York, NY 10017. Website: www.aaaa.org

American Advertising Federation, 1101 Vermont Avenue NW, Washington DC 20005.

American Marketing Association, 250 S Wacker Drive, Chicago, IL 60606. (Publishes *Directory of Market Research Companies*.) Website: www.ama.org

Market Research Association, Silas Deane Hwy, Suite 5, Rocky Hill, CT 06067. Website: www.mra-net.org

Career Opportunities in Advertising and Public Relations, (Facts on File).

Public Relations News, 27 E 80th St, New York, NY 10021-0333.

Public Relations Career Directory, R. W. Fry (ed), (Career Press Inc).

PR Reporter, PO Box 600, Exeter, NJ 03833.

Handbook of Advertising & Marketing Services, Executive Communications, Inc, 919 Third Ave, 9th Floor, New York, NY 10022-3903.

Bradford's Directory of Market Research & Management Consultants, PO Box 276, Fairfax, VA 22030-0276.

Standard Directory of Advertising Agencies, National Register Publishing, 11500 W Olympic Blvd, Suite 355, Los Angeles, CA 90064-1527.

Major employers
Among the leading companies in this field are:
Interpublic Group of Companies, 1271 Avenue of the Americas, New York, NY 10020.

The Owl Group, 466 Lexington Ave, New York, NY 10017.

A C Nielson & Co, Nielson Plaza, Northbrook, IL 60062.
Ogilvy Group, 309 W 39th St, New York, NY 10019.

Recruitment consultants
DGH, DM, International Staffing Consultants, Executive Recruitment
Services, Grafton, QD.

Aerospace
There is a strong demand for aerospace engineers despite the
decline in defence spending. The main manufacturing areas are
California, Texas and Washington State.

Useful address and publications
American Institute of Aeronautics and Astronautics. Website:
www.aiaa.org
VGM's Handbook of Scientific and Technical Careers, (NTC Con-
temporary Publishing Co).
Career Opportunities in Science and Technology, (Facts on File).

Major employers
Boeing Company, Inc, PO Box 3707, Seattle, WA 98124.
General Dynamics Corp, 3190 Fairview Park, Falls Church, VA
22042-4523.
General Electric Company, 3135 Easton Turnpike, Fairfield, CT 06431.
Lockheed Martin Corp, 6801 Routledge Drive, Bethesda, MD 20817.
McDonnell Douglas, PO Box 516, St Louis, MO 63166.
Northrop Corp, 1840 Century Park East, Los Angeles, CA 90067.
Rockwell International Corp, 2201 Seal Beach Blvd, CA 90740.
United Technologies Group, United Technologies Building, Hartford,
CT 06101.

Recruitment
Butler, CDI-Anders, TMP-MDK

Agriculture
Generally speaking there are few opportunities in this field, unless
you fancy becoming a cowboy and the low pay that comes with it.
A special visa is available for people who undertake seasonal jobs,
but many of the jobs are taken up by workers from Central
America. Pay is better if you perform as a rodeo cowboy, but the
profession is competitive and the work exhausting. If you have
cash to spare, you could consider buying a ranch or farm, but
prospects in the agricultural sector are far from rosy.

Useful addresses
National Cattlemen's Association. Website: www.ncanet.org
Dude Ranchers' Association. Website: www.duderanch.org
Professional Rodeo Cowboys' Association. Website: www.prorodeo.com
American Farm Bureau Federation, 225 Touhy Ave, Park Ridge, IL 60008. Website: www.fb.com
American Society for Agricultural Consultants. Website: www.agri-associations.org/asac
Agricultural vacancies website: www.atinet.org/atinet-bin/jobfind

Architecture

To practise architecture in the US you need to be registered with the National Architectural Accrediting Board in most states or work under a registered architect. Landscape architects tend to be concentrated in the sunbelt states.

Useful addresses
American Institute of Architects, 1735 New York Avenue NW, Washington, DC 20006. Website: www.aia.org
American Society of Landscape Architects, 636 I Street NW, Washington, DC 20001. Website: www.asla.org/asla

Banking and finance

Opportunities when they occur would tend to be for experienced people in very specialist fields, *eg* Eurobonds. There are a number of British financial institutions with branches in the US, and you could always apply for a transfer. Some financial recruitment is done for the USA in the UK.

Useful addresses and publications
American Bankers' Association, 1120 Connecticut Ave, NW, Washington, DC 20036. Website: www.aba.com
American Financial Services Association, 9919 19th Street NW, Washington, DC 20006. Website: www.americanfinsvcs.com
American Bank Directory, (McFadden Business Publications, Norcross, GA 30092-3105).
US Savings and Loans Directory, (Rand McNally).
Insurance and Financial Services Careers, (Wallace Witners, Memphis, TN 38174).

Recruitment consultants
Executive Recruitment Services, Grafton, International Staffing Consultants, Financial Recruitment International.

Construction

Nine out of ten construction managers work in the contract construction industry and the same applies to most of the other specialists in this sector. Perhaps the best plan is to subscribe to one of the American construction magazines to find out where the main areas of activity are. In the past decade the sunbelt states, especially Florida, have seen a great deal of construction activity, but one cannot say whether this will continue. If you have worked on contract for an American construction firm in the past – in the Middle East, for instance – you could ask for suggestions.

Useful addresses
American Society of Civil Engineers, 1801 Alexander Bell Drive, Reston, VA 20191. Website: www.asce.org
Associated General Contractors of América, 1957 E St, NW, Washington, DC 20006. Website: www.agc.org
Associated Builders & Contractors, 1300 17th Street, Rosslyn, VA 22209. Website: www.abc.org
United Brotherhood of Carpenters and Joiners of America, 101 Constitution Avenue NW, Washington, DC 20001.

Recruitment consultants
Brunel Energy, G&T, Grafton, International Staffing Consultants, Morson, NES Overseas, Sherwood.

Creative

The jobs outlook for artists and designers is good, and a few people go to the US to operate on a freelance basis. This is, however, a very competitive sector.

Useful addresses and publications
American Society of Interior Designers, 608 Massachusetts Avenue NE, Washington, DC 20002. Website: www.asid.org
Graphic Artists Guild, 90 St John Street, Suite 403, New York, NY 10038. Website: www.gag.org
Industrial Designers Society of America, 1142 E Walker Road, Great Falls, VA 22066. Website: www.idsa.org
Professional Photographers of America Inc, 57 Forsyth St, Suite 1600, Atlanta, GA 30303. Website: www.ppa-world.com
Career Opportunities in Art, (Facts on File).

Electronics

This is a sector which employs a large number of foreign engineers – usually on contract – and job advertisements appear from time to time in the British press. A number of these jobs are in defence-related industries and in the rapidly developing IT field.

Useful address and publications
Institute of Electrical and Electronics Engineers, 445 Hoes Lane, Piscataway NJ. Website: www.ieee.org
VGM's Handbook of Scientific and Technical Careers, (NTC Contemporary Publishing Co).
Career Opportunities in Science and Technology (Facts on File).

Major employers
Advanced Micro Devices Inc, 901 Thompson Place, Sunnyvale, CA 94086.
Amp Inc, Eisenhower Blvd, Harrisburg, PA 17105.
CTS Corp, 905 NW Boulevard, Elkhart, IN 46514.
E G & G Inc, 45 William Street, Wellesley, MA 02181.
Emerson Electric Co, 8000 W Florissant Avenue, St Louis, MO 63136.
Motorola, 1313 E Algonquin Road, Schaumburg, IL 60196.
Perkin-Elmer Corp, 761 Main Avenue, Norwalk, CT 06859.
RCA Corp, 30 Rockefeller Plaza, New York, NY 10020.
Square D, 1415 S Roselle Rd, Palatine, IL 600679.
Tektronix, PO Box 500, Beaverton, OR 97077.
Westinghouse Corp, Westinghouse Building, Gateway Centre, Pittsburgh, PA 15222.

Recruitment consultants
Beechwood, CDI-Anders, Electronics Recruitment Co, Morson, Randall Massey, TMP-MDK.

Engineering and technology

In recent years there has been a decline in the number of graduates in engineering in the US, and to make good this shortfall there should be good opportunities for foreign engineers. If your work affects life, health or property you will need to register with the state in which you operate. Salaries in industry start at around $40,000 and can reach $100,000 at senior management level.

Useful addresses and publications
National Society for Professional Engineers, 1420 King Street, Alexandria, VA 22314. Website: www.nsbp.org

Society of Women Engineers, 345 E 47th St, New York, NY 10017. Website: www.swe.org

American Institute of Chemical Engineers, 345 E 47th St, New York, NY 10017. Website: www.aiche.com

American Society of Mechanical Engineers, 345 E 47th St, New York, NY 10017. Website: www.asme.org

Institute of Industrial Engineers, 25 Technology Park, Atlanta, GA 30092-2988.

Peterson's Engineering, Science and Computer Jobs, 202 Carnegie Center, Box 2123, Princeton, NJ 08543.

JETS Guidance, 1420 King Street, Alexandria, VA 22314. (Central distribution point for information on engineering careers in the US).

Recruitment agencies
Beechwood, Brunel Energy, Butler, CDI-Anders, Executive Recruitment Services, Fircroft, International Staffing Consultants, Morson, NES, Randall Massey, Rosta, Sherwood, TMP-MDK.

Entertainment and the performing arts

As in the UK this is an overcrowded profession, with a majority of its practitioners 'resting' at a given moment. While the likes of Demi Moore and Brad Pitt may earn fabulous salaries, most people live very modestly and often have to supplement their earnings. Also, unless you happen to be a very distinguished member of the profession or belong to a very important company, you may well find difficulty in obtaining the necessary work visa.

Many of the dance companies are centred on New York. If you want to be a film extra you will probably have to register with Central Casting . . . and unless you have some very unusual features there is a long waiting list.

Useful contacts and publications
Associated Actors and Artistes of America, 165 W 46th Street, New York, NY 10036.

American Federation of Musicians, 1500 Broadway, Suite 600, New York, NY 10036. Website: www.afm.org

American Guild of Musical Artists, 1727 Broadway, New York, NY 10019.

Association of Talent Agents, 9255 Sunset Blvd, Suite 930, Los Angeles, CA 90069. Website: www.wavenet.com/-ata

Art Search – National Employment Service Bulletin for the Performing Arts, Theatre Communications Group Inc, 355 Lexington Ave, New York, NY 10017.

Theatre Careers – A Comprehensive Guide to Non-Acting Careers, J. W. Greenburg, (Holt Rinehart Winston).
Career Opportunities in the Music Industry, Shelly Field (Facts on File).
Career Opporunities in Theater and the Performing Arts (Facts on File).

Environment, forestry and nature conservation

Since the majority of jobs are with the federal or state governments, these are the organisations you need to approach. This is a particularly good sector for vacation employment.

Useful addresses and publications
Society of American Foresters, 5400 Grosvenor Lane, Bethesda, MD 20814. Website: www.safnet.org
US Department of Agriculture, Forest Service, 14th Street and Independence Avenue SW, Washington, DC 20250. Website: www.fs.fed.us
US Department of Agriculture, Soil Conservation Service, PO Box 2890, Washington, DC 20013.
US Fish and Wildlife Service, Department of the Interior, 18th and C Streets, Washington, DC 20250. Website: www.fws.gov
Bureau of Land Management, Department of the Interior, C and 19th Streets NW, Washington, DC 20240. Website: www.blm.gov
National Park Service, Department of the Interior, 18th and C Streets NW, Washington DC 20004. Website: www.nps.gov
Society for Range Management, 1839 York Street, Denver, CO 80206.
Environmental Opportunities, PO Box 670, Walpole, NH 03608.
A Complete Guide to Environmental Careers, (CEIP, 68 Harrison Ave, Boston, MA 0211).
Conservation Directory, (US National Wildlife Federation, 1412 16th Street NW, Washington, DC 20036).
Conservation Careers, Ellen Shenk (Stackpole).

Health care

(See also under **Medical** and **Nursing**).

An ageing population and advances in medical technology mean that this sector is likely to grow rapidly, especially the home health care sector. However, it is not certain that the US will produce enough qualified people to cope with the demand, in which case there will be plenty of opportunities for foreigners.

It is worth bearing in mind that in order to practise your profession, whether on a self-employed basis or in a hospital, you will normally have to be licensed by the state in which you are active. This may involve taking an exam and having approved qualifications. Osteopaths, incidentally, are in particular demand in the sunbelt states.

A number of British and Irish employment consultants recruit for the United States and are acquainted with the rules and regulations. Otherwise you should contact the appropriate body in the US for further details. Physiotherapists and nurses currently benefit from Schedule A exemption from labor certification, which means there should be no problems in obtaining the required H-1A work visa.

Useful addresses and publications
American Chiropractors Association, 1701 Clarendon Boulevard, Arlington, VA 22209. Website: www.amerchiro.org
American College of Healthcare Executives, 1 N Franklin Street, Chicago, IL 60606. Website: www.ache.org
American Dental Association, 211 E Chicago Ave, Chicago, IL 60611. Website: www.ada.org
American Dental Hygienists' Association, 444 N Michigan Ave, Suite 3400, Chicago, IL 60611. Website: www.adha.org
American Medical Technologists, 710 Higgins Rd, Park Ridge, IL 60068.
American Occupational Therapy Association, PO Box 31220, Bethesda, MD 20824. Website: www.aota.org
American Optometric Association, 243 North Lindberg Boulevard, St Louis, MO 63141. Website: www.aoa.net.org
American Osteopathic Association, 142 E Ontario Street, Chicago, IL 60611. Website: www.am-osteo-assn.org
American Podiatric (footcare) Medical Association, 9312 Old Georgetown Road, Bethesda, MD 20814-1621. Website: www.apma.org
American Psychological Association, 1200 17th Street NW, Washington, DC 20036.
American Physical Therapy Association, 1111 N Fairfax Street, Alexandria, VA 22314. Website: www.apta.org
Opticians Association of America, 10341 Democracy Lane, PO Box 10110, Fairfax, VA 22030. Website: www.opticians.org
Career Opportunities in Healthcare, (Facts on File).
Career Opportunities for Psychologists, (Facts on File).
VGM's Handbook of Healthcare Careers, (NTC Comtemporary Publishing Co).

Major employers
American Medical International, 414 N Camden Drive, Beverly Hills, CA 90201.

Charter Medical Corporation, 577 Mulberry Street, PO Box 209, Macon, GA 31298.

Hospital Corporation of America, 1 Park Plaza, Nashville, TN 37203.

Humana, Inc, PO Box 1438, Louisville, KY 40201.

Manor Care, Inc, 10750 Columbia Pike, Silver Springs, MD 20901.

National Medical Enterprises, 11620 Wilshire Boulevard, Los Angeles, CA 90025.

Recruitment consultants
Grafton, Medic International.

Hotels and catering

The industry is a plentiful source of vacation jobs, particularly in the main holiday areas where jobs as waiters and barmen are fairly easy to come by, especially if you arrive early in the season. If you are a student, see the BUNAC entry and Camp Counsellors entries in Chapter 3. This is a sector which is easy to get into and employs a large number of foreigners, some of whom are working illegally. A good way to arrange temporary jobs in advance is to peruse an international hotels directory and send off a few speculative applications.

More senior posts are difficult to come by because of visa restrictions, unless you happen to be a senior executive with a British owned international hotel chain. However, there are no such restrictions on jobs on US based luxury cruises which are handled by VIP Luxury Cruise Management Division.

This is also a sector which is ideal for the entrepreneur with cash to invest or a friendly backer.

Useful addresses and publications
American Hotel and Motel Association, 1201 New York Avenue NW, Washington, DC 20005. Website: www.ahma.org

National Restaurant Association, 1200 17th St, NW, Washington, DC 20036. Website: www.restaurant.org

Official Guide to Food Service and Hospitality Management Careers, International Publishing Co of America, 665 La Villa Drive, Miami Springs, FL 33166.

Career Opportunities in the Food and Beverage Industry, Barbara Sims-Bell (Facts on File).

Major employers
Brock Hotels Corp, 4441 West Airport Freeway, Irving, TX 75062.

Holiday Inns, Inc, 3742 Lamar Avenue, Memphis, TN 38195.
Marriott Corp, 1 Marriott Drive, Washington, DC 20058.

Recruitment consultants
Profile, VIP.

Information technology

Like many other countries America is suffering from a shortage of qualified and experienced IT specialists of all kinds, and employers have to rely on foreigners to make up the shortfall. Computer vacancies are advertised in UK computer magazines and on the Internet and there are a number of UK based recruitment consultants which handle these jobs.

Useful addresses and publications
Information Technology Association of America, 1616 Fort Myer Drive, Suite 1300, Arlington, VA 22209. Website: www.itaa.org
Career Opportunities in Computers and Cyberspace, (Facts on File).
Peterson's Engineering, Science and Computer Jobs, (Peterson's Guides, Box 2123, Princeton, NJ 08543).

Major employers
Automatic Data Processing, 1 ADP Boulevard, Roseland, NJ 07068.
Burroughs Corp, Burroughs Place, Detroit, MI 48232.
Compaq Computer Corp, 10555 SH 249, Houston, TX 75240.
Computer Sciences Corporation, 2100 E Grand Avenue, El Segundo, CA 90245.
Control Data Corp, 8100 34th Avenue S, Minneapolis, MN 55440.
Data General Corp, 4400 Computer Drive, Westboro, MA 01580.
Dell Computer Corp, 1 Dell Way, Round Rock, TX 78682.
Electronic Data Systems Corp, 7171 Forest Lane, Dallas, TX 75230.
Hewlett Packard Co, 3000 Hanover Street, Palo Alto, CA 94304.
Honeywell Inc, Honeywell Plaza, Minneapolis, MN 55408.
IBM, Old Orchard Road, Armonk, NY 10504.
Intel Corp, 3535 Garrett Drive, Santa Clara, CA 95051.
Microsoft Corp, 1 Microsoft Way, Redmond, WA 98052-6399.
Sun Microsystems Inc, 2550 Garcia Avenue, Mountain View, CA 94043.
Wang Laboratories Inc, 1 Industrial Avenue, Lowell, MA 01851.

Recruitment consultants
James Baker, Beechwood, Butler, CDI-Anders, Compuware, Computing Resource Centre, DGH, Electronics Recruitment, Forsyth, Grafton, HB, Hays IT, Randall Massey, Track International, TRC.

Insurance
The headquarters of the main American insurance companies are based in Boston, Chicago, Hartford, New York and Philadelphia, but there are possibilities of working on a self-employed basis throughout the country.

Useful addresses and publications
Alliance of American Insurers, 1501 E Woodfield Road, Schaumberg, IL 60173. Website: www.allianceai.org
Insurance Information Institute, 110 William St, New York, NY 10038. Website: www.iii.org
National Association of Insurance Brokers, 1300 I Street NW, Suite 490 E, Washington, DC 20005. Website: www.nailb.org
Society of Actuaries, 475 N Martindale Road, Schaumburg, IL 60173. Website: www.soa.org
Society of Chartered Property and Casualty Underwriters, Kahler Hall, CB/9, 720 Providence Road, Malvern, PA 19355. Website: www.aicpcu.org
Insurance and Financial Services Careers, (Wallace Witners).

Major employers
Aetna Life & Casualty Co, 151 Farmington Avenue, Hartford, CT 06156.
American International Group, 70 Pine Street, New York, NY 10270.
Cigna Corp, 1 Liberty Plaza, Philadelphia, PA 19103.
Marsh & McLennan (insurance broking), 1166 Avenue of the Americas, New York, NY 10036.

Recruitment consultant
IPS.

International organisations
The headquarters of the UN, some of its agencies and other international organisations are based in the United States. Jobs in these are not subject to visas quotas as is the case if you want to work for an American firm. Some of the posts will involve foreign travel and possibly postings outside the US. There are two kinds of posts:

- Professional posts: specialists in economics, science, data processing, etc.; translators, interpreters, précis writers, etc.

- General service posts: secretarial, administrative, information, clerical, accounting, etc.

Useful addresses

Professional Recruitment Service, UN Secretariat, 1 United Nations Plaza, New York, NY 10017. Website: www.un.org

United Nations Children's Fund (UNICEF), 866 UN Plaza, 6th Floor, New York, NY 10017. Website: www.unicef.org

United Nations Development Programme (UNDP), 1 United Nations Plaza, New York, NY 10017. Website: www.undp.org

United Nations Institute for Training & Research, 801 UN Plaza, New York, NY 10017. Website: www.unitr.org

United Nations Population Fund (UNPFA), 200 East 42nd Street, New York, NY 10017. Website: www.unfpa.org

International Monetary Fund, 700 19th Street NW, Washington, DC 20431. Website: www.imf.org/recruitment

World Bank, (including International Bank for Reconstruction and Development, International Development Association, International Finance Corporation) 1818 H Street NW, Washington DC 20433. Website: www.worldbank.org

Inter-American Development Bank, 1300 New York Avenue NW, Washington, DC 20577. Website: www.iadb.org

Law

This is a sector which is likely to experience expansion in coming years, and this is particularly true for legal assistants (paralegals). American law is similar to British Common Law, so there should be few problems in making the transition. However the Americans make no distinction between barristers and solicitors. To practise as a lawyer you may need to take the Multistate Bar Examination (MBE) and perhaps a written ethics examination as well. To obtain information about the requirements you should contact the Clerk to the Supreme Court of the state in which you will be practising or the State Board of Bar Examiners. The Law Society in London can also advise you.

Useful addresses and websites

American Bar Association, 750 North Lake Short Drive, Chicago, IL 60611. Website: www.abanet.org (Publishes *Regulation of Foreign Lawyers* which deals with the jurisdictions in a number of states.)

National Association of Legal Assistants, Inc, 1516, S Boston, Suite 200, Tulsa, OK 74119. Website: www.nala.org

National Federation of Paralegal Associations, PO Box 33108, Kansas City, MO 64114-0108.

National Employment Listing Service for the Criminal Justice System and Social Services, Criminal Justice Center, Sam Houston State University, Huntsville, TX 77341.

FBI, US Dept of Justice, Washington, DC 20535.
Website: www.lawyersearch.com
Website: www.chicago.lawjobs.com
Website: www.attorneysearch.com
Website: www. legnetwork.com

Recruitment consultants
Executive Recruitment Services, HW, QD.

Librarianship and information science
Opportunities tend to be few and far between, unless you have specialist skills that are in demand. The most fruitful areas to look at are the academic and public sectors.

Useful addresses
American Library Association, 50 E Huron St, Chicago, IL 60611.
    Website: www.ala.org
American Society for Information Science, 8720 Georgia Ave, Suite 501, Silver Spring, MD 20910-3606.

Management and management consultancy
For management positions one idea is to approach an executive search or recruitment organisation either in this country or in the US. If your own company has interests in the US you should see if it is possible to get a transfer. Another idea is to set up your own business. Management and management consultancy posts in the US are advertised from time to time in the British press. Prospects for management analysts – of whom 50% are self-employed – look particularly good.

Useful addresses and publications
American Management Association, 1601 Broadway, New York, NY 10019. Website: www.amanet.org
Association of Management Consultants, 521 Fifth Avenue, 35th Floor, New York, NY 10175. Website: www.imcusa.org
Association of Management Consulting Firms, 521 Fifth Avenue, 35th Floor, New York, NY 10175. Website: www.amcf.org
National Management Association, 2210 Ann Arbor Boulevard, Dayton, OH 45439. Website: www.nma1.org
Peterson's Business and Management Jobs, 202 Carnegie Center, Box 2123, Princeton, NJ 08543.
VGM's Handbook of Business and Management Careers, C.T. Norback, (ed) (VGM Career Books).

Recruitment consultants
Executive Recruitment Services. See also Appendix C: Executive Recruitment.

Medicine

At one time doctors and surgeons encountered few barriers to entering and practising in the US, but since 1977 they have needed to apply for labour certification (unless they are eminent in their field) and pass a visa qualifying examination or the National Board of Medical Examiners exam (Parts I and II). It is possible to do non-clinical work on a B2 visa provided it is non-remunerative, and on a J-1 visa provided it is related to your training programme. Physicians intending to become permanent residents must first work for three years on H-1B visa status.

The North East has the highest doctor-patient ratio, so your chances will be increased if you head for areas where the ratio is lower, *eg* the southern states. The US Department of Health and Human Resources can provide a list of areas where medical practitioners are in short supply.

Working as a doctor in the US can be extremely remunerative. However, medical insurance companies are now seeking to keep costs down by shifting to managed health care programmes that rely to a greater extent on medical assistants. The era of fat fees for consultations could be drawing to a close.

Useful address
American Medical Association, 515 N State St, Chicago, IL 60610. Website: www.ama-assn.org
Department of Health and Human Resources, 200 Independence Avenue SW, Washington, DC 20201. Website: www.os.dhhs.gov

Mining

(See also Oil and gas).
This is a sector which appears to be in decline. Certainly there are very few opportunities available.

Useful addresses
American Institute of Mining, Metallurgical and Petroleum Engineers, 345 E 47th Street, 14th Floor, New York, NY 10017. Website: www.idis.com/aime/
Geological Society of America, PO Box 9140, 3300 Penrose Place, Boulder, CO 80301. Website: www.geosociety.org

Minerals, Metals & Materials Society, 420 Commonwealth Drive, Warrendale, PA 15086. Website: www.tms.com

Society for Mining, Metallurgy and Exploration, PO Box 625002, Littleton, CO 80127-5002. Website: www.smenet.org

Miscellaneous trades

There could be opportunities as a self-employed person provided you can get a visa. A number of trades are heavily unionised and you may have to join a union in order to get a good job.

Useful addresses

The American Welding Society, 550 NW LeJeune Road, Miami, FL 33135.

International Brotherhood of Electrical Workers, 1125 15th St, NW, Suite 1201, Washington, DC 20005.

International Brotherhood of Painters and Allied Trades, 1750 New York Avenue NW, 8th Floor, Washington, DC 20006.

National Association of Plumbing, Heating and Cooling Contractors, PO Box 6808, Falls Church, VA 22046. Website: www.naphec.org

Nursing

(See also Health care)

There are excellent opportunities for nurses in the USA. Healthcare is an expanding sector and there is a special visa category (H-1A) for nurses which currently exempts them from the labor certification requirement. However, before you can practise in the US, in nearly every state except Arkansas, you need to pass a licensing examination. This can either be a state board exam or the CGFNS examination which is held three times a year at various locations around the world, including London. Several agencies in the UK recruit nursing staff and some US hospital companies have offices in London. There are four nursing grades:

- Licensed Practical Nurse. An LPN works under the supervision of doctor or registered nurse in hospitals, private homes, surgeries and clinics.

- Registered Nurse. The next step up the ladder. Two-thirds of RNs work in hospitals, with the rest working in nursing homes, community clinics, private clinics and industry.

- Certified Nurse-Midwife. A CNM is a registered nurse with additional training.

- Nurse Practitioner. The highest grade of all. A nurse practitioner is a registered nurse with additional training who is licensed to perform routine medical procedures.

Useful addresses
American College of Nurse-Midwives, 818 Connecticut Avenue NW, Washington, DC 20006. Website: www.midwife.org
American Nurses' Association, 600 Maryland Ave SW, Suite 100W, Washington, DC 20024-2571. Website: www.ana.org
National League for Nursing, 350 Hudson Street, New York, NY 10014. Website: www.nln.org
American Hospital Association, Division of Nursing, 1 N Franklin Street, Chicago, IL 60611. Website: www.aha.org
Commission on Graduates of Foreign Nursing Schools (CGFNS), 3624 Market Street, Philadelphia, PA 19104.

Recruitment consultants
Grafton, Medic International.

Oil and gas
There are a number of foreigners working in this sector, and job advertisements appear from time to time in the British press. Texas, Oklahoma, Louisiana, California and Alaska are the main areas for this industry. (See also **Mining**.)

Useful address
Society of Petroleum Engineers, 222 Palisades Creek Drive, Richardson, TX 75083-3836. Website: www.spe.org

Major employers
Atlantic Richfield, 515 South Flower Street, Los Angeles, CA 90071.
Chevron Corp, 475 Market Street, San Francisco, CA 94105.
Exxon Corp, 225 East John W Carpenter Freeway, Irving, TX 75062-2298.
Halliburton Co, 500 N Akard Street, Dallas, TX 75201.
Occidental Petroleum Corp, 10889 Wilshire Boulevard, Los Angeles, CA 90024.
Phillips Petroleum Co, Adams Building, Bartlesville, OK 74004.
Texaco, 2000 Westchester Avenue, White Plains, NY 10650.
Unocal, 2141 Rosencrans Avenue, Suite 400, El Segundo, CA 90245.

Recruitment consultants
ABB Lutech, Brunel Energy, CDI-Anders, G&T, International Staffing Consultants, Morson, NES, Rosta, Sherwood.

Personnel and training
There are good prospects in this area, particularly in the employment agency sector, but a foreigner would need to become fully versed in US employment legislation in order to obtain a management post. There are advantages in becoming a certified personnel consultant.

Useful addresses
American Society for Training and Development, 1630 Duke Street, PO Box 1443, Alexandria, VA 22313. Website: www.astd.org
Society for Human Resource Management, 1800 Duke Street, Alexandria, VA 22314. Website: www.shrm.org

Pharmaceuticals
The pharmaceuticals industry is very competitive and, as in the UK, there have been a number of mergers.

Useful addresses
American Pharmaceutical Association, 2215 Constitution Ave, NW, Washington, DC 20037. Website: www.aphanet.org

Major employers
Abbott Laboratories, Abbott Park, North Chicago, IL 60064.
American Home Products Corp, 685 Third Avenue, New York, NY 10017.
Dupont de Nemours & Co, 1007 Market Street, Wilmington, DE 19898.
Bristol-Myers Co, 345 Park Avenue, New York, NY 10154.
Lilly & Co, 307 East McCarty Street, Indianapolis, IN 46285.
Merck & Co, PO Box 2000, Rahway, NJ 07065.
Sterling Drug Inc, 90 Park Avenue, New York, NY 10016.
Upjohn Co, 7000 Portage Road, Kalamazoo, MI 49001.
Warner Lambert Co, 201 Tabor Road, Morris Plains, NJ 07950.

Recruitment consultants
Butler, Rosta.

Pharmacy
If you wish to practice as a pharmacist all states require that you be licensed. For this you will need a qualification from an accredited pharmacy college (some states accept foreign study programmes), to pass a state board exam, to demonstrate good character and serve an internship under the supervision of a licensed pharmacist.

Useful addresses
National Association of Boards of Pharmacy, 700 Busse Highway Park
  Ridge, IL 60068.
National Community Pharmacists Association, 205 Daingerfield Road,
  Alexandria, VAS 22314. Website: www.ncponet.org/~ncpa

Printing
There would appear to be few opportunities in this sector, and
there could be problems in obtaining a visa unless you plan to set
up your own business.

Useful address
Printing Industries of America, Inc, 100 Daingerfield Rd, Alexandria,
  VA 22314. Website: www.printing.org

Property
Estate agents (called real estate agents or realtors in the US) are
required to pass a state licensing exam. Land surveyors also need
to be licensed. There could be opportunities serving the needs of
the growing British communities in California and Florida.

Useful addresses
Building Owners and Managers Association, 1201 New York Avenue
  NW, Suite 300, Washington, DC 20005. Website: www.boma.org
International Association of Corporate Real Estate Executives, Suite
  10, 440 Columbia Drive, West Palm Beach, FL 33409. Website:
  www.nacore.org
National Association of Realtors, 430 N Michigan Ave, Chicago, IL
  60611-4087. Website: www.realtor.com

Public sector jobs
(See also **Teaching, Social services**.)
The widest range of jobs is found in the public sector at the
federal, state or local level, though some of these jobs will be
open only to US citizens. The US Office of Personnel Management
has a network of Federal Job Centres involved in
recruitment in cities throughout the country and the states have a
similar system. If you are in the US, this should be the first place
to head for.

Alternatively, you could write to the department of the federal
government, state, county or municipality which is likely to be
interested in your qualifications.

Useful addresses and publications
Federal Job Information Center, US Office of Personnel Management, 1900 East Street NW, Washington, DC 20415. Tel: 001 202 606 2700. Website: www.fedworld.gov/pub/jobs
National Employment Listing Service for the Criminal Justice System and Social Services, Criminal Justice Center, Sam Houston State University, Huntsville, TX 77341.
National Association of the Counties, 440 First Street NW, Washington, DC 20001.
International City Management Association, 777 North Capitol Street NE, Washington DC 20002. (Publishes *The Municipal Yearbook*.)
International Association of Fire Fighters, 1750 New York Ave NW, Washington, DC 20006.
National Federation of Federal Employees, 1016 16th Street NW, Washington, DC 20036.
American Federation of Government Employees, 80 F Street NW, Washington, DC 20001.
Fraternal Order of Police, 2100 Gardiner Lane, Louisville, KY 40205-2900.
Federal Employment Bulletin, PO Box 11715, Washington, DC 20008. (Fortnightly bulletin.)
Federal Career Directory (Gordon Press).
VGM's Handbook of Government and Public Services Careers, (NTC Contemporary Publishing Co).
National Directory of State Agencies, (Cambridge Information Group).
Book of the States, (Council of State Governments, Iron Works Pike, Lexington, KY 40578).

Publishing and the media
This is a competitive field, but opportunities are expected to grow as more local newspapers are established. A number of British publishing companies are active in the US, and if you are on the staff of one of these you could look into the possibility of a transfer. The US has a vast number of local radio stations, newspapers and magazines, and you could try your luck there.

Useful addresses and publications
Association of American Publishers, 71 5th Avenue, New York, NY 10003. Website: www.publisher.org
Magazine Publishers of America, 575 Lexington Avenue, New York, NY 10022. Website: www.magazine.org
National Association of Broadcasters, 1771 N St, NW, Washington, DC 20036. Website: www.nab.org
National Newspaper Publishers' Association, 3200 13th Street NW, Washington, DC 20010.

Editor and Publisher Market Guide and *Editor and Publisher International Yearbook*, 11 W 19th St, New York, NY 10011-4202.
National Directory of Magazines, (Oxbridge Communications).
Ulrich's International Periodicals Directory, (R. R. Bowker).
Career Opportunities in TV, Cable and Video, (Facts on File).
Career Opportunities in Magazine Publishing, (Facts on File).

Major employers
Capital Cities/ABC Inc, 77 W 66th St, New York, NY 10023.
Dun & Bradstreet Corp, 299 Park Avenue, New York, NY 10171.
Gannett Co, 100 Wilson Blvd, Arlington, VA 22209.
Grolier, Inc, Sherman Turnpike, Danbury, CT 06816.
Harte-Hanks Communications, 40 NE Loop 410, San Antonio, TX 78216.
Knight Ridder Newspapers Inc, 1 Herald Plaza, Miami, FL 33101.
New York Times, 229 W 43rd Street, New York, NY 10036.
Taft Broadcasting Co, 1718 Young Street, Cincinnati, OH 45210.
Time Warner, Inc, Time & Life Building, Rockefeller Cntr, New York, NY 10020.
Viacom Inc, 1515 Broadway, New York, NY 19936.

Religious occupations
(See also **Teaching and lecturing**.)
Ministers of religion and other religious workers come into a special visa category, which means it is generally easier for them to obtain a visa to enter the US than for many lay people.

Many of the American religious denominations have their counterparts in the British Isles, and if you are interested in working in the US it is likely that you will make arrangements through the church or other religious organisation to which you belong.

The Roman Catholic Church is currently experiencing a shortage of priests and is particularly anxious to increase its numbers. Judaism is experiencing a shortage of rabbis away from the main urban areas.

As religion is not taught in public sector schools, the only openings for teachers of religious instruction are in church and private schools and colleges.

Reference
Yearbook of American and Canadian Churches, (Abingdon Press).

Scientific work

The United States possesses excellent facilities for scientific research in industry, in academic institutions and the public sector, and these attract scientists from all over the world.

Useful addresses and publications

American Chemical Society, 1155 16th St, NW, Washington, DC 20036. Website: www.acs.org

American Institute of Physics, 1 Physics Ellipse, College Park, MD 20740. Website: www.aip.org

American Mathematical Society, PO Box 6248, Providence, RI 02940.

American Institute of Biological Sciences, 1444 I Street NW, Washington, DC 20005. Website: www.aibs.org

American Society of Biological Chemists, 9650 Rockville Pike, Bethesda, MD 20014. Website: www.faseb.org.asbmb

American Statistical Association, 1429 Duke Street, Alexandria, VA 22314. Website: www.amstat.org

Career Opportunities in Science and Technology, (Facts on File).

Jobs Bulletin, Association for Women in Science, 1200 New York Avenue NW, Suite 650, Washington, DC 20005. Website: www.awis.org

VGM's Handbook of Scientific and Technical Careers, (NTC Contemporary Publishing Co).

Secretarial work

There is always a need for good secretaries, though there could be problems in gaining labour certification unless you are particularly well qualified and the prospective employer is able to make out a good case for employing you. If you have residential status there are plenty of employment agencies offering both temporary or permanent employment. (See Appendix C.)

Useful addresses and publications

Professional Secretaries International, 10502 NW Ambassador Drive, PO Box 10502, Kansas City, MO 64195-0404. Website: www.psi.org

National Association of Legal Secretaries, 2250 E 73rd Street, 3005 E Skelly Drive, Tulsa, OK 74136.

Office and Professional Employees International Union, 265 W 14th Street, New York, NY 10011.

VGM's Guide to Temporary Employment, (NTC Contemporary Publishing Co).

Social services and voluntary organisations

(See also **Public sector jobs.**)

Two-fifths of social workers work in the public sector, often at the municipal or county levels. Most of the rest are employed in voluntary agencies (also called 'non-profits'). Many states have licensing or registration requirements for social workers. This is an expanding profession, partly as a result of the ageing population.

Useful organisations and publications

National Association for Social Workers, 750 1st Street NE, Suite 700, Washington, DC 20002. (Offers voluntary certification ACSW or ACBSW.)

Intercristo, PO Box 33487, 19303 Freemont Ave N, Seattle, WA 98133. (A Christian organisation which offers a job placement and job information service. It publishes a quarterly newsletter *On the Job* and operates *Prospectus*, a database of 40,000 openings in non-profit Christian organisations. However, it is not in a position to arrange jobs for people living outside the US.)

Access: Networking in the Public Interest, 1001 Connecticut Ave NW, Suite 838, Washington DC 20036. www.accessjobs.org Information on non-profit sector employment.

Employment Listings for the Social Services, 10 Angelica Drive, Framingham, MA 01701.

National Employment Listing Service for the Criminal Justice System and Social Services, Criminal Justice Center, Sam Houston State University, Huntsville, TX 77341.

Jobs and Careers with Non-Profit Organisations, Ron Krannich (Garrett Park).

Doing Well by Doing Good: The Complete Guide to Jobs in the Non-Profit Sector, Terry M McAdam (Fund Raising).

Sport, recreation and tourism

Around half of leisure workers are employed in the public sector. The rest work in commercial and voluntary organisations, some of them quite small affairs. There is plenty of seasonal vacation work available, especially at summer camps for young people. Many of these jobs are carried out by students. (see Chapter 3.) There is also an increasing need for experienced groundsmen.

Useful addresses and publications

National Recreation and Park Association, 22377 Belmont Ridge Road, Ashburn VA 20148. Website: www.nrpa.org (Publishes a twice monthly bulletin of job openings.)

American Camping Association, Bradford Woods, 5000 State Road 67 N, Martinsville, IN 46151. Website: www.aca-camps.org

Professional Golfers Association, 100 Ave of Champions, Palm Beach Gardens, FL 33418. Website: www.pgaonline.org

US Professional Tennis Association, 3535 Briar Park Drive, Houston, TX 77042. Website: www.uspta.org

Athletics Employment Weekly, Box 86, Warsaw, IL 62379.

Career Opportunities in the Sports Industry, (Facts on File).

Career Opportunities in Travel and Tourism, (Facts on File).

Major employers

Bally Manufacturing Corp, 8700 W Bryn Mawr Avenue, Chicago, IL 60631. (Amusement parks.)

Walt Disney Productions, 500 South Buena Vista, Burbank, CA 91521. (Disneyworld).

YMCA National Office, 101 N Wacker Street, Chicago, IL 60606. Website: www.ymca.net

Teaching and lecturing

If your principal objective is to gain teaching experience for up to one year in the USA, your best plan would be to go to the US on an exchange programme. Among the organisations that organise teacher/lecturer exchanges are the Central Bureau and the Fulbright Commission. Chapter 3 deals with exchanges in more detail.

For longer periods your employer will normally need to apply for labor certification, unless you are pre-eminent in your field. School teachers wishing to teach in the public sector need to have their credentials accepted by the teaching certification department of the state in which they wish to teach, and this applies to US teachers as much as to foreign ones. The addresses are given in Appendix G.

In some states, you need to be a US citizen in order to become a teacher in a state school, notably the District of Columbia, Florida, Idaho, Indiana, Maryland, Mississippi, Nevada, New Jersey, North Dakota, Pennsylvania, Nebraska, South Dakota, Texas, Washington, South Carolina and West Virginia.

Lists of schools and school districts are obtainable from the relevant state department of education (which is listed in Appendix G). Some state education departments maintain a placement bureau that you can contact, but more often than not recruitment is the responsibility of the school district or individual school. There are also teacher placement agencies which may charge a fee.

Teachers seeking posts in church schools, private schools and higher education establishments do not usually need to meet the same certification requirements as those seeking posts in public sector schools. Applications should normally be directed to the principal of the school, college or university in question.

Academic vacancies are listed on various websites including: www.volvo.gslis.utexas./edu/~acadres/geographic.html and www.chronicle.merit.edu

Useful addresses and publications

National Association of Independent Colleges and Universities, 1025 Connecticut Avenue NW, Suite 700, Washington, DC 20036.

National Association of Independent Schools, 1620 L Street NW, Suite 1100, Washington, DC 20036. Website: www.nais-schools.org

National Association of Teaching Agencies, c/o Fairfield Teacher's Agency, 797 Kings Highway, Fairfield, CT 06432. www.jobsforteachers.com

Association of School College and University Staffing (ASCUS), Box 4411, Madison, WI 53711. (Publishes the *Directory of Public Schools Systems in the US* and *A Job Search Handbook for Educators*.)

American Federation of Teachers, 555 New Jersey Avenue NW, Washington, DC 20001.

Independent Educational Services, 20 Nassau Street, Princeton, NJ 08542, 1101 King Street, Alexandria, VA 22314-2944 www.ies-searching.org (Teacher recruitment agency.)

Modern Language Association, 10 Astor Place, 5th Floor, New York, NY 10003. (Publishes job information lists.)

American Association of University Professors, 1012 14th Street, Washington, DC 20005. Website: www.agc.apc.org/aaup

The Fulbright Commission, 62 Doughty Street, London WC1N 2LS has a small library and can provide further information on the US educational system.

The Handbook of Private Schools, (Porter Sargent Publishers, Inc).

How to Get a Job in Education, Joel Levin (Adams Media).

Telecommunications

The main opportunities are in the growing mobile communications sector.

Useful address

United States Independent Telephone Association, 1801 K St NW, Suite 1201, Washington, DC 20006.

Major employers
AT & T Technologies, 550 Madison Avenue, New York, NY 10022.
GTE Corporation, 1 Stamford Forum, Stamford, CT 06904.
United Telecommunications, Inc, 2330 Shawnee Mission Parkway, Shawnee Mission, KS 66205.

Recruitment consultants
Butler, Executive Recruitment Services, Forsyth, TMP-MDK.

Transport
Not many openings in this sector for non-Americans, though some foreigners have worked in trucking on a self-employed basis.

Useful addresses and publications
Air Transport Association of America, 1709 New York Ave, NW, Washington DC 20006.
Air Line Pilots Association, 1625 Massachusetts Avenue NW, Washington, DC 20036.
American Trucking Association Inc, 1616 P St, NW, Washington, DC 20036. Website: www.trucking.org
Guide to Airline Careers, (International Publishing Co of America).

Veterinary medicine
There are good prospects for vets. However you will need a licence to practise; this is gained through taking a two day state board proficiency examination.

Useful address
American Veterinary Medical Association, Suite 100, 1931 N Meacham Road, Schaumburg, IL 60173-4360. Website: www.avma.org

Writing
(See also **Publishing and the media.**)

Useful addresses and publications
American Society of Journalists and Authors, 1501 Broadway, Suite 302, New York, NY 10036. Website: www.asja.org
Society for Technical Communication, 901 N Stuart St, Suite 904, Arlington, VA 22203. Website: www.stc-va.org (Technical writers' association.)
National Writers Union, 113 University PL, 6th Floor, New York, NY 10003. Website: www.igc.apc.org/nwu/
Writers Guild of America, 8955 Beverly Blvd, West Hollywood, CA

90048; 555 W 57th Street, New York, NY 10019. Website: www.wga.org (For TV, cinema, radio writers.)
Career Opportunities for Writers, R. Guiley (Facts on File).
Writers Market, (Writer's Digest Books).

Further information
You will find a more comprehensive list of professional and trade associations and also employers together with addresses and telephone numbers in *Business Phone Book USA* (Omnigraphics).

Appendix B
UK Recruitment Organisations

The following listing represents some of the UK based agencies that currently recruit for jobs in the United States.

James Baker Associates

105 Queens Road, Reading, Berks RG1 4DA.
Tel: 0118 950 5022
Fax: 0118 950 5056
E-mail:info@jba.clara.net
Job Sectors: IT; High technology
Type of employer: Multinationals, large national companies, consultancy organisations.
Method of Recruitment: Advertising, selection, database.
Advertising media used: *Computer Weekly, Computing*, national newspapers.
Qualifications and experience required: Technical graduates aged up to 30 with a minimum of three years' experience; normally highly specialist computer skills are required.
Additional information: Also recruits for Europe and the Middle East.

Beechwood Recruitment Ltd

221 High Street, London W3 9BY
Tel: 020 8992 8647
Fax: 020 8992 5658.
Website: www.beechwoodrecruit.com
E-mail: mail@beechwoodrecruit.com
Job sectors: Engineering, scientific, technology, sales and marketing, software and computing.
Type of employer: Most, particularly nultinationals, manufacturers and defence industry.
Method of Recruitment: Advertising; Candidate Register; Recommendation; Website.
Advertising media used: National press; Trade press; Local papers
Qualifications and experience required: Minimum degree level; 22–45 age range

Additional information: Salaries range from £15,000 to £40,000. Also recruits for other countries worldwide. (REC)

Butler International,

Kings Mill, Kings Mill Lane, South Nutfield, Redhill RH1 5NE.
Tel: 01737 822000.
Fax: 01737 823031.
Website: www.butlerinternational.co.uk
E-mail: info@butlerinernational.co.uk
Job sectors: Engineering and Information Technology
Type of Employer: Multinational industrial and manufacturing firms. Main sectors aerospace, automotive, telecommunications, chemicals, pharmaceuticals, information technology, general manufacturing.
Method of recruitment: Advertising, executive search, candidate register, referrals.
Advertising media used: Daily Telegraph, specialist magazines and journals.
Qualifications and experience: Engineers and IT specialists with HNC or BSc and a minimum of 3 years' experience. Salary range: £18,000–£80,000. Contract rates: £12–£35+ per hour.
Additional information: One of the largest specialist technical recruitment companies in the USA with 50 offices there. Over 6,000 contractors are employed at any one time. Also recruits for Europe and Middle East. US website: www.butler.com

CDI-Anders Elite (formerly Anders Glaser Wills)

Capital House, 10th Floor, Houndwell Place, East Street, Southampton SO14 5HU.
Tel: 02380 223511.
Fax: 02380 227911.
Website: www.anderselite.com
E-Mail: resource@anderselite.com
Job Sectors: Automotive, aerospace, IT, petrochemical, power generation, marine engineering.
Type of employer: Multinational engineering and construction firms
Method of Recruitment: Advertising, Candidate register
Advertising media used: National newspapers and specialist publications.
Qualifications and experience required: Minimum qualification HND, but most of the jobs are for graduates. Five years experience desirable.
Additional information: Part of the CDI Corporation, the largest supplier of temporary technical staff in the US with around 250 offices. Also recruits for Africa, Europe, Middle East and Far East. (REC)

Compuware Ltd

34 Francis Grove, Wimbledon, London SW19 4DY

Tel: 020 8288 4880.

Fax: 020 8288 4882.

Website: www:compuware.com

E-mail: cir@compuware.com

Job sectors: IT.

Type of Employer: Fortune 500 companies.

Methods of recruitment: Advertising, database, referrals, executive search.

Advertising media used: Computing, Computer Weekly, Internet.

Qualifications and experience: IT skills such as SAP, Oracle Financials, GSM, Hogan, Adabas Natural, Snalltalk, Baan/Triton.

Additional information: Also recruits for Canada, Australia and New Zealand.

Computing Resource Centre Ltd

West Lodge, 407 Uxbridge Road, London W3 9SH.

Tel: 020 8896 3110.

Fax: 020 8896 2912.

Website: www.itjobs.net

E-mail: it@itjobs.net

Job sectors: Computing (SAP).

Type of employer: Multinationals, management consultancies.

Method of recruitment: Recommendation, executive search, advertisement.

Advertising media used: The Times, Computing.

Qualifications and experience required: Hands-on SAP experience (either computer implementation or business experience).

Additional information: US office opened in 1995; also recruits for Europe.

DGH Management & Recruitment Consultants,

Broomebourne Farm, Further Quarter, High Halden, Kent TN26 3HL

Tel: 01233 850104.

Fax: 01233 850105.

Job Sectors: Sales and marketing.

Type of employer: Multinationals.

Method of Recruitment: Executive Search.

Qualifications and experience required: Degree in Science or Business preferred; age: 30–40; at least 5 years' experience in IT, data communications or telecommunications sales.

Additional information: Also recruits for Europe and the Far East.

Executive Recruitment Services
Ambassador House, 575–599 Maxted Road, Hemel Hempstead. Hertfordshire HP2 7DX.
Tel: 01442 231691.
Fax: 01442 230063.
Website: www.ers.co.uk/ers
E-mail: ers_plc@ers.co.uk
Job sectors: Business, technology, financial, communication, environmental, legal, technical, defence.
Type of employer: Various.
Method of recruitment: Advertisement, candidate database.
Advertising media used: National and specialist press.
Qualifications and experience required: Varies according to job.
Additional information: Office in Texas. Also recruits for Europe.

The Forsyth Group
4 Thorne Passage, Barnes, London SW13 0PA.
Tel: 020 8878 9189.
Fax: 020 8878 8586.
Website: www.forsythgroup.co.uk
E-mail: tfg@forsythgroup.com
Job sector: Information technology
Types of employer: Hardware and software companies involved in the Internet, Intranet, E-commerce, wireless and telecommunication sectors.
Method of Recruitment: Executive search, candidate database.
Qualifications and experience: Candidates with a highly technical background and with Internet programming skills are of particular interest for the US.
Additional information: Associate company based in Boston, New York and San Francisco. Also recruits for Europe.

G & T Associates
Suite B, William Knox House, Britannic Way, Llandarcy, Neath, West Glamorgan SA10 6EL.
Tel: (01792) 321202.
Fax: (01792) 321295.
Website: www.gtassociates.co.uk
E-mail: dm-gaskins@gt-associates.freeserve.co.uk
Job sectors: Mainly steel industry, but also oil, gas, construction, etc. Wide range of disciplines at the management and supervisory level.
Types of employer: Various.
Qualifications and experience required: Managerial or supervisory experience.

Additional information: Recruits for permanent positions and long or short-term contracts. Also recruits for Eastern Europe, India, Middle East, Far East, and South America.

Grafton International Ltd

35-37 Queens Square, Belfast BT1 3FG.

Tel: (028) 9024 2824.

Fax: (028) 9024 6429.

Website: www.grafton-group.com

E-mail: broddy@grafton-group.com

Job sectors: Sales, marketing, engineering, construction, finance, nursing, medical.

Method of Recruitment: Advertising and candidate register.

Advertising media used: Professional journals.

Qualifications and experience required: Relevant to the job.

Additional information: Candidates should contact the appropriate branch of the agency: healthcare; industrial; or technical, IT and engineering.

Hays IT

The Tythe Barn, High Street, Edlesborough, Dunstable LU6 2HS.

Tel: (01525) 222222.

Fax: (01525) 222466.

Website: www.hays-it.com

E-mail: perm@hays-it.com (permanent appointments) and contract@hays-it.com (contract appointments).

Job sectors: IT.

Method of recruitment: Advertising and candidate database.

Advertising media used: National and specialist press.

Qualifications and experience required: Qualified and experienced IT professionals.

Additional information: A business services company which recruits for posts worldwide.

HW Group (Accountancy)
HW Group (Legal)

See TMP Worldwide entry.

International Staffing Consultants Europe

PO Box 124, Eastleigh, Hants SO50 8ZE.

Tel: (012380) 651281.

Fax: (012380) 620877.

Website: iscworld.com

E-mail: isceurope@aol.com

Job sectors: Sales and marketing, finance, management, construction, oil and gas.

Method of recruitment: Advertisement, database, search.

Advertising media used: National and specialist press.

Qualifications and experience required: Qualified for middle management and above.

Additional information: Member of the world's largest and oldest placement organisation. Affiliates in USA, Canada, Australia, Singapore, Taiwan, Europe (including Eastern Europe). Also recruits for Canada, Europe and worldwide.

Medic International (Worldwide Healthcare Exchange)

The Colonnades, Beaconsfield Close, Hatfield, Herts, AL10 8YD.

Tel: 01707 259233.

Fax: 01707 259223.

Website: www.bnauk.com

Job Sectors: Medical (occupational therapists and physiotherapists).

Type of employer: Various.

Method of Recruitment: Advertising, Recommendation, Candidate register.

Advertising media used: Professional journals.

Qualifications and experience required: British qualifications normally acceptable but may need to be assessed by US Registration Board.

Additional information: Three week orientation provided; also recruits for countries worldwide. (REC)

Morson International

Stableford Hall, Monton, Eccles, Manchester M30 8AP.

Tel: 0161 707 1516.

Fax: 0161 788 8372.

Website: www.morson.com

E-mail: recruit@morson.com

Job sectors: Engineering, especially oil and gas construction, petrochemicals, aerospace.

Type of employer: Multinational.

Method of recruitment: Advertising, candidate register.

Advertising media used: National press.

Qualifications and experience required: At least a first degree or HND in engineering. Multidisciplinary experience (eg electrical, mechanical, piping, instrumentation).

Additional information: Places around 100 engineers a year in US at salaries in £25,000–£50,000 range. Canadian Office: c/o ROAN, 2155 Dunwin Drive, Unit 4, Mississauga, On. Tel: 00 1 905 820 0679. Also recruits for Europe. (REC)

NES Overseas Ltd

6 Ambassador Place, Stockport Road, Altrincham, Cheshire WA15 8DB.
Tel: (0161) 929 1313.
Fax: (0161) 926 9867.
E-mail: admin@nesoverseas.com
Job sectors: Oil, gas, petrochemical, chemical, power, water, construction and infrastructure projects.
Type of employer: Various.
Method of recruitment: Advertising, candidate register.
Advertising media used: Newspapers and specialist journals.
Qualifications and experience required: Experienced engineers and managers with qualifications ranging from C&G to graduate level.
Additional information: Part of the NES Group, one of the largest technical agencies in Europe with a branch in Orlando (Florida). Also recruits for Europe, Middle East, North Africa, Far East and South America.

Overseas Placing Unit (OPU)

Level 1, Rockingham House, 123 West Street, Sheffield S1 4ER.
Tel: 0114 259 6051/6052.
Fax: 0114 259 6040.
Website: www.jobcentreplus.gov.uk
Job sectors: All.
Type of employer: All.
Method of Recruitment: Candidate database; Job Centres.
Qualifications required: Various.
Additional Information: A specialist branch of the Employment Service (DWP) which recruits for vacancies abroad through local Jobcentres.

Profile Management & Specialist Recruitment Ltd

201 Haverstock Hill, Belsize Park, London NW3 4QG.
Tel: 020 7692 3000.
Fax: 020 7794 4229.
Website: www.pmsr.com
Job sectors: Hotels, restaurants.
Method of recruitment: Candidate database.
Qualifications required: Well qualified and experienced professionals for senior management positions.
Additional information: Recruits for positions worldwide. Branch offices in Paris and New York. New York Office: Profile International USA Inc., 885 Third Avenue, Suite 2900, New York NY 10022. Tel: (00 1) 212 829 4333. Fax: (00 1) 212 829 5505. E-mail: profileusa@msn.com (REC)

QD Legal,

See TMP Worldwide entry.

Randall Massey

Ambrose House, 30-33 Milton Road, Swindon, Wilts SN1 5JA.
Tel: 01793 614700.
Fax: 01793 619243.
Website: www.randallmassey.co.uk
E-mail: bill@randallmassey.com
Job Sectors: Electronics, IT.
Type of employer: High-tech vendors and users.
Method of Recruitment: Advertising; Executive search.
Advertising media used: Sunday Times; Daily Telegraph.
Qualifications and experience required: Degree in electronics or computer science; 25–35 years old; unique skill set (e.g. in mobile communications or semi-conductors).
Additional information: Also recruits for Europe and Hong Kong.

Rosta Engineering Ltd

144 Castle Street, Edgeley, Stockport SK3 9JH.
Tel: 0161 429 5333.
Fax: 0161 429 5322.
Website: www.rosta.com
E-mail: mail@rosta.com
Job sectors: Automotive, construction, petrochemical, pharmaceutical.
Type of employer: Various.
Method of recruitment: Advertising, candidate database.
Advertising media used: Daily Telegraph.
Qualifications and experience required: Qualified and experienced technical and engineering personnel, design personnel, administrators, managers, as well as construction supervisors, inspectors and managers.
Additional information: Also recruits for the Far East, Australia, Nigeria and Middle East. (REC)

Sherwood Engineering Recruitment

Sherwood House, 200 Sheffield Road, Tinsley, Sheffield S9 1UP.
Tel: 0114 244 6600.
Fax: 0114 244 7800.
Website: www.sherwoodrecruitment.com
Email: robert@sherwoodrec.force9.co.uk
Job sectors: Construction and process industry.
Type of employer: Multinational.
Method of recruitment: All.
Advertising media used: E-Mail, newspapers in various areas.

Qualifications and experience required: Construction and process related technical staff with overseas experience from foreman supervisor to project director level.

Additional information: Recruits for positions worldwide.

TMP Worldwide

Chancery House, 53-64 Chancery Lane, London WC1A 1QS.

Tel: 020 7406 5000.

Fax: 020 7406 5001.

Website: www.eresourcing.tmp.com

Type of organisation: Private recruitment agency.

Job sectors: Most sectors including hi-tech industry (electronics, aerospace, semiconductors, telecommunications, software). Also legal, financial and accountancy appointments.

Type of employer: Mainly multinationals.

Method of recruitment: Advertising, executive search, candidate database.

Advertising media used: Daily Telegraph, Times, Sunday Times, Electronics Weekly, Electronics Times, Computing, Law Society Gazette and other professional journals.

Candidate profile: At least a degree plus 3-4 years' experience in the relevant disciplines.

Additional information: An international consultancy which recruits for positions world wide and has offices throughout Europe. In recent years TMP has acquired the HW Group and the QD Group which specialise in legal and financial recruitment. Owns the websites www.monster.com and www.monster.co.uk.

Track International

PO Box 1, Perranporth, Cornwall TR6 0YG.

Tel: 01872 573937.

Fax: 01872 571282.

Website: www.trackint.com

E-mail: rja@trackint.com

Job Sectors: IT.

Type of employer: Various.

Method of Recruitment: Advertising.

Advertising media used: Teletext, *Computer Weekly, Overseas Jobs Express,* Internet (own site and Job Serve site).

Qualifications and experience required: Graduates in the appropriate discipline aged up to 35.

Additional information: Also recruits for Europe.

VIP International

17 Charing Cross Road, London WC2H 0EP.
Tel: 020 7930 0541.
Fax: 020 7930 2860.
Website: vipinternational.co.uk
E-mail: vip@vipinternational.co.uk
Job Sectors: Hotel and catering management.
Type of employer: Public sector and multinational companies.
Method of Recruitment: Advertising, Candidate Register, Executive Search, Recommendation.
Advertising media used: Hotel Management, Caterer, Evening Standard, etc.
Qualifications and experience required: At least 23 with appropriate qualifications and ideally junior management experience in first class establishments.
Additional information: Few management position in the US itself, but many opportunities on board US-based luxury cruises handled by VIP Luxury Cruise Management and Recruitment Division. (REC)

The following organisations also recruit for the United States but normally to a lesser extent.

ABB Lutech Resources Ltd

Knowles House, Cromwell Road, Redhill RH1 1RT.
Tel: 01293 442110.
Fax: 01293 404225.
E-mail: intech@gb.abb.com
Recruits for a few positions in process engineering, IT and the oil. gas. petrochemical and energy industries. Candidates need to be graduates with a minimum of 5 years' experience in petrochemical or oil/gas industry. Design engineering experience essential. Parent company has offices in New Jersey and Houston, USA. Also recruits for Europe, Middle East and W Africa.

Brunel Energy (formerly Alasdair Graham Associates Ltd)

Epic House, 28–32 Cadogan Street, Glasgow G2 7LP.
Tel: 0141 302 3000.
Fax: 0141 302 3001.
Website: www.brunelenergy.net
E-mail: energy@brunel-uk.com
Recruits professional engineers aged 30-55 to work in multinational oil, gas, water, power and construction companies for salaries in excess of US$50,000. Has associate office in Houston and also recruits for Australia, Middle East, SE Asia, Europe and North Africa. (REC)

DM Management Consultants Ltd

19 Clarges Street, London W1Y 7PG.
Tel: 020 7499 8030.
Fax: 020 8948 6306.
Website: www.dmmc.co.uk
E-mail: enquiries@dmmc.co.uk
A specialist in strategic marketing, direct marketing and mail order appointments. The normal requirement is for graduate senior marketing and general managers in their mid-20s, 30s and 40s.

Financial Recruitment International

Southmead, Long Hey Road, Caldy, Wirral L48 1LY.
Tel: 0151 625 0565.
Fax: 0151 625 0058.
Recruits accountants with ACA or equivalent qualification as audit seniors for banking, insurance, fund management and public practice. Also recruits for the Caribbean, Europe, Middle East and Far East.

Fircroft Group

Trinity House, 114 Northenden Rd, Sale, Cheshire M33 3HD.
Tel: 0161 905 2020.
Fax: 0161 969 1743.
Website: www.fircroft.co.uk
E-mail: recruitment@fircroft.co.uk
Recruits a small number of graduate engineers (all disciplines, especially oil and gas) with at least five years' experience for multinationals. Has a network of offices in the USA. Also recruits for the Far East and (to a lesser extent) the Middle East. (REC).

HB Associates

101 High Street, Evesham, Worcs WR11 4DN.
Tel: 01386 49856.
Fax: 01386 41925.
E-mail: hbassociates.co.uk
Recruits graduate software engineers aged 25-35 for multinational computer/IT corporations. Advertises in *IS Opportunities*, maintains a candidate register, and undertakes executive search. Associate office in Boston, USA. Also recruits for France and Germany.

IPS Group

Lloyd's Avenue House, 6 Lloyd's Avenue, London EC3N 3ES.
Tel: 020 7481 8111.
Fax: 020 7481 0994.
Website: www.ipsgroup.co.uk
E-mail: enquiries@ipsgroup.uk

Places skilled insurance and reinsurance staff qualified to ACII standard with multinational insurance brokers and companies. The majority of candidates come through recommendation. (REC)

NOTES

REC: Member of the Recruitment and Employment Confederation, 36–38 Mortimer Street, London W1N 7RB. Tel: 020 7323 4300.
ASSC: Member of the Association of Search and Selection Consultants, 24 St James's Square, London SW1Y 4HZ. Tel: 020 7839 7788.

The information in this section is based on the replies to questionnaires circulated to a number of recruitment organisations. It does not claim to be a comprehensive list, and readers should be aware that an organisation's recruitment needs may change.

Appendix C
US Recruitment Organisations

Executive recruitment

This is a select list of executive recruitment consultancies with offices in the British Isles and the United States – and often other countries too. It is important to realise that the British or Irish office listed will not necessarily recruit for jobs in the United States, nor will US branches be equipped to deal with applications from abroad. Please refer to the relevant sections in Chapters 4 and 6. For a more comprehensive list of executive recruitment consultants you should refer to Executive Grapevine's *International Directory Executive Recruitment Consultants.*

Accord Group, 10 Park Avenue, 15th Floor, New York, NY 10017; 10 Hallam Street, London W1N 6DJ. Website: www.accordgroup.co.uk

Boyden International Inc., 100 Park Avenue, New York, NY 10017; 24 Queen Anne's Gate, London SW1H 9AA. Tel: (020) 7222 9033. Website: www.boyden.com Also in Atlanta, Boston, Cleveland, Dallas, Fort Lauderdale, Houston, Los Angeles, Minneapolis, Morristown, Pittsburg, San Francisco, Stamford, Washington.

Egon Zehnder International Inc., 55E 59th St, 14th Floor, New York, NY 10022-1112; Devonshire House, Mayfair Place, London W1X 5FH. Tel: (020) 7493 3882. Website: www.zehnder.com Offices in Atlanta, Chicago, Los Angeles.

Robert Half International, 522 5th Ave, New York, NY 10036-7660; Walter House, Strand, London WC2R 0PT. Tel: (020) 7836 3545. Website: www.rhii.com 140 offices throughout US.

Heidrick & Struggles, 233 S Wacker Drive, Suite 2850, Chicago, IL 60606; 100 Piccadilly, London W1V 9FN. Tel: (020) 7491 3124. Offices in Atlanta, Boston, Cleveland, Dallas, Greenwich (CT), Jacksonville (FL), Menlo Park, Minneapolis, New York, San Francisco, Washington.

AT Kearney, Inc., 222 W Adams Street, Chicago, IL 60606-5904; Lansdowne House, Berkeley Square, London W1X 5DH. Tel: (020) 7468 8000. Website: www.atkearney.com. Offices in Alexandria (VA), Atlanta, Chicago, Dallas, Denver, Los Angeles, Miami, New York, Scottsdale (AZ).

Korn Ferry International, 200 Park Ave, 37th Floor, New York, NY 10066; 252 Regent Street, London W1R 5DA. Tel: (020) 7312 3100. Website: www.kornferry.com Offices in Atlanta, Boston, Chicago, Denver, Houston, Los Angeles, Minneapolis, Newport Beach, Palo Alto, San Francisco, Seattle, Stamford, Washington.

KPMG Search & Selection, 345 Park Ave, New York, NY 10154-0111; 1–2 Dorset Rise, London EC4Y 8AE. Tel: (020) 7311 5374. Website: www.kpmg.co.uk Branches throughout US.

Norman Broadbent International, 200 Park Ave, 18th Floor, New York, NY 10166; 54 Jermyn Street, London SW1Y 6LX. Tel: (020) 7529 1755. Website: normanbroadbent.com

PriceWaterhouseCoopers, 1177 Avenue of the Americas, New York, NY 10036; 32 London Bridge Street, London SE1 9SY. Website: www.pwcgolobal.com/executive

Russell Reynolds Associates, 200 Park Avenue, 23rd Floor, New York, NY 10166-0105; 24 St James's Square, London SW1Y 4HZ. Tel: (020) 7839 7788. Website: www.russreyn.com Offices in Atlanta, Boston, Chicago, Cleveland, Dallas, Los Angeles, Minneapolis, San Francisco, Stamford, Washington.

Spencer Stuart, 277 Park Avenue, 29th Floor, New York, NY 10172; 16 Connaught Place, London W2 2ED. Tel: (020) 7298 3333. Website: www.spencerstuart.com Offices in Atlanta, Chicago, Dallas, Houston, Los Angeles, Philadelphia, San Francisco, Stamford.

TASA Worldwide, 750 Lexington Avenue, Suite 1800, New York, NY 10022; 1–11 John Adams Street, London WC2N 6HT. Tel: (020) 7233 1234. Website: www.tasa_ww.com Office in Palo Alto.

Ward Howell International, 99 Park Avenue, New York, NY 10016; (Whithead Mann), 11 Hill Street, London W1X 8BB. Tel: (020) 7290 2000. Website: whiteheadmann.co.uk Offices in Barrington (IL), Chicago, Dallas, Encino (CA), Houston, Los Angeles, San Francisco, Stamford.

Whitney Group, 850 3rd Avenue, 11th Floor, New York, NY 10022; 17 Buckingham Gate, London SW1E 6LB. Tel: (020) 7630 9255.

Temporary help services and other employment agencies

To list all such agencies and their branches would require a book several times the size of this one. Normally, you would apply to such an agency once you have arrived in the United States, and the best policy is to thumb through the Employment Agency section of the local *Yellow Pages* to find what is available. Some telephone directories list agencies according to their specialisation. You could also access agency websites to get an idea of their requirements.

The agencies listed below are just a sample of what is available. Most of them have several branches.

Adecco Employment Personnel Services, Redwood City, CA. Website: www.adecco.com
Administaff Inc, Kingwood, TX. Website: www.adminstaff.com
CDI Temporary Services, Philadelphia, PA. Website: www.cdicorp.com
Computemp Inc, Boca Raton, FL. Website: www.computemp.com
Data Processing Resource Corp, Newport Beach CA. Website: www.dprc.com
Dunhill Personnel Systems Inc, Hauppauge, NY. Website: www.dunhillstaff.com
General Employment Enterprises Inc, Oakbrook Terrace, IL. Website: www.generalemployment.com
Interim Services Inc, Fort Lauderdale, FL. Website: www.interim.com
Kelly Services, Troy, MI. Website: www.kellyservices.com
Mactemps Inc, Cambridge, MA. Website: www.mactemps.com
Manpower Inc, Milwaukee, WI. Website: www.manpower.com
Norrell Temporary Services, Atlanta, GA. Website: www.norrell.com
Olsten Corporation, Melville, NY. Website: www.olsten.com
Peak Technical Services, Pittsburg, PA. Website: www.peaktechnical.com
Personnel Group, Charlotte, NC. Website: www.pga-inc.com
SOS Staffing Services, Salt Lake City, UT: Website: www.sosstaffing.com
Temporaries Inc, 400 North Sam Houston Pkway, Houston TX 77060. 20036.
Western Staff Services, 301 Lennon Lane, Walnut Creek, CA 94598.

Appendix D
Newspapers and Specialist Journals

Key

W: weekly; F: fortnightly; M: monthly, B. bi-monthly; Q: quarterly; A: annual.

UK expatriate newspapers and magazines

Most of these are designed for people who are planning to work and live abroad and provide useful tips on living conditions and the jobs scene. A number carry job advertisements.

Going USA, M, Outbound Newspapers, 1 Commercial Road, Eastbourne, East Sussex BN21 2XQ. Tel: (01323) 726040. Fax: (01323) 649249. Website: www.outbound-newspapers.com

*Overseas Jobs Express**, F, Premier House, Shoreham Airport, Sussex BN43 5FF. Tel: (01273) 440220. Fax: (01273) 440229. Website: www.overseasjobsexpress.co.uk

*Nexus**, M, Expat Network, PO Box 380, Croydon CR9 2ZQ. Tel: (020) 8760 5100. Fax: (020) 8760 0469. Website: www.expatnetwork.co.uk

*Home & Away**, M, Expats International, Box 24733, London SE13 7WD. Tel: (020) 8469 3419. Fax: (020) 8694 8360. Website: www.expats.co.uk

Resident Abroad and The International*, M, Financial Times Magazines, Maple House, 149 Tottenham Court Road, London W1P 9LL. Tel: (020) 7896 2525. Fax: (020)7896 2172.

*Asterisked titles carry job advertisements.

UK weekly newspapers

Newspapers in the United States tend to be extremely parochial. If you wish to keep in touch with international and British news you may find one of the following as godsend.

The Economist, Subscription Fulfilment Service, PO Box 471, Haywards Heath, RG16 3GY. Tel: (01444) 475647. E-mail: subscriptions@economist.com

The Guardian Weekly, 164 Deansgate, Manchester M60 2RR, Tel: (0161) 832 7200.

The Weekly Telegraph, PO Box 14, Harold Hill, Romford, Essex RM3 8EQ. Tel: (01708) 381000.

The Independent International, 1 Canada Square, London E14 5DL. Website: www.independent.co.uk

US national newspapers

Virtually all US newspapers are regional papers. The few exceptions are:

Christian Science Monitor, 1 Norway Street, Boston, MA 02115. Website: www.csmonitor.com

USA Today, 1000 Wilson Boulevard, Arlington, VA 22209. Website: www.ustoday.com

Wall Street Journal, 200 Liberty Street, New York, NY 10281. This has four regional editions. Website: www.wsj.com

In the USA local and regional newspapers carry a greater proportion of job advertising than the above-mentioned journals. Appendix G lists many of the leading ones state by state.

US professional and trade journals

These constitute another important medium for job advertisements in addition to providing up-to-date information on developments in your specialist field. In some cases it is possible to access large sections of particular journals via their websites.

For a more comprehensive selection of journals consult *Benn's International Media Guide, Willing's Press Guide* or *Ulrich's International Periodicals Directory*.

Advertising Age, W, Crain Communications. Website: www.adage.com

Air Conditioning, Heating & Refrigeration, Website: www.bnp.com/thenews

American Banker, D, One State Street, Plaza, New York, NY 10004. Website: www.americanbanker.com

American Printer, M, Intertec Publishing, Website: www.americanprinter.com

Architectural Record, M, McGraw-Hill. Website: www.archrecord.com

Automotive Engineering, M, 400 Commonwealth Drive, Warrendale, PA 15096.

Automotive News, Crain Communications.

Aviation Week, W, McGraw-Hill. Website: www.aviationweek.com

Broadcasting & Cable, W, Cahners. Website: www.broadcastingcable.com

Building Design & Construction, M, Cahners. Website: www.bdcmag.com

Builder, M. Website: www.builderonline.com

Business Week, W, McGraw-Hill. Website: www.businessweek.com

Chemical and Engineering News, W, Technomedia. Website: www.pubs.acs.drg/cen

Chemical Engineering, F, McGraw-Hill.

Chemical Week, W, McGraw-Hill. Website: www.chemweek.com

Civil Engineering, M. Website: www.pubs.asce.org

Communications News, W. Website: www.commnews.com

Computer World, W, CW Communications, Box 880, 375 Cochituate Road, Framlingham, MA 01701.

Construction Equipment, M, Cahners. Website: www.coneq.com

Consulting-Specifying Engineer, M, Cahners. Website: www.csemag.com

Control Engineering, M, Cahners. Website: www.controleng.com

Chronicle of Higher Education, 1255 23rd St NW, Suite 700, Washington, DC 20037. Website: www.chronicle.merit.edu

Data Communications, M, McGraw-Hill. Website: www.data.com

Design News, F, Cahners. (for design engineers) Website: www.designnews.com

Editor and Publisher, W, McGraw Hill. Website: www.mediainfo.com

Education Week, W, 4301 Connecticut Ave NW, Suite 250, Washington, DC 20008.

Electric Utility Week, W, McGraw-Hill. Website: www.mhenergy.com

Electrical World, M, McGraw-Hill.

Electronic Business, F, Cahners. Website: www.cahners.com

Electronic Design, M, Penton. Website: www.penton.com/ed

Electronic News, W, Website: www.sumnet.com/enews

Electronic Packaging and Production, M, Cahners (electronic circuits and equipment). Website: www.cahners.com

Engineering News-Record, W, McGraw-Hill. Website: www.enr.com

Farm Journal, 230 Washington Square, Philadelphia PA 19105.

Furniture Today, W, Cahners. Website: www.furnituretoday.com

Hotels, M, Cahners. Website: www.hotelsmag.com

Industry Week, W, Penton. Website: www.industryweek.com

Interior Design, M, Cahners. Website: www.cahners.com

Library Journal, F, Cahners. Website: www.bookwire.com/ljdigital

Machine Design, M, Penton. Website: www.penton.com/md/

Mechanical Engineer, M. Website: www.memagazine.org

Modern Materials Handling, M, Cahners. Website: www.mmh.com

Modern Plastics, McGraw-Hill. Website: www.modplas.com

Nation's Restaurant News, W, Website: www.nrn.com

Nursing, Website: www.springnet.com

Nursing World, M. www.nursingworld.com

Oil & Gas Journal, Website: www.pennwell.com/ogj.html

Packaging Digest, M, Cahners. Website: www.packagingdigest.com
Pharmacy Times, M, 80 Shore Road, Port Washington, NY 11050.
Plant Engineering, F, Cahners. Website: www.manufacturing.net/ magazine/planteng
Plastics News, W, Crain Communications. Website: www.plasticnews.com
Power, M, McGraw-Hill. Website: www.powermag.com
Professional Builder, W. Website: www.probuilder.com
Publishers Weekly, W, Cahners. Website: www.bookwire.com/pw
Purchasing Magazine, F, Cahners. Website: www.purchasing.com
Restaurants and Institutions, F, Cahners. Website: www.rimag.com
Telecommunications, Website: www.telecoms-mag.com
Textile World, M, McGraw-Hill. Website: www.textileworld.com
Transport Topics, Website: www.ttnews.com
Variety, F, Cahners. Website: www.cahners.com

Publishers
Cahners Publishing Company, 6 Bell Yard, Strand, London WC2. Tel: (020) 7520 5255. Website: www.cahners.com US HQ: 275 Washington Street, Newton, MA 02158.
McGraw-Hill, Wimbledon Bridge House, 1 Hartfield Road, London SW19 3RU. Tel: (020) 8543 1234. Website: www.mcgraw-hill.com
Penton Publishing, 1100 Superior Avenue, Cleveland OH 44114. Website: www.penton.com Publish a range of trade titles.
Ziff-Davis Publishing, One Park Ave, New York, NY 10016 publish a number of aerospace and IT titles. Website: www.zdnet.com

Other publications
College Outlook and Career Opportunities, B, 20 E Gregory Blvd, Kansas City, MO 64114. Website: www.product.com/top/outlook/ outlook.html
Federal Employment Bulletin, PO Box 11715, Washington, DC 20008.
Job Bulletin, M, Association for Women in Science, 2401 Virginia Avenue NW, Suite 303, Washington 20037.
Job Openings, US Government Printing Office, Washington, DC 20402.
National Business Employment Weekly, W, 420 Lexington Avenue, New York, NY 10170.
National Employment Listing Service for the Criminal Justice System & Social Services, Criminal Justice Center, Sam Houston State University, Huntsville, TX 77341.
Employment Weekly, W, CE Publications, PO Box 97000, Kirkland, WA 98083-9700. Website: www.ceweekly.wa.com

Appendix E
Job Applications

You may have discovered the ideal job opportunity, but that is only the first step on the road to landing the job. Along the way you have to convince the employer of your suitability for the post, which means presenting yourself in a positive light from the very first contact.

In a competitive jobs market modesty and reticence have to be abandoned if you are to propel yourself to the interview stage. Americans on the whole tend to be good at selling themselves, and you need to take a leaf out of their book.

Get off on the right foot with documentation that looks good and reads well. Use good quality notepaper of A4 size, and either type or word-process your correspondence unless your hand-writing is exceptionally neat and legible.

An increasing number of people now understand what it takes to make an effective application. For those who are unsure of the process this section offers a few pointers.

Answering an advertisement

The agency or employer will often request a CV, or 'résumé' in American parlance. You should include a covering letter with it as a matter of course since this gives you an opportunity to draw attention to your strong points.

The letter should set out:

- WHY you want the job
- WHAT qualifications and experience you have
- HOW you measure up to the job description.

CV or résumé?

In the United States you do not submit a CV (personal history) but a résumé, which is almost the same thing, but not quite. Generally speaking, a British style CV offers more information than an American style résumé, because federal and state laws

Tel: 011 44 71 111 9999   20 Balmoral Avenue
E-mail: jes@britnet.com   London W19 1ZZ
                                           United Kingdom

                                           February 29, 200X

Caroline North Vice-President,
Human Resources
Iowa Investment Bank, Inc.
5432 Maine Street,
Shenandoah, IA 50300
USA

Dear Ms North

I wish to apply for the post of international business manager of your organisation as advertised in the *Red Oak Daily Tribune*. I believe this is a challenging post which will offer me scope to make full use of my extensive financial skills.

Since graduating in Economics from the London School of Economics I have worked for a prestigious merchant bank in the City of London and have been promoted twice. I have gained experience in share dealing, investment management and international financing, and have made several successful foreign business trips on behalf of the bank, particularly to Brussels, Frankfurt and Paris.

With my sound knowledge of the European banking scene I believe I am well placed to assist you in your plans to increase your international profile. I am, incidentally, familiar with United States banking practice having done a three month placement with the New York firm of Goldschmidt and Silber three years back.

I very much look forward to meeting you in order to discuss your requirements in depth.

Sincerely yours,

James E Stuart

Fig. 19.   Sample application letter.

designed to combat discrimination in the workplace restrict the type of information that should be divulged to an employer (*eg* age, sex, race, religion).

American employers appreciate the much fuller British style CVs, and if you are applying to an address on this side of the Atlantic you should not hesitate to submit a full-blown CV. If you are applying within the US you should proceed with caution; to include details of your age, date of birth, sex and family status, or to enclose a photograph, might contravene state laws on equal employment rights and render your application invalid.

Your CV/résumé should be concise, typed and, if possible, tailored to the job you are after. Ideally, it should cover no more than one sheet of A4 paper. If your career has been rich and varied, you may have to compromise by providing a one-page summary of your career followed by a more extended version.

There are broadly speaking two types of résumé:

- The chronological CV/résumé which details the positions you have held in chronological (or reverse chronological) order and is by far the commoner of the two;

- The functional CV/résumé which presents your work experience in terms of skills and responsibilities.

A typical chronological CV/résumé should contain the following information.

- Your name, address for correspondence and contact telephone number(s). A fax number or E-mail address is also useful.

- Your job objective. This is often included in American résumés as a matter of course, and might be quite a good idea for a speculative application.

- Your career: positions held, employers, dates. It is quite common in the UK to begin with your present job and work backward.

- Your education and qualifications. Make sure that the latter are comprehensible to an American who may not have a clue what MIMM, FCIS, AIBA or different classes of degree stand for. People near the beginning of their careers may prefer to put details of their education and qualifications before the career section.

- Other details: membership of professional associations, public offices held, hobbies (within reason), additional skills.

Regard your résumé as your personal sales brochure and be prepared to blow your own trumpet. You need to present a positive image to potential employers.

The interview
Before the interview make sure you are fully clued up about the organisation you are going to visit. If details are hard to come by, ring up the public relations officer and ask for a brochure or a copy of the annual report.

There are certain golden rules to observe during the interview:

- be on time
- dress smartly
- be natural
- look at the interviewer
- be polite
- stay calm
- draw attention to your strengths.

Remember that you need to convince your prospective employer that:

- you have a positive attitude to the job and organisation
- you will be both punctual and regular in attendance
- you enjoy good health
- you have relevant experience
- you are a person who can be relied on
- you can adapt to the requirements of the organisation and job.

Follow up letter
Courtesy can pay dividends in the long run. After the interview it is a good idea to send a letter to the interviewer, thanking him for seeing you and confirming that you are still interested in the job. In order to speed up delivery you might consider sending your message by fax.

If you know by this time that you have not been selected, mention that you would be glad to be considered for any future vacancies that may occur.

Owen Gwynedd

Address: 20 Caernarfon Street, Llangarth, Wales LH1 1BB
(0123) 987654 (evenings and weekends):
(0123) 456789 (daytime)
Date of Birth: 30 November 1972
Birthplace: Pwllheli, North Wales
Family Status: Married with one child
Nationality: British

Education and Qualifications:
1983–90 Llywelyn Fawr School, Cardiff
5 O Levels; A Levels in Welsh, Physics
1990–92 Bleddyn ap Cynfyn Technical College, Bala
Higher National Diploma in Mechanical
Engineering
1992–93 Institute of Petroleum Studies, Aberdeen
Certificate in Drilling Rig Maintenance

Employment Record:
1993–97 Welsh Petroleum Co, Harlech, Wales
Maintenance Engineer on an offshore drilling rig
operating off the Lleyn Peninsula
1997–2000 Antrim Exploration Ltd, Ballymena, N Ireland
Chief Driller with the Abu Dhabi project
2000–now Instructor in oil rig maintenance

Interests:
Rugby Football
Choral Singing
Collecting antiques

Other Information:
Excellent health
Willingness to relocate
Clean PSV driving licence
Member of Professional Society of Oil Rig Operatives
Languages: Welsh, Arabic
Overseas experience: Spain, Abu Dhabi, Oman

Fig. 20. Sample British style CV.

Résumé of   14 Leicester Terrace
Elisabeth Mary Tudor   Raleigh
                                            Essex ES1 2YY
                                            United Kindom
                                            Tel: 011 44 911 98765
                                            E-mail: lizt@britserve.com

JOB OBJECTIVE: Features Editor

EMPLOYMENT

1999–present   Assistant Editor, *Historic Britain* magazine
                Leicester Publishing, Windsor, Berks, UK.
                Edited articles; liaised with printers and designers;
                dealt with enquiries; assisted with promotions
1998–99   Editorial Assistant,
                Boleyn Brooks, Sydney, Australia.
                Assisted with copy editing, general office duties,
                as well as promotional work.

ADDITIONAL EXPERIENCE

                Reporter for college newspaper.
                Vacation employment as assistant manager of a
                fashion boutique in Raleigh.
                Vacation employment as a market research
                interviewer.

EDUCATION

1997–98   Greenwich Polytechnic, London, UK
                Diploma in Publishing.
1993–1997   University of St Albans, UK
                BA in History
1986–1993   Shakespeare High School, Southwark, London, UK
                General Certificate of Education A Levels
                (equiv. post-high school diploma) in History, Latin,
                Mathematics and Zoology

ADDITIONAL INFORMATION

                Fluent in French and Italian
                Typing speed: 50 words a minute
                Driving licence
                Member of Guild of Publishing Assistants

Fig. 21.   Sample chronological résumé.

Richard Gloucester

HOME ADDRESS
26 Clarence Drive
Buckingham, BX90 9XX
Great Britain
Tel: 011 44 111 22222
Fax: 011 44 222 33333

CURRENT ADDRESS
9872 York Blvd
Bosworth
OK 98765
Tel: 888 999 7777
Fax: 888 999 7778

JOB OBJECTIVE
> Senior position in either the sales or training division of a progressive telecommunication company.

MANAGEMENT EXPERIENCE
> Managed Middle East sales team of Stanley Telecommunications, and increased our exports to the area by 50 per cent in three years. Supervised the installation of telephone exchanges in Yemen and Qatar.

SALES EXPERIENCE
> Planned several sales campaigns within the UK for Brakenbury Industrial which led to a considerable increase in profits.
>
> Streamlined customer after-sales service for Brakenbury which led to a significant increase in repeat orders.
>
> Sold telecommunications equipment to seven countries in the Middle East, more than doubling company turnover in this area.

TRAINING EXPERIENCE
> Instructed apprentices at Stanley Communications in basic electrical skills, gaining a national training award for the firm.
>
> Lectured part-time in telecommunications engineering at Ratcliff Technical College. Several of my students went on to higher education.
>
> Devised and directed training programme for export sales department of Brakenbury Industrial.

EDUCATION
> Higher National Diploma in Telecommunications (post high school diploma) from Rivers College, Richmond, Yorkshire, UK.
>
> City and Guilds Certificate in Supervisory Management (by correspondence).

OTHER DETAILS
> Member of Chartered Institute of Management
> Treasurer of Oxford branch of the Lions Club
> Hobbies: Football, gliding and rallying

Fig. 22.   Sample functional résumé.

Tel: (555) 666 7773
E-mail: HenryP@sunserve.com

605 Sunset Strip
Aquitaine
WV 54321

July 4, 200X

Mr R D Franklin
Adams Lincoln Inc
519 Hayes Blvd
Arcadia FL 00999
USA

Dear Mr Franklin

I am a robotics design engineer and keen to make full use of my skills and experience. As I know that Adams Lincoln is a world leader in this field, I wonder, if you expect to have any vacancies in the near future.

Let me tell you a little about myself. After graduating in computer science from Oxford University, England, I studied for a Master's degree in Robotics at York University, England. I then took a position as a development officer at the National Robotics Research Institute in Much Hadham, and was involved in pioneering the use of robots in mountain bike manufacture. One of my inventions was a runner-up in the European Robotics Awards earlier this year.

I am now keen to apply my knowledge within a commercial organisation and to learn more about the state of robotics technology in the United States. I intend to visit Florida during the coming month and would like to take the opportunity to call on you – with no obligation on either side.

I will telephone you when I arrive in the States to arrange an appointment.

Sincerely yours,

Henry Plantagenet

Enc. Résumé

Fig. 23.   Sample speculative letter.

Tel: 011 44 987 6543
E-mail: wn@britserve.com

91 Battlefield Close
Hastings HS9 7JJ, UK

December 16, 200X

Mr T Jefferson
President
Colorado Computing Services
1490 Island Road
Miles City, MT 59600
USA

Dear Mr Jefferson,

Thank you for seeing me yesterday during your visit to London. I enjoyed learning about your organisation and the new developments you are planning, and confirm that I am still keen to join your staff.

I hope that your trip proved worthwhile and you had a pleasant flight back to the US. Please let me know if you require any further information from me.

Yours sincerely

William Norman

Tel: (123) 456 7890

156 Marlborough Heights
Halle, IL 77755
7/24/0X

Mr W Wilson
Director of Human Resources
Alabama Associates
Fort Carolina, TX 12345
USA

Dear Mr Wilson,

Thank you for your letter of July 10 regarding my application for a position.

I enjoyed my visit to your firm which is clearly poised for an exciting future, and would like to thank all of those who met me.

I am naturally sorry that you saw fit to appoint another person. Nevertheless, I hope you will keep my details on file in case another vacancy occurs in the future for which I would be better suited.

Sincerely yours,
George Hanover

Fig. 24.   Sample follow-up letters.

Appendix F
Useful Addresses: United Kingdom

Aaronson & Co, 308 Earls Court Road, London SW5 9BA. Tel: (020) 7373 9516. Fax: (020) 7835 1014. (Immigration lawyers.)

Ambler Collins, Eden House, 59 Fulham High Street, London SW6 3JJ. Tel: (020) 8371 0213. Website: www.amblercollins.com (Immigration consultants)

American Chamber of Commerce, 75 Brook Street, London W1Y 2EB. Tel: (020) 7467 7400. (Has small reference library, but appointments to use it have to be made in advance.)

Amertrans, Bushey Mill Lane, Watford, WD2 4JG. Tel: (01923) 54444. (International removers.)

Animal Aunts, Smugglers' Cottage, Green Lane, Rogate, Petersfield, Hants GU31 5DA. Tel: (01730) 821529 Website: www.animalaunts.co.uk (Pet minding service.)

Association of Search & Selection Consultants, 24 St James Square, London SW1Y 4HZ. Tel: (020) 7839 7788.

Avalon Overseas, Drury Way, Brent Park, London NW10 0JN. Tel: (020) 8451 6336. Fax: (020) 8451 6419. Website: www.avalon-overseas.com (International removers.)

BBC World Service, PO Box 76, Bush House, Strand, London WC2B 4PH. Tel: (020) 7240 3456. Fax: (020) 7240 4899. Website: www.bbc.co.uk/world service (Publishes *On Air*, a monthly bulletin of BBC World Service radio programmes as well as BBC World TV and BBC Prime TV.)

Benefits Agency Overseas Branch: Tyneview Park, Whitley Road, Benton, Newcastle upon Tyne NE98 1BA. Tel: (0191) 228 7777 or (0191) 228 7878. Website: www.dss.gov.uk

Bishops Move, Overseas House, Stewarts Road, London SW8 4UG. Tel: (020) 7498 0300. Fax: (020) 7498 0749. www.bishops-move.co.uk (International removers.)

Britannia, Unit 3, Wyvern Estate, Beverley Way, New Malden, Surrey KT3 4PH. Tel: (0845) 6006661. Fax: (020) 8336 0961. Website: www.britannia-movers.co.uk (International removers.)

British American Chamber of Commerce, 8 Staple Inn, Holborn, London W1CV 7QH. Tel: (020) 7404 6400. Fax: (020) 7404 6828.

British Association for Counselling, 1 Regent Place, Rugby CV21 2PJ. Tel: (01788) 578328.

British Association of Removers, 3 Churchill Court, Station Road, North Harrow, Middlesex HA2 4HZ. Tel: (020) 8861 3331. Fax: (020) 8861 3332. Website: www.bar.co.uk

British Overseas Trade Board (BOTB), Department of Trade and Industry, 1 Victoria Street, London SW1H 0ET. Tel: (020) 7215 5000.

BUPA International, Russell Mews, Brighton BN7 2NE. Tel: (01273) 208181. Fax: (01273) 866583. Website: www.bupa.com/int (Health insurance.)

CBI Employee Relocation Council, Centre Point, 103 New Oxford Street, London WC1A 1DV. Tel: (020) 7379 7400. (Advises companies moving staff; publishes *Relocation News*.)

Centre for International Briefing, Farnham Castle, Surrey GU9 0AG. Tel: (01252) 720416. Fax: (01252) 719277. Website: www.cibfarnham.co.uk E-mail: cibfarnham@dial.pipex.com (Country briefings.)

Copsey Removals, 178 Crow Lane, Romford, Essex RM7 0ES. Tel: (020) 8592 1003. Fax: (01708) 727305. (International removers.)

Corona Worldwide (Women's Corona Society), Southbank House, Black Prince Road, London SE1 7SJ. Tel: (020) 7793 4020. Website: www.coronaworldwide.freeserve.co.uk Email: coronaww@hotmail.com (Briefings and country reports).

Culture Shock Consulting, 311 Ballard Lane, London N12 8LY. Tel: (020) 8446 2440. Fax: (020) 8446 2441. E-mail: csconsulting@bravo.net

Davies Turner, 334 Queenstown Road, London SW8 4HG. Tel: (020) 7622 9361. (International removers.)

Department of Health Leaflets Unit, PO Box 21, Honeypot Lane, Stanmore, Middx HA7 1AY. Tel 0800 555777.

Department of Health International Branch, Room 512, Richmond House, 79 Whitehall, London SW1A 2NS. Website: www.doh.gov.uk/traveladvice. (Information on elegibility to state health facilities abroad).

Department of Trade and Industry, Exports to North America Branch, Kingsgate House, 66–74 Victoria Street, London SW1E 6SW. Tel: (020) 7215 4601.

Department for the Environment, Food & Rural Affairs (DEFRA), Export of Cats & Dogs Section, 1A Page Street, London SW1P 4PO. Tel: (020) 7904 6347. PETS helpline: (0870) 241 1710. Website: www.defra.gov.uk/animalh/quarantine

Frederick De Pasquale, Visa Services Inc., Devlin House, 36 St George Street, Mayfair, London W1R 9FA. Tel: (020) 7529 1423. Fax: (020) 7529 1402. Website: www.immigrationvisas.com (Immigration attorney.)

ECIS (European Council for International Schools), 21 Lavant Street, Petersfield, Hants GU32 3EW. Tel: (01230) 268244. Fax: (01730)

267914. Website: www.ecis.org (Publishes a directory of international schools.)

ECA International, Anchor House, 15 Britten Street, London SW3 3TY. Tel: (020) 7351 7151. (Briefings and country reports.)

Europea IMG, Fivash House, 9 Denne Parade, Horsham RH12 1JD. Tel: (01403) 63860. (Medical insurance.)

Exeter Friendly Society, Beech Hill House, Walnut Gardens, Exeter EX4 4DG. Tel: (01392) 498063. (Medical insurance.)

Expat Network, Rose House, 109a South End, Croydon CR0 1BG. Tel: (020) 8760 5100. Fax: (020) 8760 0469. Website: www.expatnetwork.co.uk (Overseas jobs magazine and directory publishers; expatriate service organisation; insurance brokers.)

Expatriate Advisory Services PLC, 14 Gordon Road, West Bridgeford, Nottingham, NG2 5LN. Tel: (0115) 981 6572. Fax: (0115) 945 5076. (Financial advisers.)

Expats International, PO Box 24733, London SE13 7WD. Tel: (020) 8469 3419. Fax: (020) 8694 8360. Website: www.expats2000.co.uk (Expatriate service organisation.)

FCO Travel Advice Unit, Consular Department, Clive House, Petty France, London SW1H 9HD. Tel: (020) 7238 4129. Website: www.fco.gov.uk/travel/

Gary M. Ferman, 27 Bruton Street, London W1J 6QN. Tel: (020) 7499 5702. Fax: (020) 7236 2533. (Immgration lawyer.)

Four Corners Emigration, Freepost NWW 5817A, Cheadle SK8 1YG. Tel: (0845) 841453. Website: www.4-corners.com

Wilfred T Fry Ltd, Cresent House, Crescent Road, Worthing BN11 1RN. Tel: (01903) 231545. Fax: (01903) 200868. Website: www.wtfry.com. (Financial advisers.)

The Fulbright Commission, Fulbright House, 62 Doughty Street, London WC1N 2LS. Tel: (020) 7404 6994. Fax: (020) 7404 6874. Website: www.fulbright.co.uk

Gabbitas Educational Consultants, Carrington House, 126–130 Regent Street, London W1R 6EE. Tel: (020) 7734 0161. Fax: (020) 7437 1764. Website: www.gabbitas.co.uk. (Education advisers.)

Global International Fowarding Ltd, 16 Perivale Industrial Park, Greenford UB6 7RW. Tel: (020) 8997 4321. (International removers.)

Golden Arrow Shippers, Horsford Kennels, Lydbury North, Shropshire SY7 8AY. Tel: (01588) 680240. (Pet transportation experts.)

Richard S. Goldstein, 96A Mount Street, Mayfair, London W1X. Tel: (020) 7499 8200. Fax: (020) 7499 8300. (Immigration lawyer with office in New York.)

Goodhealth International Healthcare, 5 Lloyds Avenue, London EC3N 3AE. Tel: (0870) 442 7376. Website: www.goodhealth.co.uk. (Medical insurance.)

Healthsearch Ltd, 9 Newland Street, Rugby CV22 7BL. Tel: (01788) 541855. (Advice on medical insurance.)

Diane B. Hinch, 24 Grosvenor Street, London W1X 9FB. Tel: (020) 7917 9680. Fax: (020) 7917 6002. (Immigration lawyer with office in California.)

Homesitters Ltd, Buckland Wharf, Aylesbury, Bucks HP22 5LQ. Tel: (01279) 777049. Website: www.homesitters.co.uk (Caretaking service.)

Inland Revenue Claims Branch, Foreign Division, Merton Road, Bootle L69 9BL. Tel: (0151) 922 6363.

ISIS (Independent Schools Information Service), 35 Grosvenor Gardens, London SW1W 0BS. Tel: (020) 7798 1500. Website: www.isis.org.uk

Institute of Freight Forwarders, Redfern House, Browells Lane, Feltham, Middlesex. Tel: (020) 8844 2266.

Jaffe & Co, America House, 40 Hendon Lane, London N3 1TT. Tel: (020) 8371 0656. Fax: (020) 8371 9677. (Visa and immigration attorneys).

LaVigne, Coton & Associates, 150 Minories, London EC3N 1LS. Tel: (020) 7264 2110. Fax: (020) 7264 2107. (Immigration lawyer with offices in Florida and Las Vegas.)

Manor Car Storage, PO Box 28, Clavering, Saffron Walden, Essex CB11 4RA. Tel: (01799) 550021.

Mercers College, 14 Baldock Street, Ware, Herts SG12 9DZ. Tel: (01920) 465926. E-mail: mercerscollege@lycos.co.uk. (Correspondence courses for young people.)

National Insurance Contributions Office, Inland Revenue, International Services, Benton Park Road, Newcastle upon Tyne NE98 1ZZ. Tel: (0845) 915 4811 or (0191) 225 4811. Website: www.inlandrevenue.gov.uk

Overseas Resettlement Secretary, Board for Social Responsibility, Church House, Dean's Yard, London SW1P 3NZ. Tel: (020) 7898 1000. (Can arrange contacts at destination.)

Par Air Services, Warren Lane, Colchester, Essex CO3 5LN. Tel: (01206) 330332. Website: www.parair.co.uk (Pet shipping agents.)

Passport Agency, Globe House, 89 Eccleston Square, London SW1V 1PN. Offices in Belfast, Durham, Glasgow, Liverpool, Newport, Peterborough. Tel: (0870) 521 0410. Website: www.passport.gov.uk

PPP Healthcare, International Health Plan, Philips House, Crescent Road, Tunbridge Wells, Kent TN1 2PL. Tel: (01892) 772002. (Medical insurance.)

Recruitment and Employment Confederation, 36-38 Mortimer Street, London W1N 7RB. Tel: (020) 7323 4300. Website: www.rec.uk.com

Joel Z. Robinson, 4 Helmet Row, London EC1V 3QV. Tel: (020) 7253 2404. Fax: (020) 7253 0760. (Immigration lawyer with New York office.)

Ryslip Livestock Shipping, Ryslip Kennels, Church Lane, Binfield,

Bracknell, Berks RG42 5NL. Tel: (01344) 424144. Fax: (01344) 861460. Website: www.ryslip.com (Pet transport.)

SFIA Educational Trust Ltd, 41 London Road, Twyford, Berks RG10 9EJ. Tel: (0845) 458 3690. Website: sfia.co.uk. (Advice on children's schooling.)

Society of Pensions Consultants, Bartholomew House, 92 Fleet Street, London EC4. Tel: (020) 7353 1688. Fax: (020) 7353 9296.

State Boarding Information Service (STABIS), DFES, Pupil Support & Independent Schools, Mowden Hall, Staindrop Road, Darlington DL3 9BG. Tel: (01325) 391272. Website: www.stabis.org.uk and www.dfes.gov.uk

Stan Steinger, 96 Kensington High Street, London W8 4SG. Mobile Tel: (07956) 222572. (Immigration lawyer with offices in California and Iowa.)

Dave Tester Expatriate Insurance Services, 18a Hove Park Villas, Hove BN3 6HG. Tel: (01273) 703469. Fax: (01273) 777723. E-mail: info@expatriate-insurance.com

TSW International, 1st Floor, Jupiter House, Station Road, Cambridge CB1 2JZ. Tel: (01223) 363650. (Tax consultants.)

David Turner, 162 Regent Street, London W1. Tel: (020) 7437 7076. Fax: (020) 7437 7079. (Immigration lawyer.)

UK Expatriates Professional Advisory Services Ltd, 84 Grange Road, Middlesbrough TS1 2LS. Tel: (01642) 221211 (Tax advisers.)

United States Embassy, 42 Elgin Street, Ballsbridge, Dublin. Tel: (Dublin) 688777.

United States Embassy, 24 Grosvenor Square, London W1A 2JB. Tel: (020) 7499 9000. Website: www.usembassy.org.uk

Visa Branch, 5 Upper Grosvenor Street, London W1A 2JB. Tel: (020) 7499 7010. Visa information lines: (09068) 200290 (recorded) and (09061) 500590 (live).

US Information Service, 55/56 Upper Brook Street, London W1A 2LH. Tel: (020) 7499 9000 ext 2643 and 2638.

United States Consulate-General, Queen's House, Queen Street, Belfast BY1 6EQ. Tel: (02890) 328239.

United States Consulate-General, 3 Regent Terrace, Edinburgh EH7 5BW. Tel: (0131) 557 6023.

Universal Aunts, PO Box 304, London SW4 0NN. Tel: (020) 7738 8937. (Personal services agency.)

US Tourism Information: Tel: 0906 550 8911.

US Educational Advisory Service: see Fulbright Commission.

US Visa Consultants, 52 Maddox Street, London W1R 9PA. Tel: (020) 7317 6709. Fax: (020) 7317 6712.

WES Home School, 202 Bramhall Lane, Davenport, Stockport, Cheshire SK3 8TY. Tel: (0161) 456 8275. Website: www.weshome.demon.co.uk (Distance learning for younger children.)

Workpermit.com, 11 Bolt Court, Fleet Street, London EC4A 3DQ. Tel: (020) 7495 3999. Fax: (020) 7495 3991. Website: www.workpermit.com

Appendix G
Useful Addresses: United States

National

American Automobile Association, 1000 AAA Drive, Heathrow, FL 32746. Website: www.aaa.com

American Immigration Lawyers Association, 1400 I Street, NW, Suite 1200, Washington, DC 20005. Website: www.aila.org

Association of Executive Search Consultants, 500 5th Ave, Suite 94340, New York, NY 10010. Website: www.aesc.com

British American Chamber of Commerce, 52 Vanderbilt Avenue, 1640 5th Street, 20th Floor, New York, NY 10017. Website: www.bacc.nyc.ny.us

British American Chamber of Commerce – California, 41 Shutter Street, Suite 303, San Francisco, CA 94104 and 1640 5th Street, Suite 203, Santa Monica, CA 90401.

British Embassy, 3100 Massachusetts Ave NW, Washington, DC 20008. Website: www.britain.nyc.ny.us/bis/ukmis.htm

British Consulates-General:
11766 Wilshire Blvd, Suite 400, Los Angeles, CA 90025.
1 Sansome Street, Suite 850, San Francisco, CA 94101.
245 Peachtree Center Ave NE, Suite 2700, Atlanta, GA 30303.
400 N Michigan Ave, Suite 1300, Chicago, IL 60611.
600 Atlantic Ave, Federal Reserve Plaza, 25th Floor, Boston, MA 02210.
845 3rd Ave, New York, NY 10022.
1000 Louisana Street, Suite 1900, Houston, TX 77002.

British Consulates:
19 Observatory Circle NW, Washington, DC 20008.
1001 Brickell Bay Drive, Suite 2110, Miami, FL 33131.
55 Public Square, Suite 1650, Cleveland, OH 44113.
2911 Turtle Creek Blvd, Suite 940, Dallas, TX 75219.
999 3rd Ave, Suite 820, Seattle, WA 98104.

British Florida Chamber of Commerce, Suite 550, 2121 Ponce de Leon Blvd, Coral Gables, FL 33134.

Health Insurance Association of America, Suite 8802, 555 13th Street NW, Washington 20570. Website: www.hiaa.org

International Franchise Association, 1250 New York Avenue NW, Suite 900, Washington, DC 20005. Website: www.franchise.org

Irish Embassy, 2234 Massachusetts Avenue NW, Washington, DC 20008. Tel: 202 462 3939.

National Association of Personnel Services, 3133 Mt Vernon Ave, Alexandria, VA 22305. Website: www.napsweb.com

National Association of Temporary and Staffing Services, 119 South Saint Asaph St, Alexandria, VA 22314. Website: www.natss.com

National Park Service, Room 1013, US Department of the Interior, 18th & C Street NW, Washington, DC 20240. Website: www.nps.gov

Service Corps of Retired Executives (SCORE), 409 3rd Street SW, 6th Floor, Washington, DC 20024. Website: www.score.org

US Customs Service, 1300 Pennyslvannia Avenue, Washington, DC 20004. Website: www.ustreas.gov

US Forest Service, US Department of Agriculture, 14th & Independence Avenue, South Agriculture Building, Washington, DC 20250. Website: www.fs.fed.us

US Department of Commerce, 14th Street and Constitution Avenue, Washington, DC 20230. Website: www.doc.gov

US Department of Health & Human Services, 200 Independence Avenue SW, Washington, DC 20201.

US Department of Labor, 200 Constitution Avenue, Washington, DC 20210. Website: www.dol.gov

US Employment Service, 200 Constitution Avenue NW, Washington, DC 20210. Website: www.ajb.dni.us

US Equal Employment Opportunity Commission, 1801 L Street NW, Washington, DC 20507. Website: www.eeoc.gov

US Immigration and Naturalisation Service (INS), 424 I Street NW, Washington, DC 20536. Website: www.ins.usdoj.gov

Eastern Region: 70 Kimball Avenue, South Burlington, 1 VT 05403-6813.

Central Region: 7701 N Stemmons Freeway, Dallas, TX 75247.

Western Region: 24000 Avila Road, Laguna Niguel, CA 92607-0080.

US Internal Revenue Service (IRS), PO Box 25866, Richmond, VA 23289; Rancho Cordova, CA 95743-0001; PO Box 9903, Bloomington, IL 61799. (People living outside the US can contact IRS at the nearest US Embassy. Website: www.irs.ustreas.gov)

US Small Business Administration, 409 3rd Street SW, Washington, DC 20416. Website: www.sba.com

By state

Each section details organisations which could be useful to a job seeker or entrepreneur. You will find the leading newspapers in each state (which carry job advertisements as well as news), state and federal government offices which you may need to deal with, and chambers of commerce which may be able to advise on business opportunities and which local companies have job vacancies. Further details are available from the websites featured.

Alabama

Website: www.alaweb.asc.edu

Birmingham Post-Herald, 2200 4th Av N, Birmingham, AL 35202. Website: www.postherald.com

Huntsville Times, Box 1007, Huntsville, AL 35807-5501. Website: www.htimes.com

Montgomery Advertiser, Box 1000, Montgomery, AL 36101-1000.

Department of Economic & Community Affairs, PO Box 5690, Montgomery, AL 36103. Website: www.alaweb.asc.edu/govern/adeca.html

Department of Education, State Office Building, Montgomery, AL 36130. Website: www.alsde.edu

Department of Labor, 100 N Union St, Montgomery, AL 36130.

Department of Revenue, Gordon Persons Bldg, Montgomery, AL 36130. Website: www.ador.state.al.us

Birmingham Chamber of Commerce, PO Box 10127, Birmingham, AL 35202. Website: www.birmingham.org/the chamber

Montgomery Area Chamber of Commerce, PO Box 79, 41 Commerce St, Montgomery, AL 36101.

Alaska

Website: www.state.ak.us

Anchorage Daily News, Box 149001, Anchorage, AK 99514-9001. Website: www.adn.com

INS District Office, 620 E 10th St, Suite 102, Anchorage, AK 99513-7581.

Alaska Industrial Development Authority, 480 W Tudor Rd, Anchorage, AK 99502. Website: www.state.ak.us/gov/boards/factsheet/aidea.htm

Department of Education, Website: www.educ.state.al.us

Division of Employment Services, Department of Labor, Website: www.state.ak.us/local.akpages/labor/esd/esd.htm

Department of Labor, PO Box 1149, Juneau, AK 99802. Website: www.state.ak.us/local/akpages/labor/home.htm

Department of Revenue, PO Box S, Juneau, AK 99811. Website: www.revenue.state.ak.us

Anchorage Chamber of Commerce, 415 F Street, Anchorage, AK 99501-2254. Website: www.anchoragechamber.com

Juneau Chamber of Commerce, 1107 W 8th St, Juneau, AK 99802.

Arizona

Website: www.state.az.us

Arizona Republic, 120 E Van Buren St, Phoenix, AZ 85004. Website: www.azcentral.com

Arizona Daily Star, 4850 S Park Ave, Tucson, AZ 85714. Website: www.azstarnet.com

INS District Office, 2035 North Central Ave, Phoenix, AZ 85004.

Department of Commerce, 3800 N Central Ave, Phoenix, AZ 85007. Website: www.commerce.state.az.us

Department of Education, 1535 W Jefferson, Phoenix, AZ 85007. Website: www.ade.state.az.us

Employment Services Division, Department of Economic Security, 1717 W Jefferson, Phoenix, AZ 85007.

Department of Revenue. Website: www.revenue.state.az.us

Phoenix Metropolitan Chamber of Commerce, 201 N Central Ave, Suite 2700, Phoenix, AZ 85003. Website: www.phoenix.acn.net/

Arkansas

Website: www.state.ar.us

Arkansas Democrat, 121E Capitol St, Little Rock, AR 72201. Website: www.ardemgaz.com

Department of Education, Capitol Mall, Little Rock, AR 72205. Website: www.arkedu.k12.ar.us

Employment Security Division, Department of Labor, Capitol Mall, Little Rock, AR 72205. Website: www.state.ar.us/esd/ark_esd.html

Department of Labor. Website: www.state.ar.us/labor/labor.htm

Industrial Development Commission. Website: www.aedc.state.ar.us

Revenue Division. Website: www.state.ar.us/revenue

Greater Little Rock Chamber of Commerce, 101 Spring St, Little Rock, AR 72201. Website: www.littlerockchamber.com

California

Website: www.ca.gov

Bakersfield Californian, 1707 Eye St, Bakersfield, CA 93301. Website: www.bakersfield.com

British Weekly, 1626 North Wilcox Ave, #337, Hollywood, CA 90028.

Fresno Bee, 1626 E St, Fresno, CA 93786. Website: www.fresnobee.com

Press Telegram, 604 Pine Ave, Long Beach, CA 90844. Website: www.ptconnect.com

Los Angeles Times, Times-Mirror Square, Los Angeles, CA 90053. Website: www.latimes.com

Sacramento Bee, PO Box 15779, Sacramento, CA 95852. Website: www.sacbee.com

San Diego Union-Tribune, Box 191, San Diego, CA 92112. Website: www.uniontrib.com

San Francisco Chronicle, 901 Mission St, San Francisco, CA 94103. Website: www.sfgate.com/chronicle

San Jose Mercury News, 750 Ridder Park Drive, San Jose, CA 95113. Website: www.mercurycenter.com

Orange County Register, 625 N Grand Ave, Santa Ana, CA 92701. Website: www.ocregister.com

Union Jack Newspaper, PO Box 1823, La Mesa, CA 911944-1823.

Wall Street Journal, 6500 Wilshire Blvd, Suite 1400, Los Angeles, CA 90048. Website: www.wsj.com

British Consulates-General, 11766 Wilshire Boulevard, Suite 400, Los Angeles, CA 90025 and 1 Sansome Street, Suite 850, San Francisco, CA 94101.

British American Chamber of Commerce, 41 Sutter Street, Suite 303, San Francisco, CA 94104 and 1640 5th Street, Suite 203, Santa Monica, CA 90401.

INS District Offices, 300 N Los Angeles St, Los Angeles, CA 90012; 880 Front Street, San Diego, CA 92188; Appraisers Building, 630 Sansome St, San Francisco, CA 94111.

Economic Development Department. Website: www.commerce.ca.gov

Department of Education, 721 Capitol Mall, Sacramento, CA 95814. Website: www.goldmine.cde.ca.gov

Employment Development Department, 800 Capitol Mall, Sacramento, CA 95814. Website: www.edd.cahwnet.com

Department of Revenue, PO Box 1468, Sacramento, CA 95807. Website: www.dof.ca.gov

Los Angeles Area Chamber of Commerce, 404 South Bixel St, Los Angeles, CA 90017. Website: www.lachamber.org

Metropolitan Sacramento Chamber of Commerce, 917 Seventh St, Sacramento, CA 95814.

Greater San Diego Chamber of Commerce, 402 West Broadway, Suite 1000, San Diego, CA 92101. Website: www.sddt.com/chamberofcommerce

San Francisco Chamber of Commerce, 465 California St, San Francisco, CA 94104. Website: www.sfchamber.com

Colorado

Website: www.state.co.us

Colorado Springs Gazette Telegraph, PO Box 1779, Colorado Springs, CO 80901. Website: www.gazette.com

Denver Post, 1560 Broadway, Denver, CO 80202.

Denver Rocky Mountain News, 400 W Colfax Ave, Denver, CO 80204. Website: www.insidedenver.com

INS, 12027 Federal Office Building, Denver, CO 80202.

Office of Economic Development, 136 State Capitol, Denver, CO 80202.

Department of Education, 201 E Colfax, Denver, CO 80203. Website: www.cde.state.co.us

Department of Labor & Employment, 1515 Arapohoe St, Denver, CO 80203. Website: www.state.co.us/gov_dir/labor_dir/labor_home.html

Department of Revenue, 1375 Sherman St, Denver, CO 80203. Website: www.state.co.us/gov_dir/revenue_dir/home_rev.html

Colorado Springs Chamber of Commerce, PO Box B, Colorado Springs, CO 80901. Website: www.cscc.com

Greater Denver Chamber of Commerce, 1456 Market Street, Denver, CO 80202. Website: www.den-chamber.com

Connecticut

Website: www.state.ct.us

Hartford Courant, 285 Broad St, Hartford, CT 06115. Website: www.courant.com

New Haven Register, 40 Sargent Drive, New Haven, CT 06511. Website: www.ctcentral.com

INS District Office, 450 Main St, Hartford, CT 06103-3060.

Department of Economic Development, 505 Hudson St, Hartford, CT 06066. Website: www.state.ct.us/ecd/

Department of Education, 165 Capitol Ave, Hartford, CT 06106. Website: www.state.ct.us/sde/dirmain.htm

Department of Labor, 200 Folly Brook Blvd, Wethersfield, CT 06109. Website: www.ctdol.state.ct.us

Department of Revenue Services, 25 Sigourney St, Hartford, CT 06106. Website: www.state.ct.us/drs

Greater Hartford Chamber of Commerce, 250 Constitution Plaza, Hartford, CT 06103. Website: www.metrohartford.com

Delaware

Website: www.state.de.us

News Journal, 950 West Basin Road, Newcastle, DE 19720.

Economic Development Authority, Treadway Towers, Suite 23-B, Dover, DE 19901. Website: www.state.de.us/dedc

Department of Education, Townsend Bldg, Dover, DE 19901. Website: www.doe.state.de.us

Employment and Training Division, Townsend Bldg, Dover, DE 19903. Website: www.de.jobsearch.org

Department of Labor, 4425 N Market Street, Wilmington, DE 19802.

Division of Revenue, Department of Finance, 820 N French Street, Wilmington, DE 19801. Website: www.state.de.us/govern/agencies/revenue/revenue.htm

Central Delaware Chamber of Commerce, PO Box 576, Dover, DE 19903.

Delaware State Chamber of Commerce, One Commerce Center, Suite 200, Wilmington, DE 19801.

District of Columbia

Website: www.dcpages.ari.net

Washington Post, 1150 15th St, NW, Washington, DC 20071. Website: www.washingtonpost.com

Washington Times, 3600 New York Ave NE, Washington, DC 20002. Website: www.washtimes-weekly.com

INS District Office, 1025 Vermont Ave NW, Washington, DC 20538.

Washington International School, 3100 Macomb Street NW, Washington, DC 20008.

Economic Development Department, 441 6th Street NW, Washington, DC 20004.

Department of Education, 415 12th St NW, Washington, DC 20004.

Department of Employment Services, 500 C St NW, Washington, DC 20001.

Department of Finance & Revenue, 441 4th Street NW, Washington, DC 20001.

Chamber of Commerce of the District of Columbia, 1301 Pennsylvannia Ave NW, Suite 309, Washington, DC 20004. Website: www.dcchamber.org

Florida

Website: www.state.fl.us

Florida Times-Union, PO Box 1949, Jacksonville, FL 32232. Website: www.times-union.com

Fort Lauderdale News Sun Sentinel, 200 E Las Olas Blvd, Fort Lauderdale, FL 33301. Website: www.times-union.com

Miami Herald, 1 Herald Plaza, Miami, FL 33132. Website: www.herald.com

Orlando Sentinel, 633 N Orange Drive, Orlando, FL 32801. Website: www.orlandosentinel.com

Palm Beach Post, PO Box 24700, West Palm Beach, FL 33416. Website: www.pbpost.com

St Petersburg Times, Box 1121, 490 First Ave S, St Petersburg, FL 33731. Website: www.sptimes.com

Tampa Tribune, 202 S Parker St, Tampa, FL 33601. Website: www.tampatrib.com

British Consulate, Suite 2110, 1001 S Bayshore Drive, Miami, FL 33131.

British Florida Chamber of Commerce, Suite 550, 2121 Ponce de Leon Blvd, Coral Gables, FL 33134.

INS District Office, Room 1324, Federal Building, 51 SW First Ave, Miami, FL 33130.

Enterprise Florida Inc, Department of Commerce, 501-B Collins Bldg, Tallahassee, FL 32399. Website: www.floridabusiness.com

Department of Education, The Capitol, Tallahassee, FL 32399. Website: www.flrn.edu/doc

Labor & Employment Security Department, 2012 Capitol Cir SE, Tallahassee, FL 32399. Website: www.state.fl.us/dles

Department of Revenue, South Calhoun St, Tallahassee, FL 32399. Website: www.sun6.dms.state.fl.us.dor/

Fort Lauderdale Area Chamber of Commerce, 208 3rd Ave SE, Fort Lauderdale, FL 33302-4156.

Jacksonville Chamber of Commerce, PO Box 329, 3 Independent Drive, Jacksonville, FL 32201. Website: www.jaxchamber.com

Greater Miami Chamber of Commerce, 1601 Biscayne Blvd, Miami, FL 33132. Website: www.greatermiami.com

Tampa Chamber of Commerce, 401 East Jackson Street, Suite 2100, Tampa, FL 33602. Website: www.gtcc.usf.edu/gtcc

Georgia
Website: www.state.ga.us

Atlanta Journal-Constitution, 72 Marietta Ave NW, Atlanta, GA 30303. Website: www.ajc.com

British Consulate-General, Suite 2700, 245 Peach Tree Centre Avenue NE, Atlanta, GA 30303.

INS District Office, 77 Forsyth St, Atlanta, GA 30303.

Department of Industry & Trade, 230 Peachtree St NW, Atlanta, GA 30301. Website: www.georgia.com

Department of Education, 205 Butler St SE, Atlanta, GA 30334. Website: www.doe.k12.ga.us

Department of Labor, 501 Pulliam St SW, Atlanta, GA 30312. Website: www.dol.state.ga.us

US Department of Labor, 148 International Blvd, Atlanta, GA 30303.

Department of Revenue, 270 Washington St SW, Atlanta, GA 30334. Website: www.state.ga.us/department/dor

Georgia State Chamber of Commerce, CCN Center, Atlanta, GA 30303-2705. Website: www.forward-atlanta.com

Hawaii
Website: www.hawaii.gov

Honolulu Star-Bulletin, Box 3080, Honolulu, HI 96802. Website: www.starbulletin.com

INS District Office, PO Box 461, 595 Ala Moana Blvd, Honolulu, HI 96809.

Department of Business, Economic Development & Tourism, 250 S King St, Honolulu, HI 96813. Website: www.hawaii.gov/dbedt

Department of Education, 1390 Miller St, Honolulu, HI 96813. Website: www.k12.hi.us

Labor & Industrial Relations Department, 830 Punchbowl St, Honolulu, HI 96814. Website: www.alooha.net/edps

Department of Taxation, 425 S Queen St, Honolulu, HI 96813. Website: www.hawaii.gov/tax/ta.html

Chamber of Commerce of Hawaii, 202 Kamehamha St, Honolulu, HI 96720.

Idaho

Website: www.state.id.us

Idaho Statesman, PO Box 40, Boise, ID 83707.

Department of Commerce, Statehouse, Boise, ID 83720. Website: www.doc.state.id.us

Department of Education, Len B Jordan Bldg, 650 W State St, Boise, ID 83720. Website: www.sde.state.id.us

Department of Employment, 317 Main St, Boise, ID 83735.

Labor Department, 277 N Sixth St, Boise, ID 83720. Website: www.state.id.us.labor

State Tax Commission, 800 Park Blvd, Boise, ID 83722.

Boise Area Chamber of Commerce, PO Box 2368, 711 W Bannock, Boise, ID 83701. Website: www.boise.com

Illinois

Website: www.state.il.us

Chicago Tribune, 435 N Michigan Ave, Chicago IL 60611. Website: www.chicago.tribune.com

Peoria Journal-Star, 1 News Plaza, Peoria, IL 61643. Website: www.pjstar.com

Wall Street Journal, 1 S Wacker Drive, 21st Fl, Chicago, IL 60606. Website: www.wsj.com

British Consulate-General, 400 N Michigan Ave, Suite 1300, Chicago, IL 60611.

INS District Office, 10 W Jackson Blvd, Suite 600, Chicago, IL 60604.

Department of Commerce & Community Affairs, 620 E Adams St, 3rd Floor, Springfield, IL 62701. Website: www.commerce.state.il.us

State Board of Education, 100 N First St, Springfield, IL 62777. Website: www.isbe.state.il.us

Dept of Employment Security, 401 S State St, Chicago, IL 60605. Website: www.il.jobsearch.com

Department of Labor, #1 W Old State Capitol Plz, Springfield, IL 62702. Website: www.state.il.us/agency/idol

Department of Revenue, 101 W Jefferson St, Springfield, IL 62794. Website: www.revenue.state.il.us

Chicago Chamber of Commerce & Industry, 1 IBM Plaza, Suite 2800, Chicago, IL 60611. Website: www.chicago.org

Greater Springfield Chamber of Commerce, 3 South Old State Capital Plaza, Springfield, IL 62701.

Indiana
Website: www.state.in.us
Indianapolis News-Star, 307 N Pennsylvania Street, Indianapolis, IN 46204. Website: www.starnews.com
Business Development & Marketing Group, Department of Commerce, 1 N Capitol, Suite 700, Indianapolis, IN 46204. Website: www.ai.org/bdev
Department of Public Instruction, 227 State House, Indianapolis, IN 46204. Website: www.ideanet.doe.state.il.us
Department of Labor, 1013 State Office Bldg, Indianapolis, IN 46204. Website: www.ai.org/labor
Department of Revenue, 100 N Senate Ave, Indianapolis, IN 46204. Website: www.state.il.us/dor
Indianapolis Chamber of Commerce, 320 North Meridian St, Indianapolis, IN 46204-1777. Website: www.indychamber.com

Iowa
Website: www.state.ia.us
Des Moines Register, 715 Locust St, Des Moines, IA 50304. Website: www.dmregister.com
Department of Economic Development, 299 E Grand, Des Moines, IA 50309. Website: www.state.ia.us/government/ided
Department of Education, Grimes State Office Bldg, Des Moines, IA 50319. Website: www.state.ia.us/educate.dept.educ
Department of Employment Services, 1000 E Grand, Des Moines, IA 50319.
Department of Revenue & Finance, Hoover State Office Building, Des Moines, IA 50319. Website: www.state.ia.us/government/drf/index.html
Chamber of Commerce of Greater Des Moines, 601 Locust Street, Suite 1000, Des Moines, OA 50309. Website: www.dmchamber.com
Cedar Rapids Chamber of Commerce, 424 First Ave NE, PO Box 4860, Cedar Rapids, IA 52407. Website: www.cedarrapids.org/iowa

Kansas
Website: www.state.ks.us
Wichita Eagle-Beacon, 825 E Douglas St, Wichita, KS 67201. Website: www.wichitaeagle.com
Department of Commerce, 700 SW Harrison St, Topeka, KS 66603.
Department of Education, 120 E 10th St, Topeka, KS 66612. Website: www.ksbe.state.ks.us
Department of Human Resources, 401 SW Topeka Blvd, Topeka, KS 66603. Website: www.hr.state.ks.us
Department of Revenue, 2nd Fl, State Office Bldg, Topeka, KS 66612. Website: www.ink.org/public/kdor

Kansas City Chamber of Commerce, 727 Minnesota Ave, PO Box 171337, KS 66117. Website: www.kckacc.com

Topeka Chamber of Commerce, 120 E Sixth St, 3 Townsite Plaza, Topeka, KA 66603. Website: www.topekachamber.com

Wichita Area Chamber of Commerce, 350 W Douglas St, Wichita, KA 67202-2970. Website: www.wacc.org

Kentucky

Website: www.state.ky.us

Courier Journal, 525 W Broadway, Louisville, KY 40202. Website: www.courier-journal.com

Commerce Cabinet, Capital Plz Tower, Frankfort, KY 40601. Website: www.state.ky.us/edc/cabmain.htm

Department of Education, 500 Mero St, Frankfort, KY 40401. Website: www.kde.state.ky.us

Labor Cabinet, The 127 Bldg, US 127 S, Frankfort, KY 40601. Website: www.state.ky.us/agencies/labor/laborhome.htm

Revenue Cabinet, 200 Fair Oaks Lane, Frankfort, KY 40601. Website: www.state.ky.us/agencies/revenue/revhome.htm

Frankfort Chamber of Commerce, 100 Capital Ave, Frankfort, KT 40601.

Louisville Chamber of Commerce, 600 W Main Street, Louisville, KT 40202. Website: www.lacc.org

Louisiana

Website: www.state.la.us

The Advocate, PO Box 588, Baton Rouge, LA 70821. Website: www.theadvocate.com

New Orleans Times-Picayune, 3800 Howard Ave, New Orleans, LA 70140.

INS District Office, New Federal Building, 701 Loyola Ave, New Orleans, LA 70113.

Department of Economic Development, PO Box 94185, Baton Rouge, LA 70804. Website: www.lded.state.la.us

Department of Education, PO Box 94064, Baton Rouge, LA 70804. Website: www.doe.state.la.us

Department of Labor, PO Box 94094, Baton Rouge, LA 70804. Website: www.ldol.state.la.us

Department of Revenue & Taxation, PO Box 201, Baton Rouge, LA 70821. Website: www.rev.state.la.us

Baton Rouge Chamber of Commerce, 564 Laurel St, Baton Rouge, LA 70801. Website: www.brchamber.org

New Orleans and the River Region Chamber of Commerce, 601 Poydras Street, Suite 1700, New Orleans, LA 70130. Website: www.chamber.gnofn.org

Maine

Website: www.state.me.us

Bangor Daily News, 491 Main St, Bangor, ME 04401. Website: www.bangornews.com

INS District Office, 77 Pearl St, Portland, ME 04112.

Department of Economic & Community Development, State House Station #59, Augusta, ME 04333. Website: www.econdevmaine.com

Department of Education, State House Station #23, Augusta, ME 04333. Website: www.state.me.us/education/homepage.htm

Department of Labor, State House Station #54, Augusta, ME 04333.

Bureau of Taxation, State House Station #24, Augusta, ME 04333. Website: www.janus,state.me.us/revenue

Greater Portland Chamber of Commerce, 142 Free St, Portland, ME 04101. Website: www.portlandregion.com

Maryland

Website: www.state.md.us

Baltimore Sun, 501 N Calvert St, Baltimore, MD 21278. Website: www.sunspot.net

INS District Office, Room 124, Federal Building, 31 Hopkins Plaza, Baltimore, MD 21201.

Business & Industrial Development Department, 217 E Redwood St, Baltimore, MD 21202. Website: www.dbed.state.md.us/dbed

Department of Education, 200 W Baltimore St, Baltimore, MD 21201. Website: www.msde.state.md.us

Division of Labor & Industry, 51100 N Eutaw St, Baltimore, MD 21202. Website: www.dllr.state.md.us/labor

Treasury Department, 80 Calvert Street, PO Box 466, Annapolis, MD 21404.

Baltimore City Chamber of Commerce, 204 E Lombard Street, 3rd Floor, Baltimore, MD 21202. Website: www.wwhs.com/baltimore

Bethesda-Chevy Chase Chamber of Commerce, Woodmont Ave, Bethesda, MD 20814. Website: www.bccchamber.org

Massachusetts

Website: www.state.ma.us

Boston Globe, PO Box 2378, Boston, MA 02107. Website: www.globe.com

British Consulate-General, 600 Atlantic Avenue, Federal Reserve Plaza, 25th Floor, Boston MA 02210.

INS District Office, John Fitzgerald Kennedy Federal Building, Government Center, Boston, MA 02203.

Office of Economic Development, State House, Boston, MA 02133. Website: www.state.ma.us/econ

Department of Education, 350 Main Street, Maiden, MA 02148.

Department of Labor, 1 Ashburton Pl, Boston, MA 02108.

Department of Revenue, 100 Cambridge St, Boston, MA 02202. Website: www.state.ma.us/dor/dorpg.htm

Greater Boston Chamber of Commerce, Federal Reserve Plaza, 13th Floor, 600 Atlantic Ave, Boston, MA 02210-2200. Website: www.gbcc.org

Michigan

Website: www.migov.state.mi.us

Detroit Free Press, 321 Lafayette Blvd W, Detroit, MI 48231. Website: www.freep.com

Detroit News, 615 Lafayette Blvd W, Detroit, MI 48231. Website: www.detnews.com

Grand Rapids Press, 155 Michigan St NW, Grand Rapids, MI 49503. Website: www.mlive.com

INS District Office, Federal Building, 333 Mt Elliott St, Detroit, MI 48207.

Commercial Services Office, PO Box 30225, Lansing, MI 48909. Website: www.cis.state.mi.us/ocs

Department of Education, S Ottawa Bldg, PO Box 30008, Lansing, MI 48909. Website: www.mde.state.mi.us

Bureau of Employment Relations, Department of Labor, 1200 Sixth St, Detroit, MI 48226.

Jobs Commission, 7310 Woodward Ave, Detroit, MI 48202. Website: www.state.mi.us/mjc/ceo

Bureau of Revenue, Treasury Bldg, Lansing, MI 48909.

Greater Detroit Chamber of Commerce, 600 West Lafayette Road, Detroit, MI 48226. Website: www.detroitchamber.com

Minnesota

Website: www.state.mn.us

Star Tribune, 425 Portland Ave S, Minneapolis, MN 55388. Website: www.startribune.com

St Paul Pioneer Press Dispatch, 345 Cedar St, St Paul, MN 55101. Website: www.pioneerplanet.com

INS District Office, 2901 Metro Drive, Suite 100, Bloomington, MN 55425.

Department of Trade & Economic Development, 150 E Kellogg Blvd, St Paul, MN 55101. Website: www.dted.state.mn.us

Department of Education, 550 Cedar St, St Paul, MN 55101. Website: www.children.state.mn.us

Department of Labor & Industry, 443 Lafayette Rd, St Paul, MN 55101. Website: www.doli.state.mn.us

Department of Revenue, 10 River Park Plz, St Paul, MN 55146. Website: www.taxes.state.mn.us

St Paul Area Chamber of Commerce, 352 Minesota St, Suite N205, St Paul, MN 55101.

Greater Minneapolis Chamber of Commerce, 81 S 9th St, Minneapolis, MN 55402. Website: www.tc-chamber.org

Mississippi

Website: www.state.ms.us

Clarion Ledger, 311 E Pearl St, Jackson, MS 39201.

Department of Economic & Community Development, 1201 Sillers Bldg, Jackson, MS 39201. Website: www.mississippi.com

Department of Education, 501 Sillers Bldg, Jackson, MS 39201. Website: www.mdek12.state.ms.org

Employment Security Commission, 1520 W Capitol, Jackson, MS 39203. Website: www.mesc.state.ms.us

State Tax Commission, 102 Woolfolk Bldg, Jackson, MS 39201. Website: www.mstc.state.ms.us

Jackson Chamber of Commerce, PO Box 22548, 201 S President St, Jackson, MS 39225-2548.

Missouri

Website: www.ecodev.state.mo.us

Kansas City Star-Times, 1729 Grand Blvd, Kansas City, MO 64108. Website: www.kcstar.com

Saint Louis Post Dispatch, 9800 N Tucker Blvd, St Louis, MO 63101. Website: www.stlnet.com/postnet

INS District Office, 9747 Conant Ave, Kansas City, MO 64153.

Department of Economic Development, PO Box 1157, Jefferson City, MO 65102. Website: www.ecodev.state.mo.us/ded

Department of Elementary & Secondary Education, PO Box 480, 205 Jefferson City, MO 65102. Website: www.services.dese.state.mo.us

US Department of Labor, 911 Walnut St, Kansas City, MO 64106. Website: www.dolir.state.mo.us

Labor & Industrial Relations Dept, 421 E Dunklin St, Box 504, Jefferson City, MO 65104. Website: www.dolir.state.mo.us

Department of Revenue, Truman Bldg, 416 Belai Dr, Jefferson City, MO 65109-0708. Website: www.service.state.mo.us/dor

Greater Detroit Chamber of Commerce, 600 West Lafayette Blvd, Detroit, MI 48226.

Greater Kansas City Chamber of Commerce, 920 Main St, Suite 600, Kansas City, MO 64105. Website: www.kcity.com

St Louis Regional Commerce and Growth Association, 1 Metropolitan Square, Suite 1100, St Louis, MO 63102.

Montana
Website: www.mt.gov
Billings Gazette, 401 N Broadway, Billings, MT 59107. Website: www.bigskywire.com/gazette
INS District Office, Federal Bldg, Helena, MT 59601.
Public Education Board, 2500 Broadway, Helena, MT 59620.
Job Service Division, PO Box 1728, Helena, MT 59624. Website: www.jsd.dli.mt.gov
Department of Labor & Industry, Capitol Station, Helena, MT 59620. Website: www.dli.mt.gov
Department of Revenue, Capitol Station, Box 311, Helena, MT 59620. Website: www.mt.gov/revenue/rev.htm Billings Area Chamber of Commerce, 815 S 27th Street, Billings, MT 59107. Website: www.wtp.net.bacc

Nebraska
Website: www.state.ne.us
Omaha World-Herald, 14th and Dodge Sts, Omaha, NE 68102. Website: www.omaha.com
INS District Office, 3736 S 132nd Street, Omaha, NE 68144.
Department of Economic Development, 301 Centennial Mall S, PO Box 94666, Lincoln, NE 68509. Website: www.ded.state.ne.us
Department of Education, 301 Centennial Mall S, PO Box 94987, Lincoln, NE 68509-4987; Website: www.nde.state.ne.us
Department of Labor, PO Box 94600, Lincoln, NE 68509-4600. Website: www.dol.state.ne.us
Department of Revenue, 301 Centennial Mall S, PO Box 94818, Lincoln, NE 68509-4818. Website: www.nol.org/home/ndr
Lincoln Chamber of Commerce, 1221 North St, Lincoln, NE 68508. Website: www.lcoc.com
Greater Omaha Chamber of Commerce, 1301 Harney St, Omaha, NE 68102. Website: www.accessomaha.com

Nevada
Website: www.state.nv.us
Las Vegas Review Journal, 1111 W Bonanza Rd, Las Vegas, NV 89106. Website: www.lvrj.com
Commission on Economic Development, 600 E William, Suite 203, Carson City, NV 89710. Website: www.state.nv.us/businessop/
Department of Education, 700 E 5th St, Carson City, NV 89710. Website: www.nsn.k12.nv/us/nvdoe
Department of Labor & Training, 500 E Third St, Carson City, NV 89710. Website: www.state.nv.us/dltr/
Department of Taxation, 1550 E College Pkwy, Carson City 89706.
Carson City Chamber of Commerce, 1900 S Carson Street, Suite 100,

Carson City, NV 89701. Website: www.server2.powernet.net/ccchamber

Las Vegas Chamber of Commerce, 3720 Howard Hughes Parkway, Las Vegas, NV 89109. Website: www.lvchamber.com

New Hampshire

Website: www.state.nh.us

Portsmouth Herald, 111 Maplewood Avenue, Portsmouth, NH 03801. PO Box 780, Manchester, NH 03105.

Department of Resources & Economic Development, PO Box 856, Concord, NH 03301. Website: www.dred.state.nh.us

Department of Education, 101 Pleasant St S, Concord, NH 03301. Website: www.state.nh.us/doe/education.html

Department of Labor, 95 Pleasant Street, Concord, NH 03301. Website: www.nhwork.state.nh.us

Department of Revenue Administration, PO Box 467, Concord, NH 03301. Website: www.state.nh.us/revenue/revenue.htm

Greater Manchester Chamber of Commerce, 889 Elm St, Manchester, NH 03101.

New Jersey

Website: www.state.nj.us

Star Ledger, 1 Star Ledger Plaza, Newark, NJ 07101. Website: www.nj.com

INS District Office, Federal Bldg, 970 Broad St, Newark, NJ 07102.

Commerce & Economic Development Department, 33 W State St, CN 823, Trenton, NJ 08625. Website: www.state.nj.us/commerce/dcedhome.htm

Department of Education, 225 W State St, Trenton, NJ 08625. Website: www.state.nj.us/education

Department of Labor, CN 110, Trenton, NJ 08625-0110. Website: www.state.nj.us/labor

Division of Taxation, CN 240, Trenton, NJ 08625. Website: www.state.nj.us/treasury

Greater Newark Chamber of Commerce, 1 Newark Center, Newark, NJ 07102. Website: www.nbp.org

New Mexico

Website: www.state.nm.us

Albuquerque Journal, 7777 Jefferson St NE, Albuquerque, NM 87109. Website: www.abqjournal,com

Armand Hammer United World College of the American West, PO Box 248, Montezuma, NM 87731.

Department of Economic Development & Tourism, 1100 St Francis Dr, Santa Fe, NM 87501. Website: www.edd.state.nm.us

Department of Education, Education Bldg, 300 Don Gaspar St, Santa Fe, NM 87501-2786. Website: www.sde.state.nm.us

Department of Labor, 401 Broadway NE, Albuquerque, NM 87102. Website: www.state.nm.us/dol

Department of Taxation & Revenue, Joseph Montoya Bldg, Santa Fe, NM 87503. Website: www.state.nm.us/tax

Greater Albuquerque Chamber of Commerce, 401 Second St NW, Albuquerque, NM 87102. Website: www.gacc.org

New York State

Website: www.state.ny.us

Times-Union, 645 Albany-Shaker Road, Albany, NY 12212. Website: www.timesunion.com

Buffalo News, 1 News Plaza, Buffalo, NY 14240. Website: www.buffnews.com

New York Post, 1211 Avenue of the Americas, New York, NY 10036. Website: www.nypost.com

New York Times, 229 W 43rd St, New York, NY 10036. Website: www.nytimes.com

Democrat and Chronicle, 55 Exchange Blvd, Rochester NY 14614. Website: www.democratandchronicle.com

British Consulate-General, 845 Third Avenue, New York, NY 10022. Website: www.britain.nyc.ny.us

INS District Offices, 130 Delaware Ave, Buffalo, NY 14202; 26 Federal Plaza, New York, NY 10007.

Anglo-American School, 18 West 89 Street, New York, NY 10024.

United Nations International School, 24-50 East River Drive, New York, NY 10010.

Empire State Development Corporation, 1 Commerce Plz, Albany, NY 12245. Website: www.empire.state.ny.us

Department of Education, Education Bldg, Albany, NY 12234. Website: www.nysed.gov

Department of Labor, Harrison Campus, State Office Bldg, Albany, NY 12240. Website: www.labor.state.ny.us

Department of Taxation & Finance, Harrison Campus, Tax & Finance Bldg, Albany, NY 12227. Website: www.tax.state.ny.us

Greater Buffalo Partnerships, 300 Main Pl Tower, Buffalo, NY 14202. Website: www.gbpartnership.org

New York Chamber of Commerce & Industry, 1 Battery Park Plaza, 5th Floor, New York, NY 10004. Website: www.chamber.com

North Carolina

Website: www.state.nc.us

Charlotte Observer, 600 S Tryon Street, Charlotte, NC 28202. Website: www.charlotte.com

Durham Herald-Sun, PO Box 2092, Durham, NC 27702. Website: www.herald-sun.com

News and Observer, S McDowell St, Raleigh, NC 27602. Website: www.news-observer.com

Business & Industry Development, Department of Commerce, 430 N Salisbury St, Raleigh, NC 27603. Website: www.commerce.state.nc.us

Department of Public Instruction, 301 N Wilmington St, Raleigh, NC 27603-1712. Website: www.dpi.state.nc.us

Department of Labor, 4 W Edenton St, Raleigh, NC 27601-1092. Website: www.dol.state.nc.us/dol

Department of Revenue, 501 N Wilmington St, Raleigh, NC 27602-1348. Website: www.dor.state.nc.us/dor

Charlotte Chamber of Commerce, PO Box 32785, 129 West Trade Center, Charlotte, NC 28232. Website: www.charlottechamber.com

Raleigh Chamber of Commerce, 800 South Salisbury St, Raleigh, NC 27601. Website: www.raleigh.acn.net/chamber/

North Dakota

Website: www.state.nd.us

Forum, PO Box 2020, Fargo, ND 58107.

Economic Development Commission, Website: www.growingnd.com

Department of Public Instruction, Website: www.dpi.state.nd.us

Job Service ND, PO Box 1537, Bismarck, ND 58502.

Department of Labor, State Capitol, Bismarck, ND 58505. Website: www.tradecorridor.com/ndlabor

Tax Department, 8th Fl, State Capitol, 600 E Blvd, Bismarck, ND 58505. Website: www.state.nd.us/taxdpt

Fargo Chamber of Commerce, 321 N Fourth St, PO Box 2443, Fargo, ND 58102.

Ohio

Website: www.state.oh.us

Akron Beacon Journal, 44 E Exchange St, Akron, OH 44328. Website: www.beaconjournal.com

Cincinnati Enquirer, 4312 Elm St, Cincinnati, OH 45202. Website: www.enquirer.com

Cincinnati Post, 125 E Court St, Cincinnati, OH 45202.

Plain Dealer, 1801 Superior Ave E, Cleveland OH 44114. Website: www.cleveland.com

Columbus Dispatch, 34 S 3rd St, Columbus, OH 43216. Website: www.dispatch.com

Dayton Daily News, 44 S Ludlow St, Dayton, OH 45401. Website: www.activedayton.com

INS District Office, Room 1917, Federal Office Bldg, 1240 E 9th St, Cleveland, OH 44199.

Department of Commerce, Website: www.state.oh.us/commerce
Department of Education, Website: www.ode.ohio.gov
Bureau of Employment Services, Website: www.ohio.gov/obes
Department of Taxation, Website: www.state.oh.us/tax
Greater Cincinatti Chamber of Commerce, 441 Vine St, Suite 300 Cincinatti, OH 45202. Website: www.gccc.com
Greater Cleveland Growth Association International Trade & Business Development, 200 Tower City Center, Cleveland, OH 44115.
Columbus Area Chamber of Commerce, 37 North High St, Columbus, OH 43215. Website: www.columbus.org/gccc
Toledo Area Chamber of Commerce, 300 Madison Avenue, Suite 200, Toledo, OH 43604. Website: www.toledochamber.com

Oklahoma

Website: www.state.ok.us
Daily Oklahoman, 500 N Broadway, Oklahoma City, OK 73125. Website: www.oklahoman.com
Tulsa World, Box 1770, Tulsa, OK 74103-3401. Website: www.tulsaworld.com
Department of Commerce, 6601 Broadway Ext, Oklahoma City, OK 73116. Website: www.odoc.state.ok.us
Department of Education, 2500 N Lincoln Blvd, Oklahoma City, OK 73105. Website: www.sde.state.ok.us
State Department of Labor, 4001 N Lincoln Blvd, Oklahoma City, OK 73103. Website: www.state.ok.us/-okdol
Tax Commission, 2501 N Lincoln Blvd, Oklahoma City, OK 73194. Website: www.oktax.state.ok.us
Oklahoma City Chamber of Commerce, 123 Park Avenue, Oklahoma City, OK 73102. Website: www.okchamber.com
Metropolitan Tulsa Chamber of Commerce, 616 S Boston Ave, Tulsa, OK 74119. Website: www.tulsachamber.com

Oregon

Website: www.state.or.us
The Oregonian, 1320 SW Broadway, Portland, OR 97201. Website: www.orgonlive.com
INS District Office, 511 NW Broadway, Portland, OR 97209.
Department of Economic Development, 775 Simmer St NE, Salem, OR 97310.
Department of Education, 700 Pringle Pkwy SE, Salem, OR 97310. Website: www.ode.state.or.us
Department of Employment, 875 Union St NE, Salem, OR 97301. Website: www.emp.state.or.us
Department of Revenue, 955 Center St NE, Salem, OR 97310. Website: www.dor.state.or.us

Portland Chamber of Commerce, 221 NW Second Ave, Portland, OR 97209. Website: www.pdxcamber.org

Salem Area Chamber of Commerce, 220 Cottage St NE, Salem, OR 97301.

Pennsylvania
Website: www.state.pa.us
Harrisburg Patriot News, 812 King Blvd, Harrisburg, PA 17101.
Tribune-Democrat, 425 Locust St, Johnstown, PA 15907.
Philadelphia Daily News/Inquirer, 400 N Broad St, Philadelphia, PA 19101. Website: www.phillynews.com
Pittsburgh Post-Gazette, 34 Blvd of the Allies, Pittsburgh, PA 15230. Website: www.post-gazette.com
INS District Office, 1600 Callowhill St, Philadelphia, PA 19130.
Department of Commerce, 433 Forum Bldg, Harrisburg, PA 17120.
Department of Education, 333 Market Street, Harrisburg, PA 17108. Website: www.educ-cas.psu.edu/pde/html
Department of Labor & Industry, 1700 Labor & Industry Building, Harrisburg, PA 17120. Website: www.li.state.pa.us
Department of Revenue, Strawberry Sq, Harrisburg, PA 17101. Website: www.revenue.state.pa.us
Greater Philadelphia Chamber of Commerce, Broad & Chestnut St, Philadelphia, PA 19102. Website: www.gpcc.com
Greater Pittsburgh Chamber of Commerce, 3 Gateway Center, Pittsburgh, PA 15222. Website: www.chamber.pgh.com

Rhode Island
Website: www.state.ri.us
Providence Journal Bulletin, 75 Fountain St, Providence, RI 02902. Website: www.projo.com
Department of Economic Development, 1 Exchange St, Providence, RI 02903. Website: www.riedc.com
Department of Education, 22 Hayes St, Providence, RI 02908. Website: www.state.ri.us./stdept/sd46.htm
Department of Labor, 101 Friendship St, Providence, RI 02907. Website: www.stdept/sd15.htm
Division of Taxation, 1 Capitol Hill, Providence, RI 02908.
Providence Chamber of Commerce, 30 Exchange Terrace, Providence, RI 02903. Website: www.provchamber.com

South Carolina
Website: www.state.sc.us
Post & Courier, 134 Columbus St, Charleston, SC 29403. Website: www.charleston.net

The State-Record, 1401 Shop Rd, Columbia, SC 29201. Website: www.thestate.com

Department of Commerce, PO Box 27, Columbia, SC 29202. Website: www.state.sc.us/commerce/

Department of Education, 1429 Senate St, Columbia, SC 29201. Website: www.state.sc.us/sde

Employment Security Commission, 1550 Gadsden St, Columbia, SC 29202. Website: www.scjob.sces.org

Department of Labor, 3600 Forest Dr, Landmark Ctr, Columbia, SC 29204.

Revenue Commission, 301 Gervais St, Columbia, SC 29201. Website: www.dor.state.sc.us

Greater Columbia Chamber of Commerce, PO Box 1360, Columbia, SC 29202. Website: www.gcbn.com

Greater Greenville Chamber of Commerce, PO Box 10048, 24 Cleveland St, Greenville, SC 29603. Website: www.greenvillechamber.com

South Dakota
Website: www.state.sd.us

Argus-Leader, 200 S Minnesota Ave, Sioux Falls, SD 57012. Website: www.argusleader.com

Department of Commerce, Capitol Lake Plaza, Pierre, SD 57501. Website: www.state.sd.us/state/executive/dcr/dcr.html

Department of Education, 700 Governor's Drive, Pierre, SD 57501. Website: www.state.sd.us/state/executive/deca

Department of Labor, Kneip Bldg, Pierre, SD 57501. Website: www.state.sd.us/state/executive/dol/dol.htm

Department of Revenue, 408 E Capitol Ave, Pierre, SD 57501. Website: www.state.sd.us/state.executive/revenue/revenue/html

Sioux Falls Chamber of Commerce, 315 S Phillips, Sioux Falls, SD 57102.

Tennessee
Website: www.state.tn.us

Commercial Appeal, 475 Union Ave, Memphis, TN 38103. Website: www.gomemphis.com

The Tennessean, 1100 Broadway, Nashville, TN 37202. Website: www.tennessean.com

Department of Economic & Community Development, 320 Sixth Ave N, Nashville, TN 37219.

Department of Education, 710 James Robertson Pkwy, Nashville, TN 37243. Website: www.state.tn.us/education/

Department of Employment Security, 550 James Robertson Pkwy, Nashville, TN 37243. Website: www.state.tn.us/empsoc

Department of Labor, 710 James Robertson Pkwy, Nashville, TN 37243. Website: www.state.tn.us./labor/

Department of Revenue, Website: www.state.tn.us/labor/
Memphis Area Chamber of Commerce, 22 N Front St, PO Box 224, Memphis, TN 38101. Website: www.memphischamber.com
Nashville Area Chamber of Commerce, 161 Fourth Ave N, Nashville, TN 37219. Website: www.nashville.tnstate.edu

Texas
Website: www.state.tx.us
Austin American-Statesman, 305 S Congress Avenue, Austin, TX 78704. Website: www.austin360.com
Dallas Morning News, Box 655237, Dallas, TX 75265. Website: www.dallasnews.com
Fort Worth Star-Telegram, 400 W 7th St, Fort Worth, TX 76101. Website: www.startelegram.com
Houston Chronicle, 801 Texas Ave, Houston, TX 77001. Website: www.houstonchronicle.com
San Antonio Express-News, Ave E and 3rd St, San Antonio, TX 78205. Website: www.express-news.net
Wall Street Journal, 1233 Regal Row, Dallas TX 75247.
British Consulate-General, 1000 Louisiana Street, Suite 1900, Houston, TX 77002.
British Consulate, 2911 Turtle Creek Blvd, Suite 400, Dallas TX 75219.
INS District Offices, 8101 Stemmons Freeway, Dallas, TX 75247; 1545 Hawkins Blvd, El Paso, TX 79925; 509 N Sam Houston Parkway E, Houston, TX 77060; 8940 Four Winds Drive, San Antonio, TX 78239; 21202 Teege, Harlington, TX 78550-4667.
Department of Economic Development, 816 Congress, 12th Fl, Austin, TX 78711. Website: www.tded.state.tx.us
Texas Education Agency, 1701 N Congress Ave, Austin, TX 78701. Website: www.tea.texas.gov
Employment Commission, 101 E 15th St, Austin, TX 78778-0001.
US Department of Labor, Federal Building, 525 Griffin St, Dallas, TX 75202.
Human Services Department, Capitol Station, Austin, TX 78711. Website: www.dhs.state.tx.us
Public Accounts Department, LBJ Bldg, Austin, TX 78774.
Austin Chamber of Commerce, 901 W Riverside Drive, Austin, TX 78704. Website: www.austin-chamber.com
Greater Dallas Chamber of Commerce, 1201 Elm St, Suite 2000, Dallas, TX 75270. Website: www.gdc.com
El Paso Chamber of Commerce, PO Box 9738, 10 Civic Center Plaza, El Paso, TX 79901. Website: www.elpaso.org
Greater Houston Chamber of Commerce, 1100 Milam Bldg, 25th Floor, Houston, TX 77002.

Greater Marshall Chamber of Commerce, 213 W Auston St, PO Box 520, Marshall, TX 75670.

Greater San Antonio Chamber of Commerce, 602 East Commerce St, San Antonio, TX 78205. Website: www.sachamber.org

Utah

Website: www.state.utah.us

Salt Lake City Tribune, 143 S Main St, Salt Lake City, UT 84110. Website: www.sltrib.com

Deseret News, Box 1257, 30 E First South St, Salt Lake City, UT 84110.

Department of Commerce, 6920 State Office Bldg, Salt Lake City, UT 84114. Website: www.commerce.state.ut.us

Community & Economic Development Department, 6290 State Off Bldg, Salt Lake City, UT 84114.

Office of Education, 250 E Fifth St S, Salt Lake City, UT 84111. Website: www.usoe.k12.ut.us

Department of Employment Security, 174 Social Hall Ave, Salt Lake City, UT 84147.

Tax Commission, 210 M 1950 West, Salt Lake City, UT 84134. Website: www.tax.cx.state.utah.us

Salt Lake Area Chamber of Commerce, 175 E 400 St, Salt Lake City, UT 84111. Website: www.slachamber.com

Vermont

Website: www.state.vt.us

Burlington Free Press, 191 College St, Burlington, VT 05402.

INS District Office, PO Box 328, St Albans, VT 05478.

Agency of Development & Community Affairs, 109 State St, Montpelier, VT 05602.

Department of Education, 120 State St, Montpelier, VT 05602. Website: www.state.vt.us/education

Department of Employment & Training, Green Mountain Drive, Montpelier, VT 05602. Website: www.det.state.vt.us

Department of Labor & Industry, 7 Court St, Montpelier, VT 05602. Website: www.state.vt.us/labind

Department of Taxes, 109 State St, Montpelier, VT 05602. Website: www.state.vt.us/tax

Lake Champlain Regional Chamber of Commerce, PO Box 453, 209 Battery St, Burlington, VT 05402.

Virginia

Website: www.state.va.us

Times-Dispatch, 33 E Franklin St, Richmond, VA 23220. Website: www.gatewayva.com

Roanoke Times, 201 W Campbell Ave, Roanoke, VA 24011. Website: www.roanoke.com

Department of Commerce & Trade, 723 N 9th St, Richmond, VA 23219.

Department of Education, PO Box 2120, Richmond, VA 23216.

Employment Commission, 703 E Main St, Richmond, VA 23219. Website: www.state.va.us/vec/vec.html

Department of Labor & Industry, PO Box 12064, Richmond, VA 23219.

Department of Taxation, 2220 W Broad St, Richmond, VA 23220. Website: www.state.va.us/tax/tax.html

Hampton Roads Chamber of Commerce, 420 Bank St, Norfolk, VA 23510.

Greater Richmond Chamber of Commerce, PO Box 12280, Richmond, VA 23219. Website: www.grcc.com

Washington State

Website: www.wa.gov

Seattle Post Intelligencer, 1120 John St, Seattle, WA 98111. Website: www.seattlepi.com

Spokesman-Review, 999 W Riverside Ave, Spokane, WA 99201. Website: www.spokane.net

Morning News Tribune, 1950 S State St, Tacoma, WA 98405. Website: www.tribnet.com

British Consulate, 999 Third Avenue, Seattle, WA 98104.

INS District Office, 815 Airport Way S, Seattle, WA 98134.

Department of Trade & Economic Development, 101 General Administration Bldg, M/S: AX13, Olympia, WA 98504.

Department of Public Instruction, Old Capitol Bldg, Olympia, WA 98504. Website: www.ospi.wednet.edu

Department of Employment Security, 212 Maple Park, Olympia, WA 98504. Website: www.wa.gov/esd

Department of Labor & Industries, General Administration Bldg, Olympia, WA 98504. Website: www.wa.gov/lni

Department of Revenue, General Administration Bldg, Olympia, WA 98504. Website: www.wa.gov/dor/wador/html

Greater Seattle Chamber of Commerce, 1301 5th Avenue, Suite 2400, Seattle, WA 98101. Website: www.seattlechamber.com

West Virginia

Website: www.state.wv.us

Charleston Gazette/Daily Mail, 1001 Virginia St E, Charleston WV 25301. Website: www.wvgazette.com

Department of Economic Development, Website: www.wvweb.com/wvw/wvedc

Department of Education, 1900 Kanowha Blvd E, Charleston, WV 25305. Website: www.wvde.state.wv.us

Division of Employment Security, 112 California Ave, Charleston, WV 23505.

Division of Labor, State Capitol Complex, Bldg 3, Charleston, WV 25305.

Department of Tax & Revenue, State Capitol Complex, Charleston, WV 25305. Website: www.wvweb.net/taxrev/index.html

Charleston Chamber of Commerce, 106 Capitol St, Suite 100, Charleston, WV 25301-2610. Website: www.charleywestchamber.org

Huntington Area Chamber of Commerce, 522 Ninth St, PO Box 1509, Huntington, WV 25716.

Wisconsin

Website: www.state.wi.us

Milwaukee Journal Sentinel, PO Box 661, Milwaukee, WI 53201. Website: www.packerplus.com

Bureau of Business Expansion & Recruitment, Department of Development, PO Box 7970, Madison, WI 53707.

Department of Commerce, PO Box 7970, Madison, WI 53707.

Department of Public Instruction, 125 S Webster St, Madison, WI 53702. Website: www.state.wi.us/agencies.dpi

Job Service Division, Department of Industry, Labor & Human Relations, PO Box 7903, Madison, WI 53707.

Department of Industry, Labor & Human Relations, 201 E Washington Ave, PO Box 7946, Madison, WI 53707.

Department of Revenue, 125 S Webster, Madison, WI 53702. Website: www.dor.state.wi.us

Greater Madison Chamber of Commerce, 615 E Washington Ave, Madison, WI 53701. Website: www.greatermadisonchamber.com

Metropolitan Milwaukee Chamber of Commerce, 756 N Milwaukee St, 4th Floor, Milwaukee, WI 53202.

Wyoming

Website: www.state.wy.us

Casper Star-Tribune, PO Box 80, Casper, WY 82602. Website: www.tribune.com

Department of Commerce, 6101 Yellowstone Road, Cheyenne, WY 892001. Website: www.commerce.state.wy.us

Department of Education, 2300 Capitol Ave, Cheyenne, WY 82002. Website: www.k12.wy.us

Employment Security Commission, PO Box 2760, Casper, WY 82002.

Department of Employment, 122 W 25th St, Cheyenne, WY 82002. Website: www.wyjobs.state.wy.us

Department of Labor & Statistics, Herschler Bldg, Cheyenne, WY 82002.

Department of Revenue, 122 W 25th St, Cheyenne, WY 82002. Website:
   www.revenue.state.wy.us
Cheyenne Chamber of Commerce, 301 W 16th St, Cheyenne, WY 82001.

Note
Where two branches of a state department of labour are listed the
first is likely to provide a placement service and job advice while
the second administers and enforces the state's labour laws.

Appendix H
Bibliography

This bibliography features a number of books published in America. While some of the reference books can be consulted in some of the larger reference libraries, others may not be readily obtainable in the UK. However, it is possible to order them direct from the USA via the Internet. Among the web-based bookstores are:

www.amazon.com
www.barnesandnoble.com
www.borders.com
www.ingrambook.com

A useful source of book information is Bookwire:
www.bookwire.com

Reference books
(UK publications are asterisked)

The American Almanac of Jobs and Salaries, J. W. Wright (ed) (Avon Books).

Business Phone Book USA (Omnigraphics).

Career Guide to Professional Associations – A Directory of Organisations by Occupational Field, C. N. Shrameck (Sulzberger & Graham).

Computer Industry Almanac, Karen Jullussen (ed) (Computer Industry Alliance).

Consultants and Consulting Organisations M. and Karin Koek (Gale Research).

Directory of Executive Recruiters, James H. Kennedy (ed) (Kennedy Publications).

Directory of Franchising Organisations (Pilot Books).

Dun & Bradstreet's Directory of Service Companies (Dun & Bradstreet).

Dun & Bradstreet's Million Dollar Directory (Dun & Bradstreet).

Dun & Bradstreet's Regional Business Directory (Dun & Bradstreet).

Dun & Bradstreet's Employment Opportunities Directory (Dun & Bradstreet).

The Economist Business Travel Guide: United States (Economist Publications Ltd).*

Employment and Earnings (US Department of Labor). Monthly publication.

Handbook of Private Schools (Porter Sargent Publishers).

The Executive Grapevine International Directory of Executive Recruitment Consultants (Executive Grapevine).*

Expat Network Contact Directory (Expat Network).*

Information Please Almanac (Houghton Mifflin).

International Pay and Benefits Survey (PA Personnel Services, Hyde Park House, 60A Knightsbridge, London SW1X 7LE).*

Internships (Writer's Digest Books).

Jobs Almanac (Adams Media).

Job Hunters' Source Books, Michelle de Comte (Gale).

Job Seekers' Guide to Private–Public Companies, Charity A. Dorgan (Gale).

National Trade & Professional Associations of the United States (Columbia Books).

National Jobline Directory, Robert Schmidt (Adams Publishing).

Obtaining Visas and Work Permits, Roger Jones (How To Books).*

Occupational Outlook Handbook, US Department of Labor (VGM Career Books).

Occupational Outlook Quarterly, Bureau of Labor Statistics, US Dept of Labor. (Articles on jobs and job prospects.)

Summer Employment Directory of the United States (Writer's Digest Books).

Thomas Register of American Manufacturers (Thomas Publishing).

The Traveller's Handbook, M. Shales (ed) (WEXAS, 45 Brompton Road, London SW3 1DE).*

Ulrich's International Periodicals Directory (R. R. Bowker).

US Government Jobs (US Office of Personnel Management).

US Government Manual (Office of Federal Register, National Archives and Record Administration, Washington DC 20408).

VGM's Careers Encyclopedia (NTC Contemporary Publishing Co).

VGM's Guide to Temporary Employment (NTC Contemporary Publishing Co).

The World Almanac and Book of Facts (Funk & Wagnall).

Working Abroad, David Young (Financial Times Business Information).*

General books

(UK titles are asterisked)

Culture Shock USA (Kuperard/Times Editions).*

Culture Shock USA South (Kuperard/Times Editions).*

Doing Business in the USA, R. Starr and R. B. Donin (Oyez Publishing).*

Emerging Careers – New Occupations for the Year 2000 and Beyond, S. N. Feingold and N. R. Taylor (Garrett Park Press).

Finding a Job in the USA (Overseas Jobs Express).*

Getting a Job Abroad, (6th ed), R. Jones (How To Books).*

Getting into America, Harry Liebman (How To Books).*

How To Manage your Career, Roger Jones (How To Books).*

Jobs – where they are and how to get them, Robert Kant (CFKR Career).

Living and Working in America, (5th ed). Steve Mills (How To Books).*

Living and Working in Chicago (Kuperard/Times Editions).*

Living and Working in San Francisco (Kuperard/Times Editions).*

Living and Working in New York (Kuperard/Times Editions).*

Living and Working in the USA, David Hampshire (Survival Books).*

Long Stays in America, R. W. Hicks and F. Schulz (David & Charles/ Hippocrene).*

Teaching Abroad (3rd Edition), R. Jones (How To Books).*

Telesearch – Direct Dial to the Best Job in Your Life, J. Truitt (Books Demand).

US Business Visas, Richard S. Goldstein (Department of Trade & Industry).*

Using the Internet in your Job Search, Fred E. Jandt and Mary Nemnich (JIST).

What Color is Your Parachute?, R. N. Bolles (Ten Speed Press).

Appendix I
Using the Internet

The development of the Internet is already making life much easier for people seeking jobs overseas. This book contains hundreds of e-mail addresses and websites which will lead you directly to the information you need.

As you become more experienced in surfing the Web, you may wish to conduct your jobsearch by computer.

Here is a selection of websites which will help you to access job vacancies:

www.monster.com
www.vjf.com
www.espan.com
www.careerpath.com
(Careerpath offers newspaper job advertisements for major cities; CareerpathEXTRA offers job vacancies gathered from the websites of leading employers. The site also offers careers advice and profiles of employers.)
www.direct-jobs.com
www.ajb.dni.us
www.adamsonline.com
www.jobsamerica.com
www.cweb.com
www.yahoo.com/business_and_economy/employment/jobs
(This particular website offers a number of options which must be prefixed by /. They include:
seasonal_and_summeremployment
careermosaic
career_fields

Another idea is to tap into the websites of the individual states and go to the business_and_economy/employment option which will direct you to various job agencies. The website also provides information on housing, local taxation, social security provision, schools, etc.

You will find websites for each state in Appendix G.

eg: Alaska is www.state.ak.us

Arizona is www.state.az.us

To access individual cities try the formula:

www.ci.(name of city).(abbreviation of state).us

eg Phoenix, which is: www.ci.phoenix.az.us

In some cases the prefix 'ci' can be omitted.

eg Cleveland, which is www.cleveland.oh.us

Some cities have a different formula:

www.(name of city).com

eg Atlanta, which is www.atlanta.com

Finally here are the websites of some federal government departments and agencies you may need to contact:

Immigration and Naturalization Service: www.ins.usdoj.gov

Internal Revenue Service: www.irs.ustreas.gov

Department of Commerce: www.doc.gov

Department of Labor: www.dol.gov

Employment and Training Administration: www.doleta.gov

Social Security Administration: www.ssa.gov

Department of Agriculture: www.usda.gov

Small Business Administration: www.sbaonline.sba.gov

United States Information Agency: www.usia.gov

Index